THE EVERYTHING® GUIDE TO UNDERSTANDING SOCIALISM

Dear Reader,

I became interested in socialism by way of the British Empire. Indian cottons led me to the "dark Satanic mills" of northern England and the Industrial Revolution. The Industrial Revolution introduced me to Friedrich Engels's classic study of the lives of the working poor in England. Engels led me straight to Karl Marx. When I expanded my interests to European imperialism in general, French Algeria led me to the Paris Commune of 1830, which led me back to Karl Marx.

I soon discovered that if you spent much time reading about nineteenth-century Britain and Europe, you stumbled across socialism everywhere. Self-educated cobblers, radical dissenters, anarchist assassins, and methodical economists shared the pages with prime ministers and princes. The more I read, the more convinced I became that in the nineteenth century, socialism played the same role that yeast plays in bread dough: It made things ferment and change into something new.

Whatever your political beliefs, learning about socialism's history and beliefs is a good way to understand the present a little more clearly.

Pamela D. Toler

Welcome to the EVERYTHING® Series!

These handy, accessible books give you all you need to tackle a difficult project, gain a new hobby, comprehend a fascinating topic, prepare for an exam, or even brush up on something you learned back in school but have since forgotten.

You can choose to read an *Everything®* book from cover to cover or just pick out the information you want from our four useful boxes: e-questions, e-facts, e-alerts, and e-ssentials.

We give you everything you need to know on the subject, but throw in a lot of fun stuff along the way, too.

We now have more than 400 *Everything®* books in print, spanning such wide-ranging categories as weddings, pregnancy, cooking, music instruction, foreign language, crafts, pets, New Age, and so much more. When you're done reading them all, you can finally say you know *Everything®*!

QUESTION

Answers to common questions

FACT

Important snippets of information

ALERT

Urgent warnings

ESSENTIAL

Quick handy tips

THE EVERYTHING® GUIDE TO UNDERSTANDING SOCIALISM

The political, social, and economic concepts behind this complex theory

Pamela D. Toler, PhD

adamsmedia
Avon, Massachusetts

To my husband, Sandy Wilson, who read chapters, demanded explanations, dragged me away from my desk, and cheered me on.

An Everything® Series Book.
Everything® and everything.com® are registered trademarks of F+W Media, Inc.

Published by Adams Media, a division of F+W Media, Inc.
57 Littlefield Street, Avon, MA 02322 U.S.A.
www.adamsmedia.com

ISBN 10: 1-4405-1277-9
ISBN 13: 978-1-4405-1277-3
eISBN 10: 1-4405-2549-8
eISBN 13: 978-1-4405-2549-0

Printed in the United States of America.

10 9 8 7 6 5 4 3 2 1

Library of Congress Cataloging-in-Publication Data
Toler, Pamela D.
The everything guide to understanding socialism / Pamela D. Toler.
p. cm.
Includes bibliographical references and index.
ISBN 978-1-4405-1277-3 (alk. paper)
1. Socialism—History. 2. Communism—History. I. Title.
HX36.T63 2011
335—dc22
2011006242

The Top 10 Socialist Thinkers

1. **Eduard Bernstein** (1850–1932) was the theoretician behind Marxist revisionism, which purports that it is possible to use reform to create a socialist society.
2. **William Beveridge** (1879–1963), known as "The People's William," wrote the blueprint for the modern British welfare state.
3. **Antonio Gramsci** (1891–1937) created the concept of *cultural hegemony*, which says that a successful revolution must change a society's dominant ideas as well as its political structure.
4. **Michael Harrington** (1928–1989) was sometimes called "the man who discovered poverty." His book *The Other America* was a major influence on Lyndon Johnson's "Great Society" and the New Left of the 1960s.
5. **Vladimir Lenin** (1870–1924) transformed Marxist ideology to reflect Russian political realities. His recognition that peasants were as oppressed as any urban proletariat and represented a potential revolutionary force was the basis for later revolutions in relatively unindustrialized countries.
6. **Karl Marx** (1818–1883) and **Friedrich Engels** (1820–1895) were the Tweedledum and Tweedledee of socialism—you don't find one without the other. Together they developed the socialist theories on which Marxism is based.
7. **Pierre-Joseph Proudhon** (1809–1865) was the first person to call himself an anarchist. He developed the theoretical foundation for anarchism and syndicalism.
8. **David Ricardo** (1772–1823) was not a socialist himself. His economic theories of rent, the labor theory of value, and the iron law of wages laid the foundation for Karl Marx's analysis of capitalism.
9. **Jean-Jacques Rousseau** (1712–1778) distinguished between natural and social inequality.
10. **Sidney and Beatrice Webb** (1859–1947 and 1858–1943), founders of the English Fabian Society, developed the idea of gradualism: the transformation of society from capitalism to socialism through gradual reforms.

Introduction

AS POLITICIANS STRUGGLE TO find solutions to the worldwide economic recession that began in December 2007, the word socialism has become a political hot button. A quick Google search of "socialism in America" leads you to heated arguments on political forums, anti-socialist tirades, and equally fanatical pro-socialist defenses. The U.S. news on any particular day includes a report of Republican politicians and Tea Party activists accusing President Obama and the Democratic party of dragging America toward socialism, occasionally accompanied by a brief interview with a professed socialist saying, "no, the president is not a socialist, thank you very much." The people who attack socialism often use the word as an epithet, attaching it to any government-funded project they disapprove of—from national health care to paved roads. The people who defend socialism tend to describe it in utopian terms. On the one hand, socialism is evil. On the other hand, socialism is salvation.

But what, exactly, does socialism mean?

It's not surprising that many people are confused about what socialism means. Both its opponents and its proponents often take a position similar to that of Supreme Court Justice Potter Stewart on pornography: They know it when they see it. In fact, like democracy, socialism is an umbrella term for a wide range of doctrines, including anarchism, Marxism, social democracy, farm cooperatives, communes, and communism, that are bound together by their critique of capitalism and their commitment to the creation of an egalitarian society.

Socialism's complex history stretches back three centuries. It has inspired political realities as far apart as Robert Owen's experimental community in New Harmony, Indiana, and Joseph Stalin's brutal Russian dictatorship. Its proponents have included pragmatists and visionaries. Some have called for reform; others have called for revolution. Socialists have formed, and rejected, both political parties and trade union movements. The only thing that holds them all together is a shared concern with restructuring society in a way that corrects social and economic inequalities.

Socialism has been one of the formative forces of the modern world. In 1895, King Edward VI of England proclaimed in a speech "We are all socialists now-a-days." It was his exaggerated acknowledgement that over the course of the nineteenth century the socialist movement, in its various incarnations, changed European society and politics in fundamental ways.

The purpose of this book is to introduce you to the different types of socialism, socialists' basic beliefs, and their influence on the modern world, beginning with socialism's origins in the social turmoil of the Industrial Revolution and ending with its modern-day interpretations.

CHAPTER 1

Socialism's Beginnings

In the sixteenth century, the economic world of Europe began to change. The complicated system of rights and duties that made up the feudal system was slowly being replaced by a market economy organized on the basis of personal gain. New freedoms were accompanied by new hardships—and new social disorder. Concerned with the contrast between what was and what ought to be, political philosophers, beginning with Sir Thomas More, struggled to understand the nature of a just, stable, and efficient society. In the process, they laid the foundations for later socialist thought.

Sir Thomas More Invents Utopia

Sir Thomas More (1478–1535) wrote at the beginning of the Tudor period, a time when England was in political, cultural, and intellectual turmoil. Tudor England is often viewed in terms of its flourishing Renaissance culture and the transformative effect of the Reformation. It was also a period marked by more or less open plunder. When Henry VII took the throne in 1485, ending the thirty-year War of the Roses between the Tudors and the Yorks, he used the financial weapons of attainder and forfeiture to restore the power of the English crown and subdue the aristocracy. Fifty years later, his son, Henry VIII, seized land from Catholic monasteries and distributed it to his supporters. In the years between, their subjects competed for patronage from the Crown in the form of jobs, lands, pensions, and annuities.

The son of a prominent lawyer and judge, More studied classical languages and literature at Oxford for two years under the patronage of John Morton, then Archbishop of Canterbury. In 1494, his father called him back to London to study common law. By 1515, when he began to write his most famous work, *Utopia*, he was a successful lawyer, served as one of the undersheriffs of London, and held a seat in Parliament. He devoted his leisure time to scholarship, becoming part of the international fraternity of northern humanists led by the radical Catholic theologian Desiderius Erasmus.

eFACT

Humanist philosophers of the fifteenth and sixteenth centuries turned to the classical texts of Greece and Rome as a way of understanding man's life on earth. Northern humanists also used their Greek to study the New Testament and Church Fathers as part of a campaign to reform the Catholic Church from within.

In 1515, More traveled to Bruges as part of a delegation to negotiate a commercial treaty with the Flemish. His discussions with Erasmus and other humanists scholars while in Flanders inspired him to write the political tract that earned him a permanent place in the history of thought: *A Pamphlet truly Golden no less beneficial than enjoyable concerning the republic's best state and concerning the new Island Utopia,* better known simply as *Utopia.*

Published in Leuven in 1516, the book was an immediate success with its intended audience: More's fellow humanists and the elite circle of public officials whom he soon joined. The book went quickly into several editions and was soon translated from Latin into most European languages.

FACT

More's other claim to fame was his refusal to support Henry VIII's divorce from Catherine of Aragon and subsequent marriage to Anne Boleyn. More saw both acts as an assault on the church; Henry saw More's refusal as treason. More was tried and executed on July 7, 1535. He was canonized by Pope Pius XI 400 years later.

The Society of Utopia

More's *Utopia* is divided into two parts. The first part is written in the form of a dialogue between More and an imaginary traveler who has recently returned from newly discovered lands, including the island nation of Utopia. In comparing the traveler's accounts of the imaginary countries he visited with the actual countries of sixteenth-century Europe, More criticizes the social conditions of his day, particularly what he describes as "acquisitiveness" and "retaining" on the part of the wealthy and the "terrible necessity of hunger" that drove the poor to crimes against society.

In the second half of the tract, More describes in detail the social, political, economic, and religious conditions of an imaginary society on the island of Utopia.

ESSENTIAL

More created a new word to describe his ideal community, combining the Greek negative *ou* with *topos* (place) to create *utopia*, no-place—a pun on *eu-topos*, good place. Utopia is now used to describe a place too good to be real. In 1868, John Stuart Mill created its antonym, dystopia, to describe a place too bad to exist.

Like later reformers who shared his concerns about the negative effects of urbanization and industrialism, More proposed a small agrarian community as the prototype for the perfect society. His goal was an egalitarian society that did away with both idleness born of wealth and excessive labor due to poverty. In *Utopia*, everyone performed useful work and everyone had time for appropriate leisure. All citizens worked in both farm and town so that all acquired skills in both a trade and in agriculture. No type of work was held in higher esteem than any other and no money was required. Each family took what they produced to one of four public markets and received what they needed in return.

There was no private property. Individual family houses were assigned every ten years by lottery. Although families were free to eat meals in their homes, most preferred to eat in the common dining halls that were shared between thirty families because eating together was more pleasant than eating alone.

The government of Utopia was a combination of republic and meritocracy, in which a select few ruled with the consent of the governed. Every citizen had a voice in government and secret ballots were used so no man could be persecuted because of his vote. Each group of thirty families elected a magistrate (*philarch*). The magistrates chose an *archphilarch*, who in turn elected a prince. (Like United States Supreme Court justices, the prince was appointed for life.) Even though all citizens had a vote, not all citizens were eligible for office. Important officials could only be chosen from a limited group, who were selected because of their superior gifts.

More's Influence on Later Thinkers

More wrote *Utopia* more than 300 years before the word *socialism* first appeared in the language of social reform. Nonetheless, early socialists found much to emulate in his writing, including:

- The abolition of private property
- The universal obligation to work
- The right to an equal share of society's wealth
- The concept of equal rights under the law
- State management and control of production

The First Step Toward Equality: England Challenges the Divine Right of Kings

The death of the last Tudor monarch, Elizabeth I, in 1603 placed a new ruling family on the throne of England—the Stuarts of Scotland. The Stuart kings came with philosophical baggage that many Englishmen felt was a step backward into the Middle Ages: close ties to the Catholic Church and a strong belief in the divine rights of kings.

The English Civil War

When the second Stuart king, Charles I, inherited the throne in 1625, he immediately found himself at odds with Parliament over his annoying habit of imposing taxes without the approval of the legislature and his mild treatment of English Catholics. In 1628, Parliament passed a lengthy "Petition of Right," which listed the legislature's grievances against the king, including illegal taxation, the forced billeting of troops, the imposition of martial law, and arbitrary imprisonment. The king responded by dissolving Parliament.

For eleven years, Charles I ruled without a Parliament. He relied for advice on his French Catholic queen, Henrietta Maria, and the conservative Anglican bishop, William Laud. In 1637, Bishop Laud convinced the king to impose a pre-Reformation version of the Anglican liturgy on Calvinist Scotland. Scotland rose up in rebellion. Unable to afford the "Bishops' War," Charles I reconvened Parliament in 1640, thinking it was the easiest way to raise money quickly.

The move backfired. The new Parliament agreed to fund the war only if the king accepted severe limitations on royal power. Charles dissolved the Short Parliament after only three weeks, but was forced to convene a new Parliament only seven months later.

FACT

During Cromwell's rule, Parliament abolished the House of Lords, the monarchy, and the official Church of England. Some didn't think the reformers went far enough. One group, known as Levellers, argued that all adult males should have the vote, whether they owned property or not. Another group, the Diggers, wanted to eliminate private property altogether.

By 1642, differences between Charles I and what became known as the *Long Parliament* escalated into war between the Royalists, known as *Cavaliers*, and the supporters of Parliament, known as *Roundheads*. The English Civil War ended in 1649 with the execution of King Charles I for treason and the establishment first of the Commonwealth of England (1649–1653) and later the Protectorate (1653–1658) under Oliver Cromwell's personal rule.

The Glorious Revolution

After Cromwell's death in 1658, England was ready for a change from military rule and Puritan ethics. In 1660, Parliament invited Charles II to return from exile and become king.

Problems between monarch and Parliament began once more when Charles II's younger and openly Catholic brother, James II, inherited the throne in 1685. Within three years, James alienated every important political faction in England and repeatedly defied the laws imposing restrictions on Catholics and dissenters. Anxiety about the future of English Protestantism grew after the birth of James's son in 1688. Confronted with a Catholic heir to the throne, Whigs and Tories joined together to invite the king's Protestant son-in-law, William of Orange, to invade England. William landed at Torbay with a Dutch army in November 1688; abandoned by most of his officers, James fled to France.

Parliament offered the vacant throne to William and his wife, James's daughter Mary. This time Britain wasn't taking any chances. The offer required the royal couple to accept a Declaration of Rights that established principles of Parliamentary supremacy and denounced James II for attempting to subvert the Protestant religion and the laws of the realm. William and Mary accepted. The divine right of kings was dead in Britain.

Utopia Revised

James Harrington (1611–1677) was an aristocrat by birth and served as a Gentleman of the Bedchamber to Charles I from 1647 until the king's execution on January 30, 1649. After the king's death, Harrington retreated to his country estate to study the forces that led England to civil war.

Like Karl Marx after him, Harrington built his philosophical system on an examination of historical cause and effect. After considering the many constitutional, religious, and economic differences between Charles I and Parliament, Harrington came to the conclusion that the underlying cause for the Civil War, also known as the Puritan Revolution, was the uneven distribution of land ownership, not disagreements over the theory of the divine right of kings or the legality of Catholicism in England.

Harrington made a distinction between power and authority. Power was based on wealth, which he called the "goods of fortune," the most important of which was land. Authority was based on the "goods of the mind," namely wisdom, prudence, and courage. The best rulers combined both.

Since power was based on wealth, rather than on wisdom, property was the foundation of the state. The way property was distributed between "the one, the few, and the many" reflected the form of the government. In an absolute monarchy, the balance of property was in control of one man, the king, and mercenaries maintained the rule of law. In what Harrington called a "mixed monarchy," the nobles (the few) owned the land and controlled the military. In a commonwealth, property ownership was spread among the many and defended by citizen soldiers. Harrington concluded that if the concentration of property in the hands of a few inevitably created political instability, the only form of government that could last was an "equal commonwealth" that avoided both domination by an oligarchy and the anarchy of popular rule.

The Commonwealth of Oceana

In *The Commonwealth of Oceana* (1656), Harrington proposed a social program designed to avoid the problems that led to the English Civil War. Concerned more with social order than with social justice, his goal was to create a society in which "no man or men . . . can have the interest, or having the interest, can have the power to disturb [the commonwealth] with sedition."

Since power depends on wealth, Harrington believed that the way to ensure political stability was to prevent the concentration of property in the hands of a few families. In England, the common practice of primogeniture, in which the eldest son inherits all or most of a father's property, allowed the wealthy to accumulate and transmit property, and consequently political power, from one generation to another. In *Oceana,* a man's property was divided equally among his children at his death, so power remained widely distributed.

Harrington also deterred the development of an oligarchy through a strict division of power between the legislative and executive branches of government. Power was further separated in the legislature, which was made up of two houses with distinct responsibilities. The upper chamber, called the senate after the Roman legislature, was responsible for proposing and debating policy but had no power to enact law. The lower house was responsible for voting on the policies the upper house proposed, but was not allowed to propose or debate policy. Representatives of the upper house were drawn from a "natural aristocracy" gifted with the "goods of the mind." Representatives of the lower house were drawn from the people. Representatives for both houses were elected by indirect ballot and held their positions for fixed terms on a rotating basis. The electorate and pool from which representatives were chosen included all adult male property holders, with two exceptions. Bachelors and attorneys could vote but could not hold office because they lacked the necessary public spirit.

QUESTION

Why do some of Harrington's ideas sound so familiar?
Thomas Jefferson studied Harrington's ideas and incorporated many of them into the Constitution of the United States, including the bicameral Congress, the indirect election of the President, and the separation of powers.

Reactions to *Oceana*

Harrington's ideas made a brief entrance into the world of practical politics in the confused period after Cromwell's death in 1658. Many of those who were opposed to restoring the House of Lords unsuccessfully proposed variations of Harrington's two-house Parliament in its place.

Harrington found a new audience in the eighteenth century among Enlightenment philosophers and revolutionaries interested in the idea of a commonwealth. The French constitution of 1799 was based on *Oceana.*

The Social Contract

Like Harrington, Thomas Hobbes (1588–1679) lived during the political chaos of the Civil War, the Restoration, and the Glorious Revolution. The son of an Anglican clergyman who abandoned his family, Hobbes was raised by his uncle, a wealthy glove maker, and educated at Oxford. After graduating, he became the tutor to William Cavendish, later the Earl of Devonshire. Exposed to the clashes between king and Parliament through his employment with the Cavendish family, Hobbes became a firm Royalist. In 1640, he wrote his first work of political philosophy, a treatise defending Charles I's interpretation of his royal prerogatives. Titled *The Elements of Law, Natural and Politic*, the pamphlet was distributed in manuscript form and quoted by Royalists in Parliamentary debates on the divine right of kings. Seeing trouble on the way, Hobbes fled to Paris, where he remained for the next eleven years. (During his years in Paris, he worked briefly as a mathematics tutor for the future Charles II.)

While in self-imposed exile, Hobbes published his best-known work, *Leviathan, or the Matter, Form and Power of a Commonwealth, Ecclesiastical and Civil* (1651). In it, Hobbes laid out a new basis for the state. Instead of resting on divine appointment, political authority was the result of a social contract in which people voluntarily gave up some of their rights in exchange for security.

Hobbes believed that people are always guided by their own self-interest, and without government the natural life of man was "solitary, poor, nasty, brutish and short." Most people do not have the ability to defend themselves against competitors. With no natural common standards of behavior to which everyone agrees, life in a state of nature was "a war of every man against every man." The only way for people to protect themselves against each other was to create a government, effectively signing a social contract that gives a single man the responsibility for the safety of all and the authority to enforce the law.

Hobbes's version of the social contract required a ruler with more absolute authority than that provided by the divine right of kings. His ruler enjoyed absolute control over the army, the law, and even the interpretation of scripture.

According to Hobbes, the worst despot is better than no government or a weak government. Only when a ruler fails so completely that subjects feel they are worse off than they were in Hobbes's theoretical "state of nature" do his subjects have the right to rise up against their ruler.

Hobbes intended *Leviathan* as a handbook for rulers. He gave a specially bound copy to Prince Charles, who felt the suggestion that subjects have the right to unseat a failed ruler came a bit too close to home. The French government was equally unhappy with Hobbes's idea that the king was the supreme interpreter of scripture, which they saw as an attack on the spiritual authority of the pope. No longer welcome in France, Hobbes returned home to Britain and made his peace with Cromwell's variation of absolute rule.

The Natural Rights of Man

The son of an attorney who fought on the side of Parliament in the English Civil War, British philosopher John Locke (1632–1704) is often considered the first philosopher of the Enlightenment. He studied the standard classics curriculum at Oxford, but was more interested in the new ideas about the nature and origin of knowledge that were developed by the natural philosophers of the sixteenth century.

In 1666, several years after Charles II took the throne, Locke found a patron: Lord Anthony Ashley Cooper, later the first Earl of Shaftsbury. Locke and Shaftsbury shared numerous political positions, including support for constitutional monarchy, the Protestant succession, civil liberties, religious tolerance, and Parliamentary rule. Through Shaftsbury, Locke was actively involved in the debates over whether James II should be excluded from the succession to the throne. When his patron was arrested, tried, and acquitted of treason in 1681, Locke followed him into exile in the Netherlands.

e! ALERT

Hobbes and Locke both use the term *social contract* to discuss the basic nature of government, but they don't mean exactly the same thing. In Hobbes's version, the many trade their liberty to one strong man in exchange for safety. In Locke's, citizens give up the power of personally enforcing the laws of nature in order to avoid injustice.

Locke wrote *Two Treatises on Government* (1689) as a justification for the Glorious Revolution. In the first treatise, he refutes the divine right of kings. In the second, Locke argues that all men are born with certain natural rights, including the right to survive and the right to have the means to survive, with the corollary obligation not to harm others. Each society creates a government to protect those rights.

Locke took the rights of citizens under the social contract further than Hobbes. Since government exists by the consent of the governed and not by the divine right of kings, citizens have the right to withdraw their consent if a government fails in its duty to protect their rights.

The *Philosophes*

The eighteenth-century philosophical and scientific movement known as the Enlightenment was dominated by a group of French writers, scientists, and philosophers who called themselves *philosophes*. The *philosophes* were bound together by a core set of values that included the power of reason, the perfectibility of man, and skepticism about existing social and political institutions.

Few of the *philosophes* were philosophers in the strictest sense of the word. They wrote works in every available format on history, science, politics, economics, social issues, and the arts, applying reason to them all.

FACT

France wasn't the only center of Enlightenment thought. A parallel movement known as the Scottish Enlightenment flourished in Edinburgh and Glasgow around 1740. Its most prominent members were the economist Adam Smith and the philosopher David Hume. A "Society of gentlemen in Scotland" issued the first edition of the *Encyclopedia Britannica* in 1768 in imitation of the French *Encyclopédie*.

Individually and as a group, the *philosophes* used reason to challenge traditional assumptions about Church, state, monarchy, education, and social institutions. They did not reach a unified conclusion. Some built on Locke's idea that a prince is only the delegate for his people. Others, most notably Voltaire, supported the ideal of the enlightened despot who ruled with the intention of improving the lives of his people. Many of them ended up in jail or exile, their books banned or burned, as a result of their insistence on proving that the absolute monarch had no clothes.

The great collective work of the *philosophes* was the creation of the *Encyclopédie*, seventeen volumes of text and eleven volumes of illustrations published between 1751 and 1765. Edited by the philosopher Denis Diderot and mathematician Jean le Rond d'Alembert, with contributions from most of the important thinkers of the day, the *Encyclopédie* was meant to summarize the knowledge of its time. The *Encyclopédie*'s editors made no attempt at neutrality. In addition to technical articles on mathematics, science, traditional crafts, and technology, the *Encyclopédie* were filled with articles that criticized the French government and the Catholic Church. Both made efforts to suppress the work, and the publisher was arrested.

The Origins of Inequality

Jean-Jacques Rousseau (1712–1778) was one of the most influential of the *philosophes*. He was born in the Swiss city-state of Geneva—a small Calvinist republic surrounded by large Catholic monarchies. Rousseau left Geneva when he was sixteen. After several years as the protégé of a Swiss baroness with a taste for introducing young men to Catholicism, he found his way to Paris, where he was swept up in the intellectual circles of the *philosophes*. He was a prolific writer on a wide range of subjects, including education, botany, music, and the effects of theater on public morals.

In his political writings, Rousseau began from the position that "a people is everywhere nothing but what its government makes of it." For the most part, he felt the government botched the job.

In *Discourses on the Origins of Inequality* (1755), Rousseau distinguished between natural and social inequality. Natural inequality is based on differences in strength, intelligence, or talents. Social inequality is based solely on conventions and is the source of man's ills.

According to Rousseau, mankind was naturally good as long as he lived alone, but was gradually corrupted by society and civilization. Man's decline began from the moment the first hut was built. As man formed himself into communities, he began to make comparisons, which led to the perception of inequalities and jealousies.

The second step on the path of corruption was the invention of property. Rousseau declared, "The first man who, having enclosed a piece of ground, thought up the statement 'this is mine' and found people simple enough to believe him . . . was the real founder of civil society." The invention of property led to the need for laws and government to protect it, a false social contract imposed on the weak by the strong. The creation of government led to power, which led to further privileges and still more inequality.

In his later *Social Contract* (1772), Rousseau suggested that mankind could recover its freedom through a genuine social contract based on the general will that allowed both security and a return to man's natural freedom.

The Invisible Hand of the Marketplace

Considered the founder of modern economics, Adam Smith (1723–1790) was an important figure in the Scottish Enlightenment. In 1776, Smith published *An Inquiry into the Nature and Causes of the Wealth of Nations*, which he intended to be the first volume of a complete theory of society. *The Wealth of Nations* was the first major work of political economy.

At first glance, *The Wealth of Nations* seems like an unlikely source of socialist thought. In it, Smith examined the market economy in detail for the first time. He overturned old ideas of wealth when he identified labor, not gold or land, as the true source of wealth. He demonstrated how the law of supply and demand regulates the prices of specific goods. He examined how capital is accumulated and used. He took fascinating side excursions into the manufacture of pins, luxury goods produced under the Abbasid Caliphate, and statistics on the North Atlantic herring catch.

At its heart, *The Wealth of Nations* is an attack on the dominant economic theory of the time: mercantilism. Under mercantilism, governments created elaborate systems of regulations, tariffs, and monetary controls to protect their economies. Smith proposed a free market in which the "invisible hand" of the marketplace replaces government control and brings prosperity to all, coining the word *capitalism* to distinguish it from mercantilism. It was a newly democratic vision of wealth, based on Smith's belief that "No society can surely be flourishing and happy, of which by far the greater part of the numbers are poor and miserable."

The Foundations of Socialist Thought

The political theorists of the sixteenth and seventeenth centuries laid the foundation for later socialist thought with their enquiries into the relationship between the one, the few, and the many. Questions of equality and inequality, the distribution of wealth, the basis for authority, and the rights of man (narrowly defined) were now part of the public discourse.

CHAPTER 2

The Industrial Revolution and the New Proletariat

Modern socialism has its roots in the mills and slums of the Industrial Revolution. The ability to make goods quickly and cheaply soared as men found more and more ways to use machines to extend the productivity of a single man. Many welcomed machines and the wealth they created as the embodiment of progress. Others were troubled by the conditions under which the new urban poor lived and worked. A few began to consider ways in which the fruits of this growth in productivity could be shared more equally.

The Eighteenth-Century Population Explosion

After a century of virtually no population growth, the countries of Western Europe experienced dramatic population increases between 1750 and 1800. Many countries doubled in size. In some countries, the growth continued through the nineteenth century. The population of Great Britain, for instance, doubled between 1750 and 1800 and then tripled between 1800 and 1900.

FACT

The Industrial Revolution was paralleled by an agricultural revolution in Great Britain. New horse-drawn machinery, better fodder crops, extensive land drainage projects, and scientific stockbreeding increased agricultural productivity. But improved farming had a social cost. Between 1760 and 1799, large landowners fenced in between 2 and 3 million acres of common land that small farmers used for grazing.

There were several reasons for the sudden increase. Medical advances and improved hygiene limited the devastation caused by epidemic diseases and plagues. The introduction of new food crops, most notably the potato, provided a better diet for the poor and reduced the incidence of famine. The combination of greater public order and fewer civil wars meant that life was less hazardous. The net result was a lower death rate and soaring populations.

The growing population, with a rising proportion of children to raise and older people to care for, put increased pressure on every aspect of society. Many peasants were no longer able to provide land for their children, who were forced to look for other ways to make their living. Small artisans in the cities suffered similar problems, unable to provide places for their children in their own workshops.

The exact relationship between population growth and industrialization is unclear, though the two are clearly intertwined. (Even countries that were late to industrialize shared in the general population increase, and its related problems.) What is clear is that the growth in population increased the demand for both food and manufactured goods and provided an abundance of cheap labor to produce them.

Weaving Becomes a Modern Industry

The Industrial Revolution began in the English textile industry. Textiles had been an important part of the English economy for centuries. On the eve of the Industrial Revolution, England's fine wools were famous. Linen production was expanding into Ireland and Scotland. Only the cotton industry was small and backward, unable to compete with Indian calico and muslin on either quality or price.

Weaving was a domestic industry in the first half of the eighteenth century. Except in Manchester, where self-employed weaver-artisans belonged to highly organized trade societies, most weavers were also farmers. In many households, weaving was done in the seasons when there was little work to do on the farm. Often the entire family was involved. Children sorted, cleaned, and carded the raw fibers, women spun the yarn, and men wove the cloth.

The first changes were small. John Kay's flying shuttle, introduced in the 1730s and widely adopted in the 1750s and 1760s, allowed the weaver to speed up. Lewis Paul's carding machine, patented in 1748, made it easier to prepare fibers for spinning. Both inventions intensified a supply problem that already existed: Spinners were the bottleneck in the system. It took three or four spinners to supply yarn for one weaver working a traditional loom. When the fly-shuttle allowed a weaver to speed up, the yarn shortage became acute. The problem was worse in the harvest season, when women could make the same wage more easily by working in the fields.

James Hargreave's spinning jenny, patented in 1770, solved the yarn supply problem. Family spinning wheels were quickly replaced by small jennies, which were relatively cheap to buy and simple enough for a child to operate. In its earliest form, the jenny had eight spindles. By 1784, eighty spindles were common. By the end of the century, the largest jennies allowed one man, helped by several children, to operate as many as 120 spindles at once.

As spinning jennies grew bigger, spinning began to be moved into factories, but the new factory system did not replace the cottage-based textile industry immediately. At first, families built extensions onto their cottages where they could operate looms and jennies on a larger scale. Mill owners provided home-based spinners with raw cotton and handloom weavers with spun yarn. Because weavers could count on uninterrupted supplies of yarn, they could afford to weave full time instead of as a supplement to farming.

A Brief Period of Prosperity for Weavers

From the 1770s through the 1790s, a skilled weaver could earn three times the average farm laborer's weekly wages. With weaving no longer a part-time job, weavers began to move into towns. The new weaving communities that developed had strong leanings toward Wesleyanism and political Radicalism, both of which fostered values of independence and self-education. Every weaving district had its self-taught poets, botanists, and geologists. Writing in 1828, when hand loom weaving was almost dead, William Radcliffe, a spinner who became a factory owner, described these weaving communities nostalgically:

> *Their dwellings and small gardens neat and clean—all the family well clad—the men with each a watch in his pocket and the women dressed to their own fancy—the church crowded to excess every Sunday—every house well-furnished with a clock in elegant mahogany or fancy case—handsome tea services in Staffordshire ware . . . Birmingham, Potteries, and Sheffield wares for necessary use and ornament . . . many cottages had their own cow.*

Prosperity did not last long. The trade soon became over-crowded. Wages began to drop as early as 1798.

The Birth of the Factory System

The real change in the English weaving industry began in 1769, when Richard Arkwright patented the water frame, which improved both the speed and quality of thread spinning. Unlike the jenny, Arkwright's water-powered spinning frame was designed to be a factory machine.

A few years later, Samuel Crompton's mule combined the principles of the jenny and the water frame, producing a smoother, finer yarn that allowed English cotton to compete with Indian goods in terms of quality.

In 1795, Arkwright's patent was canceled, making the water frame available without restrictions for anyone who could afford the capital investment. That same year, a steam engine was used to operate a spinning mill for the first time. Large-scale factory production was now feasible.

Improvements in spinning technologies were followed by carding, scutching, and roving machines that replaced the tedious hand labor of preparing fibers for spinning. Each technical improvement moved the textile industry further away from the domestic system. By 1812, one spinner could produce as much yarn in a given time as 200 spinners could have produced using hand spindles.

FACT

Parliament passed the first child labor law in 1802. Aimed at "apprenticeship" of orphans in cotton mills, it had no enforcement provisions—and little effect. The use of child labor was largely unchecked until the Factory Act of 1833, which set the legal work age at nine and limited children between nine and thirteen to a forty-eight hour workweek.

The factory system was more than just a new way to organize work, it was a new way of life. Factories were dark, loud, and dangerous. The discipline and monotonous routine of the mill was very different from the workday of farmer or hand weaver. Both agricultural workers and weavers often worked fourteen-hour days. But agricultural work was varied and seasonal and independent weavers controlled their own schedules. In the factories, the same fourteen hours included few breaks plus a long walk to and from home at each end of the day. Supervisors discouraged workers from song or chatter—either of which were hard to hear over the noise. As more women and children were hired, the fathers of families were thrown permanently out of work.

The Growth of Factory Towns

As long as the new spinning mills were powered by water, they were scattered throughout northern England, located wherever falling water was available. Many of these mills were in places so isolated that their owners had trouble attracting enough labor, so they employed groups of children from London orphanages as "apprentices." With the introduction of steam power, it was possible to locate mills anywhere. Most were built near sources of coal and labor.

The key industrial cities grew at an astonishing rate in the first half of the nineteenth century, fueled by the internal migration of displaced workers, artisans, and shopkeepers in search of opportunities. The most rapid growth occurred in factory cities, like Manchester, Liverpool, and Birmingham, but port cities also grew as a result of expanded overseas trade. As governments took on more responsibilities, administrative cities swelled in size. Some older towns, untouched by the new industries or bypassed by the railroads, declined in size. By 1850, more than half the British population lived in cities.

A Change in Landscape

The new cities were ugly to the nineteenth-century eye: raw as a new suburb and dark with the soot from burning coal. Contemporary observers were appalled by the impact of what poet William Blake described as the "dark, Satanic mills," on the physical landscape. Critic John Ruskin foresaw an England "set as thick with chimneys as the masts stand in the docks of Liverpool with no meadows . . . no trees, no gardens." Socialist artist William Morris feared that all would "end in a counting house on the top of a cinder heap, with the pleasures of the eyes having gone from the world." It took a foreigner, that keen-eyed observer Alexis de Tocqueville, to equate the physical ugliness of the mill towns with their effect on the people who worked in them: "Here civilization makes its miracles, and civilized man is turned back almost into a savage," he wrote after a visit to Manchester. "From this foul drain the greatest stream of human industry flows out to fertilize the world. From this filthy sewer pure gold flows. Here humanity attains its most complete development and its most brutish."

The Power Loom and the Decline of Wages

Weavers' wages, already driven down by the increase in weavers, took another hit when power looms were introduced on a large scale in the 1820s. Handlooms required skill to operate. Power looms did not.

QUESTION

Who were the Luddites?
In 1811 and 1812, masked bands of displaced textile workers attacked mills and destroyed the machines that were threatening their livelihood, calling themselves Luddites, after a possibly mythical leader named Captain Ned Ludd. The bands were careful not to attack villagers or damage other property and often had tacit local support. The government responded by making machine breaking punishable by death.

Independent skilled weavers began to be replaced by unskilled factory labor, mostly women and children. Demobilized soldiers from the Napoleonic wars, unemployed farm workers, and Irish immigrants swelled the work force and drove wages down further. Because there were few other jobs available, wages remained low even when the market for British textiles boomed. Between 1820 and 1845, the cotton industry's production quadrupled; the wages it paid remained unchanged.

Handloom weavers clung to their independence in spite of the relentless pressure on their wages. A few weavers managed to hold on to their status as artisans because they had special skills. Many weavers were in constant debt to the mill owners who supplied them with yarn, an arrangement similar to that between landowners and sharecroppers in the American South after the Civil War. Most weavers lived on the edge of starvation, working longer and longer hours to earn less and less. A Parliamentary Select Committee investigating the condition of the weavers in 1835 found that many could not afford food of even the cheapest kind, were clothed in rags, slept on straw, and worked sixteen hour days.

A Second Wave of Industry

The industrialization of Britain's textile industry created a demand for tools, machines, and power that spurred the development of improvements in forging steel and mining coal. The original wooden machines were replaced with faster and more specialized machinery, built from metal by a nascent machine tool industry.

Steam engines provided a source of reliable and continuous power. First used for hauling coal from mines, the new technology was adapted to other industries as well. Soon steam engines were used in grain mills, sugar refineries, and the great British potteries. The need for improved transportation led to the expansion of the canal system and the later development of roads and railways.

The Creation of the Urban Proletariat

The Industrial Revolution created a new class of urban poor, as populations shifted from the countryside to the cities. The first generation that moved to the city often retained their rural roots, returning to their villages at harvest or for family celebrations. Over time, ties to ancestral villages broke and city dwellers saw themselves as substantially different from those who remained behind in the village.

ESSENTIAL

> The Industrial Revolution also created a new class of wealthy manufacturers. A few were weavers and spinners who worked their way up from artisan to mill owner. Most started as small landowners or businessmen. They were a volatile element in a changing society: sometimes competing with wealthy landowners for power and status, sometimes joining with them to fight social change.

The transition from countryside to the city was often difficult. Living conditions in the cities were horrific for the poor. Cities were unable to handle the influx of new residents. Sewers were open in working-class districts and water supplies were inadequate. Older cities paved the streets in the mid-eighteenth century, but in new cities the streets were often no better than rutted paths. Existing housing was divided and re-divided to create space; families often had only one room, or shared a room with another family. New housing was equally cramped and often badly built.

The increases in hygiene and medicine that contributed to the population explosion of the late eighteenth century city had no impact on the great industrial cities; disease and epidemics flourished. The mortality rate was high. And yet the cities continued to grow.

Contemporary Commentators

By the middle of the nineteenth century, the conditions under which the industrial workers lived began to attract the attention of social observers. Some of them documented the life of the new urban poor, most notably Friedrich Engels, in *The Condition of the Working Class in England* (originally published in German in 1845 and translated into English in 1888), and Henry Mayhew, in *London Labour and the London Poor* (1851–1862). Novelists such as Charles Dickens and Mary Gaskell reached much larger audiences with their accounts of life in the mills.

The Rise of Working-Class Radicalism

The working classes did not wait for middle-class reformers to come to their rescue. Members of the working classes began to call for reform at the end of the eighteenth century, appealing to Parliament for minimum wage laws, apprenticeship regulations, child labor laws, and other protections for laborers, forming early versions of trade unions, and going on strike.

They soon came to the conclusion, as middle-class reformers had earlier in the century, that the only way to affect real change was to reform the method of electing representatives to the House of Commons. As long as the landed classes controlled both houses of Parliament, there was no hope for reform.

Working-class radicals formed organizations called corresponding societies, which were designed to allow reformers from all over the country to stay in touch with each other. The most famous of these was the London Corresponding Society, formed in 1792 by radical shoemaker Thomas Hardy. Similar societies existed in industrial towns throughout Great Britain. As long as the corresponding societies remained local, the government left them alone. In 1793, a Scottish reform group attempted to bring representatives of many reform organizations to a meeting in Scotland. The leaders were arrested, tried for sedition, and sentenced to fourteen years' transportation. The leaders of a second attempt to organize a national reform meeting led to charges of high treason.

Reactions to the French Revolution

The French Revolution brought the march toward reform to a halt. The aristocracy was interested in repressing the rise of "Jacobin" conspiracies; manufacturers were interested in keeping wages low. Alarmed by the French example, and the enthusiasm with which it was greeted by some British radicals, the landed classes and manufacturers joined together against the radicals. Existing legislation related to apprenticeship, wage-regulation, and conditions in industry was repealed. Existing laws against conspiracy were re-enforced by the Combination Acts of 1799 and 1800, which made it illegal for workingmen to "combine" to ask for higher wages or shorter work hours, or to incite other men to leave work.

Peace and Poverty

England suffered a severe depression at the end of the Napoleonic war as a result of the transition to a peacetime economy. The sudden drop in government spending and the loss of wartime markets for British grain and manufactured goods brought with them falling prices, unstable currency, and widespread unemployment.

Dominated by landowners in both the House of Lords and the Commons, Parliament passed protective tariffs on grain as a way of solving the country's economic woes. The new Corn Laws protected landowners' incomes but forced urban laborers to pay a higher price for bread when times were already hard.

Workers reacted with strikes and bread riots across England. Moderate and radical reformers called for the repeal of the Corn Law and for parliamentary reform in large public meetings. In 1817, the government attempted to de-fang the reform societies by temporarily forbidding all public meetings, suppressing all societies not licensed by the government, and suspending the Habeas Corpus Act, so that prisoners could be held without trial.

These severe measures brought only a temporary lull in popular demonstrations. In 1819, Britain's economic problems became worse. Reformers once again held mass meetings in the larger industrial cities. The most famous of these became known as the Peterloo Massacre. In August 1819, 60,000 workers gathered on St. Peter's Field in Manchester to hear radical orator Henry Hunt (1773–1835). Fearful that a large group of reformers would turn into a large group of rioters, the local magistrate ordered a squadron of cavalry into the peaceful crowd to arrest Hunt. Eleven people were killed and several hundred were injured.

The government moved quickly to deter future demonstrations. Hunt and eight other organizers of the Manchester meeting were arrested and charged with holding "an unlawful and seditious assembling [sic] for the purpose of exciting discontent." Parliament passed the Six Acts: a series of drastic restrictions intended to eliminate unauthorized public meetings, suppress the radical press, and make it easier to convict popular leaders.

The Working-Class Movement Takes Another Path

The radical movement subsided after 1820, thanks to increased government repression and an economic upturn. For the next decade, the working-class movement focused less on reform and more on building cooperative institutions: trade unions, friendly societies, mutual aid societies, and Workingmen's Institutes. By 1832, when Parliament passed a reform act that gave the vote to much of the middle class, strong, self-consciously working-class institutions were in place to take up the battle.

The Industrial Revolution in Continental Europe

At first, the Industrial Revolution was a British phenomenon. Britain was determined to hold on to its manufacturing lead and made it illegal to export machinery or manufacturing technology. Skilled workers were not allowed to emigrate. It took a full generation for the Industrial Revolution to spread from Great Britain to the rest of Europe, or at least to Belgium, France, and the United States.

Other European powers lagged even further behind. Some parts of Germany, for example, did not begin industrial expansion until unification in 1870.

CHAPTER 3

The First Socialist Revolution

In 1789, the French people rose up chanting the slogan "Equality, Fraternity, Liberty." One revolutionary, François-Noël Babeuf, thought the French Revolution didn't go far enough. Yes, feudal titles and privileges were overturned as a result of the revolution, but one element of the *Ancien Régime* remained intact: the right of private property. According to Babeuf, the only way to guarantee equality was to abolish individual ownership of property and divide the wealth equally between all citizens. In 1796, Babeuf and the "Conspiracy of Equals" began to plot the first socialist revolution.

The French Revolution, Part I

In 1787, after almost forty years of growth, the French economy was a total mess. People at every level of society were complaining. Longstanding feudal privileges for the nobility and Catholic clergy meant that commoners, known as the Third Estate, bore the largest tax burden. A serious increase in the population drove the price of food up at the same time that wages were going down. Newly wealthy merchants and manufacturers resented the social and political privileges enjoyed by the clergy and nobility. The nobility couldn't be taxed, but they could be pressured into loaning the king large amounts of money—money it didn't look like he was able to repay. Even Louis XVI was under duress: Half the government's annual expenditure was interest on debt.

ALERT

> One of the most common misconceptions about revolutions is that they occur in times of economic depression. In fact, revolutions often occur during relative prosperity when the rising expectations of classes in the middle of society are not met.

The Estates-General and the National Assembly of France

Ironically, it was the prosperous nobility who took the first step in what became the French Revolution. In 1787 they refused to loan the king any more money and demanded restrictions on royal spending. Pressured by the nobility, Louis XVI reluctantly convened an assembly of the Estates-General, which had not met since 1614.

The nobility expected to control the Estates-General with the help of representatives of the clergy. Instead, some members of the lower clergy joined forces with the representatives of the Third Estate, who were mostly prosperous members of the bourgeoisie. On June 17, 1789, this new coalition proclaimed themselves representatives of the nation instead of individual Estates, and renamed the Estates-General the "National Assembly of France." On June 27, the king instructed representatives of the nobility and clergy to join the new legislative body, and the National Assembly began its self-appointed task of writing a constitution.

FACT

The Estates-General was formed in the fourteenth century as an advisory body to the French king. It included representatives from the three "estates" of French society: the Catholic clergy were the First Estate, the nobility was the Second Estate, and the Third Estate included the commoners, from wealthy merchants down to beggars on the street.

Storming the Bastille

Two weeks later, popular demonstrations broke out in the streets of Paris, spurred in part by rumors that the king was planning a military coup against the Assembly, and in part because conditions grew worse for urban artisans and wage-earners between 1787 and 1789. Energized by rabble-rousing speeches given by a brilliant young orator from the National Assembly, Maximilien Robespierre, a hungry mob attacked a grain shipment from the country. On July 14, the crowds went after a larger target: the medieval fortress called the Bastille, which was used as a prison and royal armory. With the help of military deserters, the crowd stormed the prison, decapitated its commander, who fired on the crowd after agreeing to negotiations, and released its prisoners. Paris was in rebel hands. The violence soon spread to the countryside, where peasants rose up against local lords.

ALERT

The Bastille was a symbol of royal despotism. Under the *Ancien Régime*, state prisoners could be held without trial with only a sealed warrant signed by the king. When the crowd stormed the fortress, they expected the dungeons to be filled with long-forgotten political prisoners. Instead, they found only seven prisoners: five ordinary criminals and two madmen.

At first, the National Assembly considered striking back. Instead, in a single late night session on August 4th, the Assembly abolished all the feudal rights and privileges of the *Ancien Régime*. On August 27th, they issued a statement of general principles titled the *Declaration of the Rights of Man and of the Citizen.* Its central idea was that all citizens should enjoy certain "natural rights" equally.

One of those "natural rights" was the individual right to own property. François-Noël Babeuf disagreed.

François-Noël Babeuf

Unlike most of the leaders of the French Revolution, François-Noël Babeuf (1760–1797) came from humble origins and knew poverty firsthand. His first job was digging canals, but he didn't dig ditches for long because he had some education. By 1787, he was a successful *feudiste*: an eighteenth-century version of a skip-tracer who researched government archives for nobles who wanted to be sure they collected all the fees and concessions they were entitled to.

The National Assembly put Babeuf out of business when they abolished all feudal privileges, but he soon found new ways to use his old skills on behalf of the Revolution. After a brief stint in Paris, he returned to his native Picardy, where he became involved in agitations against the old regime's taxes on salt and alcohol, founded a newspaper, and proposed a radical program of agrarian reform, including redistribution of land. He was zealous in his self-appointed role as a spokesman for peasants entangled in the legal claims that were created by the abolishment of feudalism; so zealous, in fact, that he was arrested more than once by the local authorities.

FACT

During the French Revolution, men often took names from Roman history as a way of expressing their political fervor. Babeuf took the name Gracchus. Tiberus and Gaius Gracchus were Roman tribunes in the second century B.C.E. who tried to pass land reforms that redistributed patrician land holdings to the plebeians.

Babeuf in Paris

In 1793, charged with fraud as a result of his land reform efforts, Babeuf fled to Paris to escape arrest. Once in Paris, he attached himself to Robespierre, who was one of the leaders of the newly formed French Republic. With Robespierre's patronage he got a job in the Bureau of Subsistence of the Commune, which was responsible for provisioning French military volunteers in Paris. Always a clever clerk, he soon found a discrepancy in the bureau's accounts.

Revolution and the abolition of privilege did nothing to relieve hunger among the lower classes in the cities. The European powers declared war on the Republic of France. The need to requisition foodstuffs for the army led to food riots in Paris. Babeuf believed that the authorities deliberately created a famine in order to profit from the demand for grain. With suspiciously convenient timing, the fraud charges from Picardy caught up with Babeuf just as he demanded a commission of investigation. Babeuf was once again arrested and the commission of investigation was suppressed.

His arrest turned out to be good luck for Babeuf. In jail for eight months, Babeuf escaped the worst of the Reign of Terror and the subsequent backlash against Robespierre and the Jacobins.

The French Revolution, Part II

From 1789 to 1792, France operated as a constitutional monarchy with political power concentrated in the hands of the National Assembly. Many of the nobility, feeling that the new government was increasingly radical, fled the country. The royal family tried to escape as well, in June 1791. They were captured at Varennes and brought back in disgrace. The king was accused of plotting counter-revolution with Austria.

The Creation of the First French Republic

If the nobility felt the new government was too radical, others felt it was too conservative. *The Declaration of the Rights of Man* proclaimed, "men are born and remain free and equal in rights." The Constitution of 1791 abandoned that principle and divided Frenchmen into two classes of citizens, active and passive, based on the amount of property taxes they paid. Only active citizens could vote.

An increasingly radical minority of Parisians were outraged that the Assembly betrayed its promises. The Jacobins, led by Robespierre, were only the most well-known of the radical political "clubs" that were formed throughout the city. These clubs advocated overthrowing the monarchy and establishing a republic. Because the dues were high, membership was limited to the professional classes, but the clubs were able to reach a wider audience through popular pamphlets and newspapers. Soon the populace began to demand that the king be dethroned.

On August 10, 1792, Paris rose again, this time in response to a Prussian threat to restore Louis XVI to full sovereignty. A revolutionary Commune seized control of the municipal government and imprisoned the royal family. In response, the legislative assembly summoned a National Convention, elected by manhood suffrage, to decide the fate of the king and draft a new constitution. The Convention's first acts were to abolish the monarchy and establish the First French Republic.

Members of the Convention soon realized that they were controlled by the *sans-culottes* and not the other way around. Before they held their first meeting, thousands of royalists were killed in a series of uprisings known as the September Massacres. Under pressure from the *sans-culottes*, who expected the new government to produce real change, Jacobin radicals began expelling moderates from the Convention.

eV FACT

Members of the political clubs abandoned the fancy knee breeches worn by upper-class men, known as *culottes*, in favor of the long trousers worn by working men. Politically militant members of the Paris working classes began to call themselves *sans-culottes*.

The Reign of Terror

By the spring of 1793, the Republic was under pressure from inside and out: war with the monarchs of Europe, insurrection in the countryside, and food riots in the cities. The Constitution of 1793 was no sooner ratified when the Jacobins, led by Robespierre, set it aside in favor of revolutionary law, which they claimed was a wartime security measure. Revolutionary law took the form of the Committee of Public Safety, which began its rule by arresting and executing the remaining moderate representatives in the Convention. The Committee had three basic goals:

- Win the European war
- Suppress the enemies of the Republic
- Establish what they called the "Republic of Virtue," based on the teachings of the Enlightenment *philosophes*

In practice, the Committee pursued all three goals by hunting down "enemies of the people" and sending them to the guillotine. People were convicted on reasons that ranged from conspiring against the Republic to showing sympathy for a guillotine victim.

ALERT

People often describe the Reign of Terror as an early example of class warfare, in which the middle and lower classes hunted down the aristocracy and clergy. In fact, only 15 percent of the thousands that were killed between June 1793 and July 1794 were aristocrats. The rest were commoners who supported the king and clergy.

Estimates of the number of people killed during the period known as "the Reign of Terror" vary between 16,000 and 40,000. The Terror reached its height in June 1794, when almost 1,300 people were guillotined in Paris in one month. Robespierre finally went too far when he executed popular leader Georges Danton for "insulting Justice." On July 27, Robespierre was arrested on the floor of the legislature and executed with twenty-one of his followers.

Liberty Does Not Guarantee Equality

Released from jail in June 1794, at the very end of the Reign of Terror, Babeuf began publishing a newspaper, *The Tribune of the People*. In it, he wrote about two basic themes: the size and injustice of the gap that separated the rich from the poor and the appropriate use of political power. He attacked first the Jacobins and later their successors, the Thermidorians and the Directorate, for their violent repression of the people of France. He denounced the new constitution of 1795, which replaced universal suffrage with voting rights based on substantial property qualifications. He argued for the abolition of private property and the redistribution of goods. He called for class warfare—the first known use of a term often attributed to Karl Marx.

Soon the police were after Babeuf again. For a time, he published his paper underground. He was arrested, released, arrested again. In prison, he continued to formulate a social doctrine based on equal distribution of land and income.

The Conspiracy of Equals

In 1796, back out of prison, Babeuf formed a political organization, the Conspiracy of Equals, which was dedicated to completing what its members believed were the aims of the French Revolution. In their eyes, the revolution did away with inequalities of power and rank, but not inequalities based on property and knowledge.

Equality and France's Future

Their goal, proclaimed in a *Manifesto of the Equals*, was "Equality! The first wish of nature, the first need of man." They believed in complete egalitarianism. Inequality of any kind, in any degree, was the source of all crime and vice. It was necessary to "remove from every individual the hope of ever becoming richer, or more powerful, or more distinguished by his intelligence." An egalitarian society would not only eliminate want, it would lead to "the disappearance of boundary-marks, hedges, walls, door-locks, disputes, trials, thefts, murders, all crimes . . . courts, prisons, gallows, penalties . . . envy, jealousy, insatiability, pride, deception, duplicity, in short all vices."

Members of the Conspiracy also developed a blueprint for what French society would look like under their rule. They envisioned a centrally controlled, planned society organized around the principle of strict equality. Cities would be taken apart and the population divided into villages. The government would supply all the necessities of life. There would be equal education. Everyone who was physically able would work, each taking a turn at unpleasant or demanding jobs. People would even eat at communal tables. In order to insure equal opportunity for all,

> *The country takes possession of every individual at birth and never quits him till death. It watches over his first moments, secures him the nourishment and cares of his mother, keeps out of his reach everything that might impair his health or enervate his constitution, guarantees him against the dangers of a false tenderness, and conducts him, by the hand of his parent, to the national seminary [same-sex boarding schools where all children would be raised] where he is to acquire the virtues and intelligence necessary to make him a good citizen.*

In short, the Conspiracy of Equals envisioned a society that combined elements of Thomas More's *Utopia* with George Orwell's Big Brother.

Already dealing with serious threats from the Royalist right, the ruling Directorate was taking no chances with something that looked like a resurgence of the old Jacobin political clubs. A military contingent headed by the young General Napoleon Bonaparte was sent to shut the organization down; Bonaparte is said to have put the padlock on the door himself.

Babeuf Plans a Revolution

Driven underground, the Conspiracy of Equals began to plot a coup. Their plans were an odd mixture of blood bath, dictatorship, and utopia. They envisioned one day of revolutionary frenzy on the part of the Parisian poor followed by a period of dictatorial rule until the work of the revolution could be completed. Apparently having learned nothing from Robespierre's mistakes, the Equals appointed a seven-member Insurrectionary Committee of Public Safety to direct what they saw as the final stage of the revolution that began in 1789.

The "Insurrectionary Act"

As a first step, the Equals adopted an "Insurrectionary Act," which they intended to distribute through the city to ignite the rebellion. The act called for citizens to take up arms and seize the national treasury, the post, the homes of ministers, and "every public or private building containing provisions or ammunition." No one would be allowed to leave Paris without a signed order from the Insurrectionary Committee.

After the citizens seized the city, anyone opposing the revolution would be suppressed by force. Opposition was widely defined. Anyone who took action as a public official would be put to death immediately, as would anyone trying to sound an alarm and any foreigners found in the streets. Bakers were ordered to continue making bread, which would be distributed for free to the people. If they refused, they would be hung from the nearest lamppost, along with anyone who hoarded food or refused to give up flour to the common good.

Once the initial uprising was stabilized, all of Paris would gather in the Place de la Revolution to elect a new National Assembly and a provisional government. Even with the new government in place, the Insurrectionary Committee would hold onto the power "until the complete accomplishment of the insurrection." The Equals realized this might be misunderstood as a personal desire for power, but they were willing to take the risk because so many of the people were led astray by what Babeuf called "the horrible cunning of the Patriciate."

ESSENTIAL

Babeuf identified an obstacle to revolution that later socialist thinkers called *false consciousness*: the idea that workers could be co-opted by the perceived possibility of upward mobility into supporting a social system that was against their own interest.

The Next French Revolution?

The Equals proved to be surprisingly effective at practical revolution. Over the course of months, they created a clandestine organization of several thousand people, organized in cells, who were committed to overthrowing the Directorate and restoring the Revolution. They recruited a chief agent in each of Paris's twelve *arrondissements*, who was charged with passing information to the workshops and barracks in his district, identifying sympathizers among the remains of *sans-culotte* radicalism, and locating food and provisions.

The Equals papered the city with flyers and posters declaring that the purpose of the Revolution was to destroy all inequality and that the Revolution was therefore not complete. They read revolutionary newspapers, including Babeuf's *Tribune,* out loud in open-air meetings, on street corners, and in cafes. Female members sang revolutionary songs at the *Bain Chinoise*, a cafe that was a well-known gathering place for radicals.

Babeuf's Revolution Fails

On May 10, 1796, shortly before the planned uprising, an informant revealed the Equals' plans to the police. The leaders were arrested. Babeuf was carried through the streets to the Vendôme in an open cage.

The arrest of the Conspiracy of Equals did not end their efforts to influence French politics. The Directorate gave the conspirators the public trial required by the French judicial system. (By contrast, the Equals intended to summarily kill the leaders of the Directorate if their uprising succeeded.) Babeuf used the trial as a forum in which to expound his egalitarian beliefs to the public.

Babeuf's Trial

The trial went from February 20 through May 26, 1797, occasionally disrupted when the prisoners broke into choruses of the *Marseillaise*. Babeuf's defense lasted for six sittings of the court. He argued that it was the Republic that was on trial rather than the Conspiracy of Equals. Comparing the Equals to the crowd who stormed the Bastille, he claimed there could be no conspiracy against an illegitimate authority. It was the Directorate who were the criminals: they had subverted the ideals of the Revolution, restoring feudal privileges and setting aside the constitution of 1793. He declared himself the philosophical heir of Diderot, Rousseau, and other members of the Enlightenment, and ended his defense with the statement that "when Jesus spread his message of human equality, he too was treated as the ringleader of a conspiracy."

The jury returned a mixed verdict. Fifty-six of the sixty-five defendants were acquitted. Seven were sentenced to deportation. Babeuf and another member of the central Committee were sentenced to death. When Babeuf heard the verdict, he stabbed himself with a dagger made from a tin candlestick that one of his sons smuggled into prison. The gesture was a failure. He wounded himself badly, but did not die. The following morning, May 27, 1797, Babeuf was sent to the guillotine. The first socialist revolution had failed.

Babeuf's Influence

Babeuf's revolution was a failure, but it was not forgotten, thanks largely to the efforts of Filippo Michele Buonarroti, one of the seven members of the Conspiracy of Equals who was deported after the trial. An expatriate Italian and great-nephew of Michelangelo, Buonarroti devoted the next forty years to keeping the revolution alive. In 1828, he published an account of the failed revolution, *Conspiracy for Equality.* Printed in Brussels, the book circulated illegally in France, where socialist historian G. D. H. Cole says it "came to rank almost as a Revolutionists' Handbook" for leaders of the Paris uprisings in 1830 and 1848; was translated into English for the Chartists in 1838; and found its way into Karl Marx's hands in 1844.

François-Noël Babeuf is generally considered to have been the first revolutionary socialist. The details of his planned society made little impact, but later socialist thinkers were influenced by two elements of his thought:

- The need for communal ownership of property
- The belief that a small group of elite revolutionaries could overthrow an oppressive government for the good of the masses

Karl Marx and Friedrich Engels acknowledged his importance in their first collaborate work, *The Holy Family* (1844), and later in the *Communist Manifesto* (1848). In 1919, the founding manifesto of the Communist International, also known as the Comintern, placed Babeuf at the beginning of their intellectual lineage: "We Communists, united in the Third International, consider ourselves the direct continuators of the heroic endeavors and martyrdom of a long line of revolutionary generations [starting] from Babeuf."

CHAPTER 4

The Paradox of Free Market Socialism

In *The Wealth of Nations*, Adam Smith declared that everyone would benefit equally as an economy expanded if only the invisible hand of the marketplace was allowed to operate. Forty years later, David Ricardo looked at an economy that was growing under the influence of the Industrial Revolution but was still ruled by protectionism. Not only were the benefits of growth unequally distributed, but those who received the greatest share did the least to deserve their reward.

David Ricardo

David Ricardo (1772–1823) was the son of a Jewish stockbroker who immigrated to London from the Netherlands shortly before Ricardo's birth in 1772. After a brief period of study in Amsterdam, Ricardo began to work for his father on the London Stock Exchange when he was fourteen. When he converted to Unitarianism and then eloped with his Quaker neighbor, Priscilla Anne Wilkins, at the age of twenty-one, his father disinherited him. His mother never spoke to him again. With a new wife and no job, Ricardo went into business for himself on the stock exchange with the help of friends and £800 in capital. He built up a substantial fortune over the next ten years, estimated at the time of his death as between £675,000 and £775,000. He retired in 1814, at the age of forty-two, "sufficiently rich to satisfy all my desires and the reasonable desires of all those about me." He moved to a country estate where he devoted himself to the study of literature, science, and the new subject of economics.

Ricardo became interested in questions of political economy in 1799 when he first read Adam Smith's *The Wealth of Nations.* At first Ricardo only dabbled in the subject, finding it "an agreeable subject for a half hour chat." He published his first work on the subject ten years later, a pamphlet in favor of basing currency on precious metals.

Ricardo's contribution to the raging bullion controversy brought him to the attention of some of the hottest political and economic thinkers of the day, including Jeremy Bentham, Thomas Robert Malthus, and James Mill. Suddenly Ricardo was playing with the big boys.

ESSENTIAL

Along with Malthus and Mill, Ricardo was one of the founding members of the Political Economy Club in 1821. Economics was a new discipline, not yet taught at universities. Discussing economic and political reform was considered dangerously radical. Founded as a forum for discussing the fundamental principals of economics, the Political Economy Club was part professional association, part seminar.

The Corn Laws

Ricardo's major contributions to economics were inspired by the 1815 debates over the British Corn Laws. The Industrial Revolution created a new class of wealthy industrialists and merchants who found themselves competing with the landed aristocracy for wealth, social prestige, and political power. The price of food became a focal point for the struggle between aristocrats and the rising industrial classes.

As England's population grew, the demand for grain exceeded supply. The shortage was made worse by the trade embargoes and blockades of the Napoleonic wars and a series of bad harvests between 1805 and 1813. Prices, and profits, soared. At first, large landholders were the only people to benefit from the new demand for grain. Then merchants began to import inexpensive grains from Europe, bringing prices back down. It was a perfect example of Adam Smith's law of supply and demand: High demand leads to high prices, which leads to competition, which leads to lower prices.

In order to protect incomes that depended on the price of their crops, the landed classes sidestepped Smith's invisible hand of the marketplace. Because they dominated both houses of Parliament, they were able to push through protective tariffs designed to keep low-priced European grains out of the English market. The Corn Law of 1815 imposed sliding taxes on imported grain that were tied to the domestic price of grain.

ALERT

The word "corn" means different things in Great Britain and the United States. In Britain, the foodstuff that Americans call *corn* is "maize" or "Indian corn." The word *corn* refers to any of the edible grasses, also known as "grain." Typically, an English-speaking European uses "corn" for the dominant grain in his region. For the British, that's wheat.

Business interests began to organize against the Corn Laws. Unlike the landed proprietors, industrialists wanted cheap grain for their workers since the price of food drove the price of wages. Cheap grain meant lower wages and higher profits. (No one except working-class radicals argued that cheap grain would improve the life of workers. The assumption was that laborers would be paid no more than a subsistence wage regardless of what bread might cost.) Petitions against the Corn Laws flooded into Parliament, which responded by forming committees to investigate. Before the committees could report, Napoleon was defeated, the blockades were stopped, and grain prices returned to normal levels. The Corn Laws remained in effect.

Ricardo Responds to the Corn Laws

Ricardo's first major publication, *Essay on the Influence of a Low Price of Corn on the Profits of Stock* (1815), was written in opposition to the new grain tariffs. In it, he argued that raising the import duties on grain increased the rents of country gentlemen but decreased the profits of manufacturers, resulting in a net loss to the nation.

Ricardo agreed with Adam Smith: Economies tend to expand. As capitalists build new factories, the demand for labor increases, temporarily increasing wages. According to what Ricardo called the "iron law of wages," increased wages result in an increase in population. As the population increases, so does the demand for food. Eventually, existing farms are not able to produce enough food. The only way to produce more food for more mouths is to bring new, less fertile land under cultivation, or spend more capital and labor on land already under cultivation. Either solution increases the cost of producing food, raising the cost of grain and consequently the cost of wages. Only the landlord benefits. The industrialist suffers directly in reduced profits. Labor suffers indirectly as lower profits lead to lower production and a reduced demand for labor. Ricardo, always quick to plug the idea of free trade, concludes that the obvious solution is to cut the landlord out of the equation and import cheap grain.

The Three Components of Wealth: Rent, Wages, and Profit

Four years later, Ricardo expanded this thesis in his major work, *Principles of Political Economy and Taxation* (1819). The central question of the book is how wealth is produced and distributed. Ricardo argues that there are three classes in any community who are involved in the production and distribution of wealth: landlords, labor, and owners of capital. Assuming the wealth of any nation is finite, none of the three classes can gain a larger portion of the total product except at the expense of one or both of the others.

ESSENTIAL

Ricardo's analysis of the conflicting interests of landlords, employers, and workers influenced Karl Marx's theory of class struggle. Building on Ricardo's idea that wealth is finite, Marx identifies the primary conflict between labor and capital as the division of profit. Marx predicts that capital will gain an increasing share of profit until labor rebels, bringing capitalism to an end.

Together, rent, wages, and profit are the components that make up wealth, with population growth or decline as the force that defines their relative share. Rent tends to increase as population grows, due to higher costs of cultivating more food. At the same time, profits vary inversely with wages, which rise or fall with the cost of necessities. If food is expensive, wages and rent go up, while profits fall. With the population clearly on the rise, Ricardo held that landlords would receive an increasing share of the national income at the expense of the capitalists, leading to economic stagnation.

The Role of the Free Market

Ricardo agreed with Adam Smith that a free market is better for the economy than protectionism, both at the national and international level. The debates over the Corn Law left Ricardo convinced that "The interest of the landlords is always opposed to the interests of every other class in the community." As long as the landholding classes were able to control the price of grain, they were the only ones who would benefit from the economic expansion produced by industry. Free trade meant that capital and labor would get their share.

The Labor Theory of Value

Ricardo builds on Adam Smith's premise that labor, not land or gold, is the true source of wealth. He argues that how much an item is worth is based on one of two things:

- Some are valuable because they are scarce, like a rare painting or the Koh-i-Noor Diamond or tickets to the Super Bowl.
- The value of most items is based on the amount of labor it takes to get them.

Although the law of supply and demand may affect the price of goods for short periods, over the long run the price of goods produced and sold under competitive conditions reflects the labor cost of producing them. Ricardo calls the correlation between labor and value the "natural price" of goods. The relative value of two objects depends on the amount of labor needed to produce them.

Ricardo's Concept of *Rent*

In Ricardo's economic model, *rent* isn't the amount paid to lease a dwelling, a car, or a farm. Ricardo uses rent in a specialized way to discuss the income landowners derive from the land.

Because not all land is equally productive, the same men and equipment can produce more bushels of grain on fertile soil than they can produce on a field of the same size that has less fertile soil. Since the wage and capital costs are the same, the field that produces more grain also produces more profit for the landowner. The difference between the amounts produced on the two fields is *rent*.

The "Iron Law of Wages"

Ricardo argued that that there was no point in trying to improve the wages of workers. The Malthusian population dynamic suggests that populations will always expand to meet available food supplies. The law of supply and demand applied to labor created an eternal cycle in which higher wages resulted in larger families, followed by increased competition for jobs and an inevitable drop in wages.

ESSENTIAL

Ricardo's model builds on the Malthusian principle of population growth. Developed by Reverend Thomas Robert Malthus (1766–1834), the Malthusian principle states that in the absence of famine, war, disease, or other disaster, population increases outstrip increases in the production of food. Malthus's theory led Thomas Carlyle to name economics "the dismal science."

The tendency of the market to keep wages at a subsistence level was simply a variation on the labor theory of value. The natural price of a car tire is tied to the cost of producing the tire. The natural price of labor is tied to the cost of producing labor: the price of the food and other necessities required to support a laborer and his family at a subsistence level. If the price of food increases, the natural price of labor increases; if the price of food falls, the natural price of labor falls.

Since the revenue from the sale of manufactured goods is split between profits and wages, capital has no incentive to give labor more than a cost of living increase, which in the early nineteenth century meant enough to buy bread.

FACT

During the Corn Law debates, the great London banker Alexander Baring summarized the iron law of wages this way: "The labourer has no interest in this question: whether the price be 84 shillings or 105 shillings a quarter [ton of wheat], he will get dry bread in the one case and dry bread in the other."

Ricardian Socialists

In some ways, the greatest of the Ricardian socialists is Karl Marx, who took the underlying assumptions behind Ricardo's economic model and spun them out to their logical conclusions. Marx made one basic change to Ricardo's system. Claiming that by 1830 the bourgeoisie had captured the political power in England and France, he removed landlords from the equations, creating a two-sided class struggle between capital and labor.

Marx himself points out that he wasn't the first socialist thinker to adopt and adapt Ricardo's theories. In the first half of the nineteenth century, a handful of English working-class radicals became known as "Ricardian socialists." The title is unintentionally ironic; instead of following Ricardo, they used his assumptions and analysis to overturn his conclusions.

QUESTION

What did Ricardian socialists have in common with the Political Economy Club?
At first glance, not much. Members of the Political Economy Club were drawn from the worlds of politics, finance, trade, and administration. With one exception, the Ricardians worked with their hands. But they all read and were influenced by the same books, most notably David Hume and Adam Smith.

Ricardian socialists adopted the labor theory of value while rejecting the elements of Ricardo's model that claimed capital, too, was productive. (Thomas Hodgskin argued that capitalists were parasites who diverted the fruits of labors' productivity to unproductive consumption.) They claimed that if labor is the source of all value, then labor has an ethical claim on everything it produces. Their mechanisms for accomplishing this varied. Some saw free trade as the road to socialism, arguing that the laws of economics would transform society when unrestricted by arbitrary legal systems. Others called for the development of trade unions to transform the system of distribution, central ownership of the means of production, or a system of national cooperatives.

Among the Ricardian socialists, the most important were William Thompson, John Gray, Thomas Hodgskin, and Francis Bray. Bray in particular reached a large audience with his book *Labour's Wrongs and Labour's Remedy, or the Age of Might and the Age of Right*, which was printed as an inexpensive weekly serial in 1838 and 1839. In it he argued that the existing system of unequal exchange of labor for wages should be replaced with central ownership of the means of production, organized as a worker-controlled joint stock company.

CHAPTER 5

Practical Utopias

The egalitarian dreams, and nightmares, of the French Revolution did not last. With a Bourbon king back on the French throne, a new generation of reformers, French and British alike, considered the nature of a society based on economic justice and cooperation. As a group they were interested in total transformation of society, without the delays of reform or the violence of revolution. Although the details of their solutions were very different, each created a blueprint for a model community and found followers eager to put his ideas into place.

The Bourbon Restoration and the July Revolution

The utopian socialists devised their plans against a backdrop of reaction and revolution.

The Bourbon Restoration

After Napoleon Bonaparte abdicated in 1814, the allied Great Powers restored the Bourbon monarchy to the throne of a reluctant France. The new regime started off with a thud when the newly crowned Louis XVIII described the new constitution as a gift from the king to the French people. Republicans and moderates alike braced to a return to the bad old days of the *Ancien Régime*.

Louis XVIII ruled France from 1814 to 1824, with a short break when Napoleon Bonaparte escaped from the island of Elba and led the French army in a mad dash across Europe that lasted for 100 days. Louis ruled as a constitutional monarch, always aware of the need to compromise between the revolutionaries of the left and the reactionary ultraroyalists on the right.

The trouble started when Louis's younger brother, Charles X, inherited the throne in 1824. As the duc d'Artois, Charles was the unofficial leader of the ultras. Made up of landowners, the aristocracy, conservative church leaders, and former émigrés, the ultras were totally opposed to the egalitarian principles of the Revolution. The ultras wanted to regain the political and social dominance they had lost. Charles wanted a return to the values of the *Ancien Régime*, including the divine right of kings and the authority of an established church.

The July Revolution

The election of 1830 brought the tensions between Charles X and republican France to a head. Opposition candidates swept the election, winning 65 percent of the seats in the Chamber of Deputies. According to the constitution, Charles should have dismissed his cabinet and accepted a moderate minister. Instead, he issued a series of decrees on July 26 that suspended freedom of the press, dissolved the newly elected chamber, reduced the size of the electorate, and allowed him to rule by decree.

Paris exploded. For three days, known in France as *les Trois Glorieuses*, workers, students, and members of the petty bourgeoisie manned the barricades alongside former members of the National Guard, which Charles disbanded in 1827. On July 29, army units began to join the rebels. On July 30, Charles X offered to cancel the July ordinances and accept a moderate cabinet. It was too late. Paris was in the control of the rebels, who were negotiating over who would lead the new regime.

As always in revolutionary French politics, there were two factions. The constitutional monarchists supported the claim of the king's cousin, Louis-Philippe, the duc d'Orleans, popularly known as "Louis the Pear" as a result of a well-known caricature by political cartoonist Honoré Daumier. The republicans supported General Lafayette, the emblematic hero of the American and French Revolutions. Lafayette himself made the final decision. At seventy-three, the former revolutionary preferred the security of a constitutional monarchy to the risk of another Jacobin government. With Lafayette's blessing, France offered the crown to Louis-Philippe.

Henri de Saint-Simon and the Scientific Elite

Henri de Saint-Simon (1760–1825) was a French aristocrat whose family claimed descent from the first Holy Roman Emperor, Charlemagne. Brought up to believe that he was destined for great things, he spent his early years in search of the next big idea. He fought on the side of the colonies in the American Revolution, winning the Order of Cincinnatus. At the end of the war, he traveled to Mexico, where he tried to convince the Spanish Viceroy to build a transoceanic canal through Lake Nicaragua. He became involved in an abortive Dutch plot to drive the British out of India, then traveled to Spain with a plan for linking Madrid to the sea.

Back in France, he flung himself into the Revolution. He renounced his title, refused the office of mayor in his hometown in favor of a non-aristocratic candidate, ran revolutionary meetings, captained the local unit of the National Guard, and successfully speculated in real estate that the government seized from the Catholic Church.

In 1793, Saint-Simon was arrested as a result of a mistaken identity. While in prison, he had a vision. Charlemagne appeared and told him that it was his destiny to be as great a philosopher as Charlemagne was a warrior.

Once out of jail, Saint-Simon set out to turn himself into a great thinker. When his self-designed education was at an end, he began to write. He published his books himself and sent them to influential thinkers of the day, hoping to interest them in his views. When he ran out of money, he took a clerical job and relied on the kindness of a former servant for his room and board. He copied his books by hand when he could no longer afford to have them printed.

Saint-Simon Diagnoses Society's Problems

While much early socialist thought was a reaction against the miseries caused by the Industrial Revolution, Saint-Simon embraced science and industry as the keys to human progress. He believed that the laws of social development could be discovered by studying history. He came to the conclusion that history alternates between periods of equilibrium and imbalance. Societies change as a result of struggle between the productive and unproductive classes: slaves and masters, serfs and lords, plebeians and patricians. The Middle Ages was a period of equilibrium, followed by the social disruption of the Reformation and the Revolution. Now society was poised for another period of equilibrium based on science and industry. The only thing that stood in the way was the semi-feudal power relationships that still existed in French society.

Unlike other socialist thinkers, Saint-Simon does not describe class struggle in terms of haves and have-nots. For him the conflict is between the productive classes and the parasites. Saint-Simon identified the vast majority of society in his own time as part of the productive "industrial/scientific" class, in which he included both workers and factory owners. Only the nobility and the clergy, who represented the last vestiges of feudal privilege, were unproductive. As long as the unproductive classes remained in power, they were a barrier to economic and social progress. For society to change, the modern productive classes had to recognize their common interests and band together.

Rule by the Scientific Elite

In his vision of the ideal society, Saint-Simon was still going for the big idea. Unlike other utopian socialists, who based their transformation of society on small groups, Saint-Simon envisioned a universal association that would incorporate the developed world. He wanted to organize society for the benefit of the poor, but distrusted democracy. Instead he proposed a cooperative commonwealth in which scientists, leaders of industry, and artists would replace the aristocracy and the military as the rulers of society.

ALERT

Saint-Simon wrote the famous dictum "from each according to his ability, to each according to his need" to describe the distribution of wealth in his proposed society. Often attributed to Karl Marx, the phrase later became one of the distinguishing marks between socialism and communism.

Saint-Simon divided mankind into three classes: the *savants*, the propertied, and the unpropertied. The *savants*, including artists of all kinds as well as scholars, would be responsible for the moral and spiritual well-being of society, the role formerly held by the church. Actual governing and administration would be done by the propertied classes, specifically the captains of industry. The primary goal of society would be the material and intellectual improvement of the unpropertied, who would remain at the bottom of society until their own talents allowed them to rise.

Late in his life, Saint-Simon decided his perfect society needed an ethical component. His first suggestion was a scientific religion that he called the Church of Newton, in recognition of Sir Isaac Newton's seminal role in the development of science. He later turned to what he called the New Christianity.

Saint-Simonism after Saint-Simon

During his lifetime, Saint-Simon acquired only a small group of followers. After his death, his disciples, led by Prosper Enfantin (1796–1864) and Saint-Amand Bazard (1791–1832), took Saint-Simon's ideas and elaborated them into a detailed reform program based on the concept of the industrial productive classes and the importance of planning. They took reform one major step further than Saint-Simon and proposed the abolition of personal property. The right of inheritance would disappear; the state would inherit all property. The means of production would become state property, with a central system of administration.

Bazard and Enfantin also developed Saint-Simon's idea of a new Christianity, adding twists that Saint-Simon had never dreamed of. For a time, Saint-Simonism took on the trappings of a religious cult, complete with flowing robes and Enfantin in the role of spiritual father. "Pere" Enfantin and some of his followers founded a model community based on Saint-Simon's ideas and Enfantin's own thoughts on the subject of free love. In 1832, the Saint-Simonians were charged with preaching doctrines dangerous to public morality and "Pere" Enfantin was sentenced to two years in jail and a 100-franc fine.

At its height, in the early 1830s, Saint-Simonism had roughly 40,000 adherents in France. The group was more influential than its numbers suggest. It appealed primarily to those portions of the professional middle class who saw themselves as members of his scientific elite, mostly engineers, scientists, military officers, and businessmen taken with Saint-Simon's emphasis on the expansion of industry. Many of them were involved in the economic development of France under the Second Empire, including the formation of the French railroad system and the creation of the *Crédit Foncier*, a national mortgage bank opened by Napoleon III to provide development capital at reduced interest rates.

Saint-Simonism was declared illegal in 1833, but a few isolated circles remained in existence until the 1870s.

Fourierism

Charles Fourier (1772–1837) was the son of a cloth merchant. He lost his inheritance during the French Revolution and narrowly escaped the guillotine when the revolutionary troops besieged Lyons. During his career as a traveling salesman in the silk industry, he saw first hand the misery suffered by the silk workers in the first steps toward the Industrial Revolution.

FACT

The original meaning of *phalanx* was an infantry formation developed by Philip of Macedonia, in which soldiers stood in close order with shields touching and spears overlapping. In the seventeenth century, the word came to mean any small, closely knit group of people. Fourier combined the word *phalanx* with *monastery* to get *phalanstery*.

Fourier did not believe social or economic inequalities were the source of human misery. Instead, he thought that most problems were the result of the society's misuse of people's "passions." Everyone has something they like to do. Every passion is good for something. If each passion could be put to its proper use the "reign of Harmony" would prevail.

Fourier proposed the establishment of small communes, called phalanxes or phalansteries, which would allow society to make the best use of all human passions. Based on the number of personality types he believed existed, Fourier calculated that the optimum size of each phalanx would be about 1,600 people, a number that would get all necessary work done by assigning every passion to its proper job. (For instance, since small boys love dirt, they would have the job of disposing of the community's garbage.)

Despite the communal nature of the phalanxes, Fourier did not propose to abolish private property. Instead, each phalanx would be organized as a joint-stock company, in which individuals could invest. Everyone in the phalanx would be guaranteed a minimum subsistence and would have the opportunity to become an investor. Beyond their minimum subsistence, members would be paid based on the worth of an individual's contribution to the community. Unpleasant work would be paid for at a higher rate than work that was pleasant but useful. Useful work would pay more than work that produced luxuries. Any profits that the phalanx made would be distributed based on relative value, with five-twelfths going to labor, four-twelfths to capital, and three-twelfths to talent.

FACT

The most famous Fourierist phalanstery was Brook Farm, which was founded outside of Boston in 1841 by a circle of Transcendentalist ministers, reformers, and writers, including the young Nathaniel Hawthorne, Margaret Fuller, and the Alcott Family. Hawthorne wrote a novel based on the experience, *The Blithdale Romance* (1852).

Fourierism in Practice

After Fourier's death, his ideas found two champions who did a better job of promoting Harmonism than Fourier ever did: Victor-Prosper

Considérant and Victor Brisbane. Considérant established a single phalanx in France, which failed, and a second in Texas, *La Reunion*, which flourished for several years.

Brisbane was more successful. He brought Fourierism to the United States from France in 1840. With the help of Horace Greeley, editor and owner of the *New York Tribune*, Brisbane was able to introduce Fourier's theories to thousand of households across the northern states. His articles inspired the creation of more than forty phalansteries in the United States. Many of the communities combined Fourierism with Transcendentalism, Swedenborgianism, Perfectionism, or Spiritualism. Most lasted only a few years. The longest-lived of the Fourierist communities was the North American Phalanx, which practiced Fourierist principles from 1843 to 1855.

ESSENTIAL

Best known for the phrase "Go west, young man, go west," Horace Greeley (1811–1872) was the opinionated founder-editor of the *New York Tribune*. He supported a wide and eclectic range of causes, on and off the page, including free public schools, producer's cooperatives, free speech, the emancipation of slaves, civil rights for freedmen, and western expansion.

Étienne Cabet and the Icarian Movement

Étienne Cabet (1788–1856) was born in Dijon. The son of a cooper, he took full advantage of the opportunities for social mobility brought about by the French Revolution. After the revolution, he remained committed to the ideals of Liberty, Equality, and Fraternity. With the Bourbons once again on the throne of France, he became a member of the French branch of the anti-monarchical Carbonari Society. When Louis-Philippe was placed on the throne, Cabet was made the attorney general of Corsica, but he was too much a child of the French Revolution to be happy even with a constitutional monarchy.

In 1834, Cabet published an article attacking Louis-Philippe's government. He was tried for *lèse-majesté*, the criminal act of bad-mouthing the king. He was acquitted the first time. When he immediately opened an anti-monarchical paper, *L'Populaire*, he was arrested again and sentenced to exile. He spent the next five years in England, where he read Thomas More's *Utopia*. More's imaginary society inspired Cabet to write his own utopian novel, *Voyage to Icaria* (1840).

Icaria

Cabet's Icaria was "a society founded on the basis of the most perfect equality." He did less well on the concept of liberty. In his attempt to mitigate the ills of inequality in modern society, Cabet designed a society that included a progressive income tax, no right of inheritance, state regulation of wages, national workshops, public education, control of marriages to promote selective breeding, and a single, government controlled newspaper. Regulations enforced uniformity in all aspects of life, including clothing.

Icarianism in France

Cabet's novel was unexpectedly popular with the French working classes. France had changed while Cabet was in England. Like the British working class before them, French workers were suffering with the early stages of the Industrial Revolution. Unemployment and bread prices were both rising. Cabet's ideas seemed to offer hope for a better future.

Cabet did not hesitate to capitalize on the situation. He re-opened *L'Populaire* and organized Icarian chapters in every major provincial city. By 1847, Cabet acquired a following that has been variously estimated between 200,000 and 400,000 adherents, mostly skilled artisans who were fearful of both the possibility of violent revolution and the impact of modern factories on their position.

Allons en Texas!

Conditions in France grew worse through the "hungry '40s." Crops failed. Unemployment increased. Bread prices reached a new high. To Cabet's discomfort, Icarians were very vocal participants in bread riots and other demonstrations across France. What's more, the police were keeping a careful eye on the editors of radical newspapers. Cabet began to fear he would once again be imprisoned or exiled.

He suggested a plan to create a small Icarian community in America as early as 1843. In the spring of 1847, he decided the time had come. A headline in *L'Populaire* announced *Allons en Icarie! (Let's go to Icaria!)* Working through a broker Cabet purchased 1 million acres of land, sight unseen, in the new state of Texas, which reportedly was eager for immigrants. When the first sixty-nine Icarians arrived, they found they were swindled. After several false starts, the group established themselves in 1849 at Nauvoo, Illinois, recently abandoned by the Mormons.

With responsibility for an actual community, Cabet leaned toward the authoritarian side of the society he described in *Voyage to Icaria* rather than the democratic. He became such a tyrant that in 1856 a majority of the Icarians voted him out of the community. He died soon afterward in St. Louis, Missouri. In 1895, the remaining Icarians realized they were small American farmers like everyone around them and liquidated the community.

Robert Owen and New Harmony

Utopian socialism wasn't limited to France. Across the channel, industrialist and social reformer Robert Owen (1771–1858) was also drafting a blueprint for an ideal society.

Owen entered the world of reform as a successful self-made factory owner who preached that employers had social responsibilities to their workers. The son of a Welsh saddle maker and ironmonger, Owen left home at the age of ten and worked his way up in the world. By the time he was twenty, he was the manager of a Manchester cotton factory that employed 500 workers. As a supervisor, he was increasingly disturbed by the gap between "the great attention given to the dead machinery, and the neglect and disregard of the living machinery."

Owen became convinced that people's characters were shaped by the circumstances in which they live. If their circumstances were changed, changes in their behavior would necessarily follow. Because mankind was essentially good, but was corrupted by a bad environment:

> *. . . the members of any community may by degrees be trained to live without idleness, without poverty, without crime and without punishment; for each of these is the effect of error in the various systems prevalent throughout the world. They are all necessary consequences of ignorance.*

Success at New Lanark

Owen first practiced his innovative ideals in the mill town of New Lanark, Scotland, where he bought existing cotton mills in 1799. When he first arrived in New Lanark, the population:

> *. . . possessed almost all the vices and very few of the virtues of a social community. Theft and the receipt of stolen goods were their trade, idleness and drunkenness their habit, falsehood and deception their garb; . . . they united only in a zealous systematic opposition to their employers.*

In addition to drunken, unreliable adults, his crew included children between five and ten years old who were placed there by orphan asylums.

Owen set out to transform New Lanark, both in the mills and in the town. He limited the returns paid to his partners and put the balance of profits back into the community in improvements. He paid his workers higher wages than any of his competitors, reduced the length of the work day, and instituted a system of rewards and punishments based on quality of work and attitude. He improved the housing, building small cottages in neatly organized neighborhoods. He replaced the shoddy, expensive goods that were sold in the company store with good-quality materials that were priced at little more than cost. He opened a school for the children that included music and dance as well as reading and writing, and occasionally taught there himself. Any resistance to his changes disappeared when he took the unprecedented step of paying full wages when American trade embargoes cut off his cotton supply during the War of 1812, forcing him to reduce production.

QUESTION

Nature or nurture?
Victorian scientist Francis Galton coined the phrase "nature versus nurture" in 1874 to describe the long-standing argument among social theorists over whether heredity or environment is more important in shaping a person's character. Owen, and many later socialists, believed that nurture was the deciding factor.

By 1815, New Lanark was a model example of the company town. A regular flow of visitors, including the future Tsar Nicholas I of Russia, came to the village to see the living proof of Owen's claim that squalor and misery were not the necessary result of industrialization. The side effect of improving the lives of his workers was increased productivity: The mills at New Lanark were enormously profitable.

Owen Wants to Do More

Owen was certain that his principles would work in a much larger community. His efforts to convince other employers, the Church of England, and the government to adopt the New Lanark system on a wider scale met with hostility. He was horrified when a less than diplomatic diplomat finally told him that ruling classes didn't want the masses to be well educated and well fed because then it would be impossible to control them.

After failing to win support for the creation of New Lanark clones, Owen became more radical. Already known as an advocate for shorter working days and the abolition of child labor, Owen began to flood Parliament and the newspapers with tracts promoting a plan for social reorganization on a grand scale. In place of the existing system of private property and profit, he proposed the creation of Villages of Cooperation. Each village would be a self-sufficient unit of between 500 and 1,000 people that combined agricultural and industrial production. Every family would have a private apartment, with common sitting rooms, studies, and kitchens. He also suggested that money be replaced with "labour notes," which would represent the time spent at work.

In 1822, Owen formed the British and Foreign Philanthropic Society to raise the £96,000 needed to set up one experimental Village of Cooperation. When the society failed to raise the money, Owen decided to devote his personal fortune to proving the value of his ideas.

New Harmony

After touring the Continent in search of opportunities to spread his ideas beyond Great Britain, Owen decided that Europe was past saving. The United States was the obvious place to build a new society.

In 1824, he purchased the town of New Harmony, Indiana, and 30,000 surrounding acres of land from the Rapperites, a German religious sect that successfully founded a communal Christian republic in the American wilderness and was ready to move to a location further west. Eight hundred settlers poured into New Harmony over the course of a few weeks. On July 4, 1826, Owen opened the community by issuing *Declaration of Mental Independence*, from the three great oppressors of mankind: "Private Property, Irrational Religion, and Marriage."

Owen soon returned to England and left New Harmony to run itself. Without Owen's paternalistic influence, the community lasted less than three years. In 1828, Owen sold the land to individuals at a loss.

Owenite Communities Without Owen

New Harmony was a failure, but the Owenite movement remained alive. Followers established at least a dozen Owenite communities in America and Great Britain.

One of the most interesting was Nashoba, founded in 1825 by Scottish-born social reformer Frances Wright on the Wolf River in Tennessee. Wright intended to prove that education and a change of environment could have the same transformative effect on slaves as they had on the proletariats of New Lanark. Wright planned to purchase slaves, educate them, and free them. The plan failed because the community could not produce enough income to pay back the debts incurred in buying the slaves.

The Cooperative Movement and Trade Unionism

Back in England, Owen discovered that one of his ideas had a significant amount of working-class support. Working cooperative societies were being formed around the country, as well as producers' and consumers' cooperatives. By 1830, more than 300 such cooperative societies were in operation.

FACT

One spin-off from Owen's cooperative movement was an enduring success: the consumer cooperative movement founded by the Rochdale Society of Equitable Pioneers in 1844. Formed by twenty-eight weavers and other artisans to buy food, the Rochdale Society developed a set of operating principles that remain the foundation for consumer cooperatives around the world.

Inspired by his unexpected success as a leader of the cooperative movement, Owen plunged into trade unionism. He founded the Grand National Moral Union of the Productive and Useful Classes, soon shortened to the Grand National; leaders of the early trade unions believed Owen was a man who would speak for their interests and rallied under the Grand National's banner. By 1833 the Grand National was a nationwide organization with 500,000 members that included virtually every important union in England. From the union leaders' viewpoint, the Grand National's primary goal was an eight-hour workday. From Owen's perspective, the goal was a total transformation of society based on Owen's Villages of Cooperation.

The Long-Term Influence of Utopian Socialism

In *The Communist Manifesto*, Karl Marx dismissed the generation of reformers who grew up during the French Revolution and Napoleonic wars as "utopian socialists." He argued that their carefully planned societies took no account of the laws that governed human development, unlike his own work, which he described as "scientific socialism."

Although their experiments in creating model communities failed, the utopian socialists of the early nineteenth century provided a vocabulary and framework for later socialist thought, including that of Marx himself. Modern socialist thought borrows heavily from Robert Owen's emphasis on environmental determinism and Henri de Saint-Simon's historical analysis of societies and the concept of class struggle. The utopians' shared ideals of cooperative effort and their creation of small-scale communities contributed to anarchist political theory as well as the communal traditions of the *kibbutz* movement, the American counterculture of the 1960s and 1970s, and the cooperative movement.

CHAPTER 6

The Revolutions of 1848

On January 12, 1848, the people of Palermo, Sicily, rose up against their ruler, Ferdinand II. It was the first of almost fifty revolutions that rocked Europe in the first four months of 1848. Armed rebellions occurred in France, Austria, Prussia, and most of the smaller German and Italian states. There was no single revolutionary organization or movement. No concerted effort across state lines. But the revolutions all had a strong family resemblance as middle classes, proletariat, and peasantry united against absolutism and the remains of feudal privilege.

The "Hungry '40s"

Economic conditions in Europe deteriorated throughout the 1840s. The widespread failure of grain crops between 1845 and 1847 created food shortages across Europe, made worse by the potato blight in 1845. Grain prices increased between 100 and 150 percent over the course of two years, drastically affecting the standard of living for both peasants and workers in the cities, who typically spent seventy percent of their income on food. Food riots were common, escalating into violence directed at local landlords, tax collectors, and mill owners.

FACT

Ireland wasn't the only country hit by the potato blight in 1845, but it was the hardest hit. Cromwell's soldiers pushed the native Irish into western Ireland in the seventeenth century. The land was too wet to grow grain, so they lived almost entirely on potatoes. When the crop failed in 1845, they had no food reserves.

The crisis in agriculture was accompanied by industrial and financial collapse. Overproduction led to falling prices for manufactured goods, business failures among shopkeepers and wholesale merchants, and widespread unemployment. Bankruptcies and bank closings increased.

Europe in Upheaval

A month after the revolt in Palermo, the Paris mob overthrew Louis-Philippe's constitutional monarchy. The February Revolution in France triggered rebellions across central Europe. In the German states, uprisings appeared first in the Austrian Empire, then in many of the lesser German states, and finally in Prussia. At the same time, revolutions spread through the Italian peninsula, from Palermo into Sardinia, Tuscany, the Papal States, and finally into those parts of Italy that were under Austrian control.

Although the rebellions had their roots in the economic disasters of the "Hungry '40s," they quickly escalated into reaction against the suppression of liberalism, constitutionalism, and nationalism that marked European politics in the post-Napoleonic era. Socialists flocked to the German states in particular to take part in what is sometimes described as the "revolution of the intellectuals."

Frightened monarchs learned from Louis-Phillipe's mistakes and gave in to revolutionary demands for constitutions, representative assemblies, and an expansion of personal freedoms. Only the unlucky Louis-Philippe lost his throne, through some of the more unpopular ministers were sent into exile.

By the end of April, Tsar Nicholas I of Russia, writing to Queen Victoria, could say with only slight exaggeration, "What remains standing in Europe? Great Britain and Russia." For a brief time, it appeared that the revolutionaries won.

ALERT

Tsar Nicholas wasn't entirely accurate in his assessment. Spain and the Scandinavian countries went untouched while Great Britain suffered its own mild version of revolution in the form of a Chartist revival. The People's Charter, a six-point petition for many of the freedoms demanded by European revolutionaries in 1848, had been presented to Parliament unsuccessfully twice before, in 1838 and 1842.

The February Revolution in France

In 1848, Louis-Philippe, the "citizen king" who took the throne following the revolution of 1830, still ruled France. The first years of his reign, known as the July Monarchy, were a clear victory of popular sovereignty over absolute monarchy. Social and political power shifted from the traditional aristocracy to the wealthy bourgeoisie, whom Louis-Philippe resembled in tastes and habits. Censorship was abolished and the National Guard restored. The Catholic Church was no longer the official religion. The voting age was reduced and the property qualification lowered, effectively doubling the electorate.

Nonetheless, there was plenty of warning that trouble was on the way. Food shortages, a rising cost of living, and widespread unemployment led to an increasing number of working-class demonstrations during the winter of 1847–1848. At the same time, the middles classes were frustrated by their desire to play a larger role in French politics. Bills to further extend suffrage and the right to hold office were repeatedly introduced in the Chamber of Deputies, and repeatedly ignored by Louis-Philippe's chief advisor François Guizot (1787–1874).

In 1847, frustrated in their efforts to pass changes through normal legislative means and forbidden by law from holding political meetings, opposition leaders organized dinner parties to promote the cause of reform. Seventy banquets were held over the course of the winter, attended by members of the parliamentary opposition and republicans who accepted the institution of the constitutional monarchy. The campaign was scheduled to end with a bang: a procession followed by a large banquet on February 22 in Paris. The evening before the banquet, fearing violence, Guizot's government banned both the dinner and the procession.

The Revolt

The following day, crowds of students and workers gathered in the streets. At first the police were able to disperse the crowds without difficulty. As the day went on, the crowds began to push back.

The revolt lasted only four days. At first Louis-Philippe refused to take the demonstrations seriously. On the second day, members of the National Guard joined the demonstrators and the crowd erected barricades in the streets. By the end of the day, things escalated too much for the king to ignore. He had two choices: bloodshed or appeasement. Louis-Philippe saw the mob in action during the revolutions of 1789 and 1830. He chose appeasement and dismissed Guizot in favor of a liberal minister. The gesture was a classic example of too little, too late. By the 24th, things got so bad in the capital that the king abdicated in favor of his ten-year-old grandson, the Count of Paris, and fled to England.

A New Government

With the revolutionaries in control of Paris and the king in flight, the Chamber of Deputies set aside an attempt by the king's daughter-in-law, the duchesse d'Orleans, to have herself named regent for the Count of Paris.

Instead the Chamber selected a provisional government of moderate republicans for the newly born Second French Republic. At the same time, the radical republicans chose their own provisional government. After more negotiations, the two bodies reached a compromise and added three members of the radical faction to the moderate government, including socialist political philosopher Louis Blanc.

ESSENTIAL

Jean-Joseph-Charles-Louis Blanc (1811–1882) believed workers had a basic right to work and earn a decent living. He suggested the formation of "social workshops" as a step toward a fully cooperative society. His book, *The Organization of Labor* (1839), influenced the demands of Paris laborers in the Revolution of 1848.

Over the course of four months, the division between the moderate and radical factions of the provisional government deepened. The moderates, supported by a majority of the French people, were primarily concerned with the questions of political reform that Louis-Philippe and his ministers refused to consider. The radicals, backed by working-class Paris, wanted social reforms, particularly improved conditions for the working class.

The Right to Work

One of the primary demands of the Paris mob during the February Revolution was the right to work. Having helped established a new government, they expected it to provide work for everyone who wanted it.

The provisional government announced the establishment of "National Workshops" based on Blanc's proposal in *The Organization of Labor.* Blanc proposed autonomous cooperative workshops, controlled by the workers themselves, as the first step in a socialist transformation of society. Under the direction of the conservative minister of public works, Alexandre Marie, the National Workshops became a relief project designed to keep the Paris mob from rising in revolt again. Enrollment in the National Workshops grew from 10,000 in March to roughly 120,000 in June. Many of the unemployed were put to work on road construction projects. Since there were more unemployed than there were roads to build, the surplus laborers were paid a small stipend.

National Elections

The split between Paris and the rest of France was demonstrated clearly on April 23, when the new republic went to the polls to elect representatives to the National Assembly, which would draw up the constitution. Out of 900 seats, 500 went to moderate republicans and only 100 to the radicals. To everyone's surprise, the remaining 300 seats went to avowed monarchists, some of whom supported the recently overthrown July Monarchy and others the Legitimist Bourbon dynasty that was ousted in 1830. Alarmed by radical threats to personal property, the peasants and the bourgeoisie had united against the radical republicans and the Paris proletariat.

June Days

The workers of Paris took to the streets once more on May 15. At first, it looked like a repetition of the February Revolution. The crowd stormed the hall where the delegates were meeting, listened to speeches by the leaders of two of the revolutionary clubs, moved on to the Hôtel de Ville, and elected a provisional government.

Unlike Louis-Philippe, the newly elected executive committee of the Second Republic acted decisively. The National Guard cleared the assembly hall and reoccupied the Hôtel de Ville. Several of the leaders were jailed and the revolutionary clubs were closed down.

On June 22, hoping to forestall further violence from the left, the government closed the National Workshops, which were essentially a proletarian army waiting for a leader. The decision backfired. Suddenly cut off from the payroll, thousands of workers took up arms.

The brief alliance between the workers and the lesser bourgeoisie was over. The assembly declared martial law in the capital and gave General Louis Cavaignac, the former governor of Algeria, full authority to bring the protest to an end. Cavaignac allowed the fighting to spread, then moved in with heavy artillery aimed at the barricades. At the end of three days, an estimated 10,000 were dead or wounded and 11,000 demonstrators were taken prisoner. Cavaignac used his emergency powers to carry out vigorous reprisals against the suspected leaders of the insurrection. Most of the 11,000 prisoners were deported to Algeria.

Revolution in the German States

The news of the successful revolution in France unleashed a series of smaller revolutions through the thirty-eight states of the German Confederation. As in France, the revolutionaries were a confused mixture of middle-class liberals looking for greater participation in government, urban workers and artisans angered by the effect of industrialization on their livelihood, and peasants rising up against inadequate land allotments and remnants of feudal dues and obligations. Most of the German rulers, willing to learn from Louis-Philippe's mistakes, promised to institute constitutions and other reforms before the revolutionaries even had a chance to organize.

ESSENTIAL

In 1815, the independent German states took the first step toward eventual unification. The German Confederation was a loose alliance formed for mutual defense. The confederation had no central executive or judiciary. It also had no way to enforce cooperation among its members, an oversight that the two largest members of the Confederation, Prussia and Austria, used to their advantage.

The Frankfurt Parliament

During 1848, liberals from all over Germany made a concerted effort to unify the German states into a single political unit. The Frankfurt Parliament was created by a group of middle-class German liberals who were inspired to action by the March revolts across Germany. They issued invitations to attend a preliminary parliament, which then arranged for delegates to a pan-German national parliament to be elected from all the German states.

The overwhelming majority of the delegates were university-educated members of the upper bourgeoisie. Very few members had experience in practical politics. None of them were members of the working classes.

FACT

At the beginning of the uprising in Prussia, Karl Marx and Friedrich Engels moved to the Prussian city of Cologne, where they founded and edited the liberal newspaper *Neue Rheinische Zeitung*. Because Marx had previously renounced Prussian citizenship, he was easily deported. Engels remained in Prussia and took an active part in the uprising.

The delegates met in the free city of Frankfort for the first time on May 18, 1848. Journalists came from all over Europe for the opening ceremonies. Delegates and spectators believed they were witnessing the birth of a new nation, Germania. Once they settled down to work, the delegates discovered that while they agreed their goal was a united German state, they disagreed not only on its form of government, but its boundaries. Supporters of "Little Germany" wanted a unified state that would include only Prussia and the smaller German states. Supporters of "Big Germany" wanted to add the German provinces of Austria.

The delegates had a further problem. The Frankfort Parliament claimed to be a government speaking for the entire German people, but it was not recognized as such by the existing German governments or their princes. Misled by the temporary weakness of the Prussian and Austrian governments, besieged in their capitals by revolutionaries, the delegates assumed the two states would follow the Parliament's lead and allow their states to be absorbed in new German nation. They were wrong.

The new Austrian emperor, Francis Joseph I, made it clear that he had no intention of giving up the non-Germanic portions of his empire for the dubious privilege of being incorporated into the new German state. The delegates then offered the crown of "emperor of the Germans" to Friedrich Wilhelm IV of Prussia. At first Friedrich Wilhelm stalled. He couldn't accept the crown without the consent of the princes of the other German states. When twenty-eight of the princes agreed to accept the constitution under his rule, the Prussian king rejected what he called "a crown picked up from the gutter" and ordered the Prussian delegates to resign from the Parliament.

The Prussian delegates were soon followed by those from Austria and a number of the lesser states. The Frankfort Parliament was reduced to its radical members, who tried to inspire the German people to continue the battle. Revolts occurred in a few of the lesser states in May 1849, but they were quickly suppressed, in many cases by Prussian troops.

Revolution in the Austrian Empire

The 1848 uprisings in the Austrian empire had a different character than those in Prussia and the lesser German states because Austria was not exactly a German state. The beginnings of industrialism in Vienna and other major cities created the usual patterns of social change, creating a growing bourgeoisie and a small urban proletariat. Peasants, who made up the overwhelming majority of the population, began to chafe against the demands of the *robota,* a type of labor rent owed to their landlords. But the real threat to the Austrian empire came from its multiethnic character.

The Hapsburg dynasty of Austria ruled an empire that included eleven different nationalities: Croats, Czechs, Germans, Italians, Hungarians, Poles, Romanians, Serbs, Slovaks, and Slovenes. In the 1840s, these minority groups, most notably the Magyars of Hungary, began to have aspirations for national autonomy within the empire.

Beginnings of a Revolt

The first responses to the news of the February Revolution in France were surprisingly mild. Students in Vienna sent a petition to the emperor requesting freedom of speech and the abolition of censorship. Hungarian nationalist Louis Kossuth addressed the Hungarian Diet, calling for an imperial constitution that would give virtual autonomy to Hungary. The students in Vienna quickly amended their petition to include a demand for a constitution.

On March 13, a clash between the army and a group of student demonstrators resulted in bloodshed. The emperor, Ferdinand I, called off the troops and announced his consent to the demands in the student petition.

Ferdinand's willingness to adopt moderate reforms did not answer the larger issue of ethnic autonomy. The emperor was soon on the defensive throughout the empire. The uprising in Vienna quickly spread to Prague, Venice, Milan, and Budapest. A war for liberation broke out in the empire's

Italian possessions. In Budapest, the Hungarian Diet adopted the decrees known as the March Laws, which created an independent Magyar state that was joined to the empire only through its allegiance to the emperor. Inspired by the Hungarian example, Czech nationalists in Prague demanded their own constitution and virtual autonomy. In June, the first Pan-Slav Congress assembled in Prague and proposed that the Austrian empire be transformed into a federation of nationalities.

Second and Third Uprisings

Back in Vienna, Ferdinand reneged on his promise for a constitutional assembly and promulgated a constitution on his own. It was not liberal enough to satisfy the radical elements in the city. When the emperor then attempted to disband the National Guard and dissolve the radical student organization, Vienna suffered a second uprising by students, workers, and members of the National Guard. The imperial family was forced to flee the capital.

From May to October, Vienna was in the hands of the revolutionaries, but the imperial army remained loyal to the Hapsburg dynasty. While the emperor appeared to cooperate with the constituent assembly's efforts to draft a constitution, conservative statesmen and military leaders encouraged the military commander in Prague, General Alfred Windischgrätz, to drill his troops in preparation for recapturing the capital.

FACT

> Austria's failure to resolve the problems of a multi-ethnic empire ultimately led to the assassination of the Archduke Franz Ferdinand in 1914 by a Serbian nationalist. The archduke's death triggered the tangled alliances that threw Europe into World War I.

A radical demonstration in Prague gave Windischgrätz an excuse to call for reinforcements and ruthlessly suppress the Czech revolutionary movement. When the general moved toward Budapest, Viennese radicals staged a third uprising. Windischgrätz used the violence as a pretext to bombard

Vienna with artillery. The city was captured in early October, many radical leaders were executed, and the constituent assembly was exiled to Moravia.

With Vienna back in the government's hands, only the Hungarian revolt remained unchecked. Austria finally defeated the Hungarian rebels in August 1849, with help from Czar Nicholas, who feared that Hungarian success might set off a similar revolt in Poland.

A New Emperor

After recapturing Vienna, the counter-revolutionary leaders staged their own version of rebellion. Convinced that the only way to restore the Hapsburgs to power was to replace Emperor Ferdinand I with a more decisive ruler, government leaders pressured the elderly emperor to yield the throne to his eighteen-year-old nephew, Francis Joseph I.

In March, 1849, Francis Joseph I promulgated a new constitution that reaffirmed the unity and integrity of the Hapsburg Empire, but did not deal with the question of ethnic nationalism. One of the few lasting results of the 1848 revolution in Austria was the emancipation of the peasants from the *robota*.

The Impact of the 1848 Revolutions on Socialism

By 1849, the revolutions were defeated. Many radical revolutionaries felt they gained nothing. The political situation in many countries was actually more repressive than it had been before the revolts. Those constitutions that were granted were suspended or watered down until they were worthless. Revolutionary leaders were imprisoned or exiled. The freedoms for which they fought were systematically denied. With few exceptions, rulers still sat on the thrones they occupied at the beginning of the uprising. France toppled the bourgeois monarchy of Louis-Philippe and voted for a new emperor in his place, Louis-Napoleon. The German states emerged from the upheavals with neither unity nor democracy. The ethnic minorities of the Austrian empire did not achieve their dreams of national autonomy. Italy was in fragments. French anarchist Pierre-Joseph Proudhon summed up the feeling of many: ". . . we have been beaten and humiliated . . . scattered, imprisoned, disarmed, and gagged. The fate of European democracy has slipped from our hands."

The defeat of the revolutions by reactionary forces changed the character of European socialism and the working-class movement. Before 1848, working-class radicals were often allied with the middle class against the traditional ruling classes. They fought together in many places at the beginning of the uprisings. As the revolutions progressed, the bourgeoisie aligned themselves with the old order, alarmed by the extremism of the mob and the perceived threat to private property.

In 1850, Karl Marx made a speech to the Central Committee of the Communist League in which he elaborated a principle of permanent revolution that he derived from the experiences of 1848. Marx told his fellow radicals that, in the case of a bourgeois revolution, if the bourgeoisie are not strong enough to hold on to power, a revolutionary workers' party should give its support to petty bourgeois forces in their struggle against a reactionary government. They should even let them take power. The task of the workers would be to make the revolution permanent until the proletariat has conquered state power. The concept of permanent revolution would play a role in the Russian Revolution in 1917.

CHAPTER 7

Karl Marx and Friedrich Engels

Together, Karl Marx and Friedrich Engels produced the most significant theory in the history of socialism. They were the first socialist thinkers to present the possibility of a socialist state as a realizable goal rather than a utopian dream. Instead of creating a detailed prescription for a future society, they used the disciplines of German philosophy, French political thought, and English economics to understand how capitalism works. They came to the conclusion that the fall of capitalism would result from its internal contradictions.

The "Odd Couple" of Socialism

From 1844 to Marx's death in 1883, Marx and Engels were political and intellectual collaborators. By Engels's own account, Marx was the originator and Engels was the popularizer. He always played second fiddle and was "happy to have had such a wonderful first violin as Marx."

It was an enormously productive and unlikely partnership. The two men came from very different backgrounds and had very different personal styles. Engels was well organized, well dressed, and charming. Marx was sloppy, careless about his appearance, often surly and given to feuds with former associates. Marx wrote about social changes in terms of abstract social developments; Engels created detailed and compassionate pictures of how the working class lived.

Karl Marx

Karl Marx (1818–1883) was born into a middle-class Jewish family in the city of Trier, on the border between Germany and France. Both of Marx's parents came from distinguished rabbinical families. His father, Hirschel Marx, was the first member of the family to leave the rabbinate. When the French seized Trier during the Napoleonic Wars and relaxed some of the restrictions on Jews, Hirschel became a lawyer. When Trier came under Prussian control in 1815, Jews were once more excluded from holding public office, including the law. Already deeply assimilated to German culture, Hirschel changed his name to Heinrich and had his entire family baptized. In time, he rose to the level of *Justizrat* (roughly equivalent to Queen's Counsel in the British system) and became head of the Trier bar.

University Years

Marx spent a year at the University of Bonn, where he indulged in the typical beer-swilling and saber-rattling behavior of a German university student of the time. He was soon in trouble with the university authorities for drunkenness and riotous behavior and with the police for subversive ideas. In the fall of 1836, with his father's whole-hearted approval, he transferred from the party-school atmosphere of Bonn to the more serious University of Berlin. In order to please his father, Marx officially studied the law, but soon neglected it in favor of the hottest subject of the day: philosophy. For a time he became a member of the group of German intellectuals who called themselves the "Young Hegelians." When he graduated in 1841 with a doctorate in philosophy, he was considered the ablest philosophy scholar of his generation.

FACT

After the death of German philosopher Georg Hegel in 1831, his followers split into two groups. The "Old Hegelians" defended his conservative belief that Prussia represented the apogee of historical development. The "Young Hegelians" used the revolutionary possibilities of Hegel's dialectic to critique religion, state, and society.

Marx as Editor, Husband, and Socialist Thinker

Denied an academic job because of his political views, Marx moved to Cologne, the center of the industrialized Rhineland, where he became the editor of the liberal newspaper, the *Rheinische Zeitung.* At the newspaper, he was exposed to problems for which Hegel provided no solutions, beginning with the debate over a bill designed to abolish the centuries-old communal privilege of picking up fallen wood in the forest. Marx had a new task: applying German philosophical thought to the realities of contemporary Germany.

When the government censor closed the *Rheinische Zeitung* in 1843, Marx accepted an offer to edit another radical paper, the *Deutsche-Franzosiche Jahrbucher,* and moved to Paris with his new wife.

In the 1840s, Paris was the center of both revolutionary politics and socialist thought. Marx met a number of critical socialist thinkers there, many of whom he would later quarrel with. He also began two new scholarly projects: a historical account of the French Revolution and an extended critique of Hegel's philosophy of law and the state. By the end of 1843, he combined Hegel's dialectic with the historical model of the French Revolution to create a new concept of history as a process of transformation fueled by the struggle between two classes. In a capitalist society, the wage-dependent proletariat would be the catalyst for change.

Marx didn't stay in Paris for long. In 1844, the Prussian government issued a warrant for his arrest. Expelled from Paris, the Marx family moved to Brussels, where they lived until 1848.

Friedrich Engels

Unlike Marx, Friedrich Engels (1820–1895) had personal experience with both capitalism and the effects of industrialization on the lives of the working class. The son and grandson of successful German textile manufacturers, Engels was born in the industrial town of Barmen, home to the first spinning machines in Germany. Caspar Engels was determined that his son would learn the textile business and join the family firm.

Furthering His Education

In 1838, his father pulled Engels out of school and sent him to Bremen to work as a clerk in an export office, the nineteenth century equivalent of getting an MBA. Away from his father's Protestant fundamentalism, Engels spread his wings and set out to educate himself. He read voraciously: philosophy, history, science, and the novels that were a forbidden frivolity at home. He wrote poetry, theater and opera reviews, and did travel sketches. He joined a singing society, composed some music, and attended concerts by Liszt. He also visited a ship that was sailing for America and was appalled by the difference between the first class cabin and steerage. The first class cabin was "elegant and comfortably furnished, like an aristocratic salon, in mahogany ornamented with gold." In steerage, people were "packed in like the paving stones in the streets."

QUESTION

Who is Moses Hess?

Moses Hess (1812–1875) was a German journalist and socialist and an early proponent of Socialist-Zionism. He is believed to be responsible for several memorable phrases in *The Communist Manifesto,* including the slogan "religion is the opiate of the masses." Faced with German anti-Semitism in the 1860s, he became convinced that the basic struggle is between nations, not classes.

In 1841, Engels left Bremen to complete his year of military service in Berlin. Still eager to educate himself, he chose Berlin because he hoped to attend lectures at the university while fulfilling his service requirements. Like Marx before him, he soon fell in with the Young Hegelians. He also met Moses Hess, who convinced him that communism was the logical outcome of the Hegelian dialectic.

Manchester, England

The following year, Engels was sent to Manchester, where his father had a financial interest in a large textile factory. He worked in the factory as a clerk for almost two years

Engels devoted his evenings to his own interests. Shocked by the conditions under which the English working classes lived and worked, he began to explore the city. He soon became involved with a young Irishwoman who worked in the Ermen & Engels factory, Mary Burns. (They married two years later.) With her sister, Mary became his guide to the parts of the city that a German manufacturer's son would never have found on his own. Together, they met with trade unionists, socialists, and other radicals. In what was left of his days, he studied the English political economists, including David Ricardo.

Engels used the material he gathered to write two articles on social and economic conditions in Manchester that appeared in Marx's *Deutsche-Franzosische Jahrbucher.* (He later returned to the subject in his classic study of urban conditions during the Industrial Revolution, *The Condition of the Working Class in England.*) The articles included an early version of the Marxist critique of classical economics that stands at the heart of *Das Kapital.*

ESSENTIAL

Karl Marx dubbed the British school of political economics that began with Adam Smith and reached its maturity in the writing of David Ricardo and John Stuart Mill "classical economics." Marx's critique of capitalism builds on their ideas about economic growth, free trade, and the labor theory of value, and uses many of the same model-building tools.

A Friendship with Marx

On his way home to Barmen in 1844, Engels stopped in Paris to see Marx, whom he met earlier in Cologne. The brief stop stretched into ten days of continuous conversation. Engels later wrote, "When I visited Marx in the summer of 1844 we found ourselves in complete agreement on questions of theory and our collaboration began at that time."

Hegel's Dialectic

Hegelian philosophy was the dominant philosophical system in Germany in the 1830s and 1840s. The central idea in Hegelian thought is the dialectic, which is often summed up in three words: thesis, antithesis, synthesis. Put simply, the conflict between two opposing views (thesis and antithesis) result in change (synthesis.) The dialectic is a dynamic process: Once a synthesis is produced, it becomes a thesis, which inevitably brings forth its own antithesis.

In *The Philosophy of History* (1822–1823), Georg Wilhelm Hegel (1770–1831) applied the concept of the dialectic to the development of history, demonstrating how conflicting intellectual forces turn old societies into new. In his view, history was the story of the progressive development of humanity from a state of savagery toward the ultimate goals of reason and freedom through the action of what Hegel called the *World Spirit*. The great men of history were those whose personal aims coincided with the dialectical movement of their times.

In the years following his death, Hegel's followers split into two camps. The right, or "old Hegelians," used Hegelian philosophy to support religious orthodoxy and conservative political policies. The left, or "young Hegelians," saw the dialectic as fundamentally revolutionary and used it to attack religion first and later the Prussian state.

Historical Materialism

Marx agreed with Hegel that history is a dialectical process and that change is consequently inevitable, but he didn't believe that the motive force for change was Hegel's abstract World Spirit. According to Marx, the history of civilization is the history of class conflicts and the end result will be communism.

Marx identifies five stages of economic development in history: primitive communism, slavery, feudalism, capitalism, and communism. In each of these stages, except for communism, there are inherent contradictions that make revolution inevitable. At some point in each stage of development, the dominant mode of production (thesis) in a society comes into conflict with the society's existing relationships (anti-thesis), which are in themselves a product of the mode of production. What was once productive turns into fetters. Social revolution follows, creating a social system based on a different mode of production (synthesis).

ESSENTIAL

Marx believed that the revolutionary crisis that would finally end capitalism would be the culmination of a long evolutionary process within society. This meant that premature attempts to bring about revolutionary change, like the French Revolution, were doomed to failure.

This succession of conflicts will end with the arrival of communism. Since there will no longer be private ownership of the means of production, there will no longer be the tension and contradictions of class divisions to fuel the dialectical movement of history. After capitalism falls, there will be a period of transition to this new society called the "dictatorship of the proletariat," followed by the first stage of communism.

Economic Determinism

In any society, the entire social structure of ideas, laws, institutions, and beliefs, which Marx called the *superstructure*, grows out of the prevailing economic system. Every society has a ruling class that controls the means of production, and consequently controls the dominant ideas and institutions in that society. The state is designed to serve the interests of the dominant class in society. The economic system determines not only how people live, but what they think and feel. In short, "It is not the consciousness of men that determines their existence, but, on the contrary, their social existence determines their consciousness." Once the modes of production change, the entire superstructure changes, including man's consciousness. A slave is different from a serf, and a serf is different from an industrial laborer not only because their legal status is different, but because their entire world view is different.

The Communist Manifesto

In November 1847, the London-based League of the Just commissioned Marx and Engels to write a manifesto for publication. Engels wrote the first draft: a policy-wonk's account of the contemporary industrial situation. Marx rewrote it, transforming Engels's policy paper into a powerful piece of political propaganda.

FACT

The League of the Just, later renamed the Communist League, was a German offshoot of the secret societies dedicated to the ideals of Babeuf that appeared in France in the 1830s. Its members were mainly expatriate German craftsmen, with the addition of a few young intellectuals, including the future leader of the German Social Democratic Party, Ferdinand Lassalle.

The Communist Manifesto begins with a paranoid shiver:

> *A spectre is haunting Europe—the spectre of Communism. All the powers of old Europe have entered into a holy alliance to exorcise this spectre: Pope and Tsar, Metternich and Guizot, French Radical and German police spies.*

Having hooked his audience, Marx explains that the fundamental problem with what he dismisses as "utopian socialists" is that they assume social change can be imposed on a society by well-intentioned members of the upper classes. He then provides in quick succession:

- His new theory that history is a succession of class struggles between exploited and exploiters

- An analysis of contemporary European society
- A program for revolutionary action that bears a striking resemblance to that of Babeuf

At the end of forty impassioned yet logical pages, Marx leaves his reader with the famous call to action, "The workers have nothing to lose but their chains. They have a world to win. Workers of all lands, unite!"

The final version was published in London in February 1848—just before the outbreak of revolutions began in France. Several hundred copies were distributed to League members, but the organization never bothered to put it on sale. By 1872, the *Manifesto* was translated into Russian and French and issued in three editions in the United States and twelve in Germany.

Marx and Engels in the Revolution of 1848

Shortly after *The Communist Manifesto* was published, the compost hit the fan in France. With Revolution in the air, the Belgian authorities decided that Marx was an undesirable alien and asked him to leave the country. As one door closed, another opened; Marx returned to France at the invitation of the new republican government.

Within weeks of the March uprising in Prussia, Marx and Engels were on their way to Cologne, Marx traveling on a temporary French passport because he gave up his Prussian citizenship several years before. (His application for British citizenship was denied because he gave up his Prussian citizenship.) Once in Cologne, they set up a revolutionary newspaper, the *Neue Rheinische Zeitung*.

At first, the paper championed a democratic alliance with the liberal bourgeoisie. In the spring of 1849, after the bourgeoisie-dominated Frankfort Assembly offered the crown of a united Germany to Friedrich William IV of Prussia, the paper openly called for social revolution on the part of the workers and peasants, and attacked the bourgeoisie for compromising with the aristocracy.

Shortly after the paper became more radical in tone, Marx was given twenty-four hours to leave Prussia. He made his way back to Paris, where he found himself once again unwelcome in the aftermath of the bloody

June Days. He would be allowed to remain in France only if he remained far from Paris. He chose instead to take refuge in Great Britain. London was Marx's home for the rest of his life.

With Marx gone, Engels closed down the paper. He remained in Prussia, where he took an active part in the final stages of the uprising. As the revolution drew to a close, Engels escaped to Switzerland and then made his way back to England.

After the Revolution

By the end of 1849, the revolutions in Europe were over and Marx and Engels were both settled in England. Engels went back to work in his father's factory, first as a clerk and later as a partner. For the next 20 years, he led a double life in Manchester: member of the business elite by day, revolutionary by night.

Marx and his family settled in London. He spent his working days in the British Museum reading room, where he wrote prolifically and educated himself in economics with the help of Parliamentary Blue Books and Engels's first-hand experience of British industry. His only regular income was writing articles on the European political situation for Horace Greeley's *New York Tribune* at the rate of £1 per article. He depended heavily on Engels, who often ghostwrote the *Tribune* articles and gave him money with a generous hand. It is one of history's ironies that the Engels's family's factory in Manchester supported Marx as he studied and wrote about the downfall of capitalism.

The First International (1864–1876)

In 1864, Marx was invited to the inaugural meeting of a new socialist organization in London, the International Working Men's Association, later known as the First International. At that first meeting, Marx was elected to the provisional committee and named chairman of the committee charged with drafting the group's constitution. He soon became the organization's leader. In 1870, Engels sold his shares in the Manchester factory and moved to London, where he joined Marx on the General Council of the First International and took over the job of corresponding with the new socialist parties that were growing up across Europe.

The group was truly international in scope, with representatives from almost every element of the European left, from trade unionists to anarchists. It soon became a unifying force in the labor movements at the end of the nineteenth century. Quickly outlawed in Germany, Austria, France, and Spain, the First International also became the symbol for the power of the radical left, credited with international influence far out of keeping with its actual numbers.

The diversity of opinions within the First International was the source of strain almost from the start, but it was 1871 before the first serious cracks appeared. Paris once more erupted into rebellion. Over the course of ten weeks, thousands died and much of the city was destroyed. Marx wrote an account of the Paris Commune on behalf of the organization that depicted the violence as the first stage of a proletarian revolution. Right-wing papers used the pamphlet to depict Marx, and by implication the First International, as instigators of the rebellion. British trade union leaders refused to endorse the pamphlet and two of the most important resigned from the organization.

QUESTION

How did Marx react to newspaper attacks in 1871?
He was delighted. He wrote to a friend, "'I have the honour to be AT THIS MOMENT THE BEST CALUMNIATED AND MOST MENACED MAN OF LONDON. That really does one good after a tedious twenty years' idyll in the swamp."

Already shaken by disagreements about the Paris Commune, the association split in two in 1872 as a result of ideological battles between Marx, who believed in centralized socialism, and anarchist Mikhail Bakunin.

Das Kapital

Marx published the first volume of his masterpiece, *Das Kapital*, in 1867. He described his purpose in writing the work as laying bare "the economic law of motion of modern society." In it, Marx examined the models of the classical economists in terms of his theory of class struggle. The result is an analysis of the economic injustices of the capitalist system and contradictions in the system that would create its ultimate fall.

eFACT

The Imperial Russian censor approved a Russian translation of *Das Kapital* for publication in 1872 on the grounds that "It is possible to state for certainty that very few people in Russia will read it and even fewer will understand it."

Marx's Critique of Capitalism

According to Marx, the class conflict that will bring an end to capitalism rests in the contradictory economic interests of the bourgeoisie and the proletariat. The basic conflict between the two rests on the value of labor. The labor theory of value, as defined by David Ricardo, argues that the value of a product is determined by the amount of labor needed to produce it. Before capitalism, economies were based on the exchange of useful products. Under capitalism, products became commodities to be bought or sold for a profit. Labor has also become a commodity, but its price is not as great as the value of the product it creates. Marx called the difference "surplus value."

Surplus Value

Under capitalism, those who own the means of production, like factory owners, produce commodities for sale in the market in order to make a profit. To do so, they need two kinds of capital:

- Constant capital, such as raw material, machinery, and buildings, which does not change its value during production
- Variable capital, i.e., labor, which does change its value during production

Profit comes through the variable value of labor. The base value of a laborer is her wage. If she works for eight hours and produces enough goods to cover her wage in the first four hours in the day, everything that she produces in the second four hours is surplus value. Surplus value is the source of the capitalist's profits and his ability to invest in new machinery and technology.

The basic economic struggle between labor and capitalist was over what Marx called the "rate of surplus value," or more negatively the "rate of exploitation." Owners wanted to increase the rate through longer hours and/or lower wages. Labor wanted to decrease the rate through shorter hours or higher wages.

e! ALERT

Those feminine pronouns aren't an attempt at political correctness. Surplus value was an even bigger issue for women than men. In the 1830s and 1840s, more than half of the factory workers and coal miners were women. Children of both sexes earned roughly the same wage. After the age of sixteen, women earned roughly one-third of a man's wage.

According to Marx, the struggle over the rate of surplus value revealed an inherent flaw in capitalism. In order to remain competitive, capitalists needed to modernize their machinery, which required them to increase their investment in constant capital at the expense of labor's share of the surplus value. More efficient production meant more commodities reached the market, but reduced wages meant laborers could not afford to buy more goods, causing a crisis of overproduction. At each crisis of overproduction stronger companies would force weaker competitors out of business. With fewer companies in business, unemployment would rise and wages would go down, causing more poverty among the proletariat. Lower wages meant the businesses that survived were able to keep a larger share of surplus value as profit. Eventually, the economy would recover as a result of the new capital that business owners accumulated and the cycle would resume. Each crisis would be more serious, leading to the eventual breakdown of capitalism and the rise of communism in its place.

Class Consciousness

According to Marx, every stage of society is divided into two classes, those who control the means of production and those who sell their labor. Throughout history, the relationship between the two has always been one of exploitation and domination: "Freeman and slave, patrician and plebeian, lord and serf, guild-master and journeyman, in a word, oppressor and oppressed stood in constant opposition to each other." As in the historical stages before it, the structure of capitalism has created a natural antagonism between its two fundamental classes: bourgeoisie and proletariat. Class struggle would end with the destruction of capitalism, because communism would be a classless society.

Engels Completes Marx's Work

Speaking at Marx's grave in 1883, Engels described Marx's place in history:

> *As Darwin discovered the law of evolution in organic nature, so Marx discovered the law of evolution in human history . . . that human beings must first of all eat, drink, shelter and clothe themselves before they can turn their attention to politics, science, art and religion.*

Having spent the previous thirty-five years making sure that the Marx family members, in fact, were able to eat, drink, shelter, and clothe themselves, Engels devoted the rest of his life to editing and published the remaining two volumes of *Das Kapital*.

CHAPTER 8

The Paris Commune of 1871

In 1871, the Franco-Prussian War brought the Second Empire of France to a humiliating end. The newest version of the National Assembly was prepared to re-establish the monarchy, again. Angry at both events, the workers of Paris took to the streets in protest, seized command of the city, and founded their own short-lived government. Watching the rise and defeat of the Paris Commune from London, Marx described it as the first proletarian revolution. Later historians have suggested that it was the last convulsion of the French Revolution of 1789.

The Second Empire

Prior to the Revolution of 1848, Napoleon Bonaparte's nephew, Louis-Napoleon Bonaparte (1808–1873), tried to take the French throne by force twice. Each time the would-be king was stopped and sent into exile.

When the revolution broke out in 1871, Bonaparte hurried to Paris to place his claim again. The provisional government was no happier to see him than their predecessors were in 1836 and 1840, but he was not entirely without supporters. When the time came, the small Bonapartist party nominated him for a seat in the National Assembly. He was elected deputy by Paris and three other districts but refused to take his seat because conditions were so unsettled. In September, he was elected again, this time by five districts.

Bonaparte began to campaign for the presidency as soon as he arrived in Paris to take his place in the assembly, evoking the glamour of the Napoleonic legend and indiscriminately promising to protect the interests of all voting groups. In December 1848, he was elected by an overwhelming majority to a four-year term as president of the Second Republic, the only candidate to receive votes from all classes of the population.

Bonaparte had no interest in being president. Instead he had his eye on his uncle's old job as emperor. He spent his first year in office in a power struggle with members of the National Assembly, most of whom favored a return to the Bourbon or Orleans monarchies. When the Assembly refused to revise the constitution to allow his re-election, Bonaparte staged a *coup d'etat* on December 2, 1851.

With the support of the military, Bonaparte squashed republican resistance in Paris, dissolved the Assembly, put a new constitution in place, and restored universal manhood suffrage. Later that month, a direct popular vote elected Bonaparte to a ten-year term as president and ratified the new constitution. A year later, he took the title of Emperor Napoleon III, an act that was also ratified by the voting public.

"Napoleon the Little"

France enthusiastically supported Napoleon III in the restoration of empire, expecting a revival of Napoleonic glory. If they didn't get glory, at least they got comfort. Under Napoleon III's rule, France enjoyed two decades of domestic prosperity for the middle and upper classes. Surrounded by Saint-Simonian advisors, the emperor threw the state's resources at encouraging industrial development, resulting in increased industrialization, the creation of a national railroad system, imperial expansion in Asia and Africa, and Baron Haussman's transformation of Paris into what author Théophile Gautier called "a crazy tinsel circus of all fleshly pleasures and all earthly magnificence." The emperor even remembered to throw a bone to the working classes in the form of lower tariffs on food.

Not satisfied with domestic success, Napoleon III wanted to re-establish France's position as a powerful player in Europe. Derided by Victor Hugo as "Napoleon the Little," the emperor recognized that he wasn't the military equal of his uncle and positioned himself as the champion of nationalist aspirations throughout Europe. First he encouraged an unsuccessful Polish rebellion against Russia. Then he involved himself in the national unification movements in Italy and Germany, picturing loose confederations of weak nations that would turn to France for protection. As a result of his efforts, he damaged French relations with both Russia and Austria and helped replace weak neighbors with the powerful new states of Germany and Italy.

The Franco-Prussian War

Looking at Napoleon III's foreign policy track record, one member of the National Assembly, Adolphe Thiers, concluded, "There are no mistakes left to commit." He was wrong. On July 19, 1870, the emperor crowned his diplomatic errors in Europe by declaring war on Prussia.

The immediate cause of the Franco-Prussian war was a diplomatic flap over the succession to the Spanish throne in 1870. A member of the Prussian royal family was a candidate for the vacant throne. The French saw this as Prussian interference in a French sphere of influence and successfully leaned on the Prussians to have the prince remove his name from consideration. Instead of enjoying his diplomatic success, Napoleon III pressed his luck by trying to add more conditions to the deal, ones that King Wilhelm found unacceptable. Bismarck edited Wilhelm's telegraphed description of his meeting with the French ambassador to make it look like the king insulted the ambassador, then leaked the doctored message to the press, deliberately manipulating Napoleon III into a declaration of war.

By July 30, Bismarck had almost 500,000 men in the field, drawn from both the Prussian army and those of its allies among the smaller German States. The French mustered less than half that number, badly organized, badly equipped, and badly led by Napoleon III himself, who really wasn't the military leader that his uncle was. The Germans soon had one French army bottled up at Metz, near the German border in Lorraine, and another cornered slightly to the west at Sedan. On September 1, the French were decisively beaten at the Battle of Sedan and the Germans captured Napoleon III and a large portion of the French army.

The Siege of Paris

When the news reached Paris three days later, republican members of the Assembly proclaimed the establishment of a new republic and set up an emergency government of national defense. On September 19, German forces surrounded Paris.

For the first six weeks of the siege, Paris enjoyed an almost festival mood. The city stayed in contact with the outside world through the use of hot-air balloons and carrier pigeons.

FACT

Léon Gambetta, a Paris attorney and the new minister of war and the interior, escaped from the besieged capital in a hot-air balloon on October 7 and organized a resistance movement in the provinces. Under Gambetta's leadership, untrained and undersupplied guerilla forces successfully harassed the German supply lines but were unable to get a relief force through to Paris.

With the onset of cold weather, conditions grew harder and the festive mood evaporated. The winter of 1870 proved to be one of the coldest on record in the nineteenth century—so cold that the Seine froze solid for three weeks. The price of fuel quadrupled. Smallpox, typhoid, and pneumonia ran through the population. Communications with the world outside the city became less reliable when it became too cold for the pigeons to fly. More than 200,000 refugees poured into the city ahead of the German troops, only to find no housing or livelihood. Business ground to a halt, creating massive unemployment and leaving small middle-class businesses in ruins. The provisional government declared a moratorium on the payment of debts and rents as an emergency measure.

Worst of all, food supplies ran low. Early in the siege, voices from the left, including socialist agitator Auguste Blanqui, argued for mandatory food rationing. Assuming in October that the siege would end quickly, the government chose to ration meat instead of grain and left the city to the vagaries of the free market.

Those people who had money and foresight stockpiled food in the early days of the siege. Most scrambled to find food. Municipal authorities did what they could. The mayors in the city's working-class *arrondisements* opened soup kitchens and employed women to sew uniforms for the National Guard.

ALERT

> The threat of starvation did not affect everyone equally. The wealthy bought horsemeat and, when the Paris zoo could no longer feed its animals, elephant, kangaroo, and yak. Rat salami became a delicacy and butchered cats were sold as "gutter rabbits." The average working-class family couldn't even afford to eat rat.

In early January, the Germans upped the pressure by bombarding the city. Rumors spread that the government had stockpiles of food in the forts surrounding Paris. The number of radical political clubs in the city increased, spawning a resurgence of revolutionary socialism. Revolutionary organizations placarded the city with posters denouncing the government's handling of the war and demanding that it relinquish its authority to the people of Paris.

With Paris in a state of starvation, and no relief in sight from either Gambetta's guerillas or the other European powers, the provisional French government signed an armistice on January 29, 1871.

Peace at Any Price?

Bismarck refused to enter into final peace negotiations with the provisional government. At the Prussian chancellor's insistence, the armistice agreement required the French to elect a new National Assembly.

On February 8, France held a hastily organized election based on universal manhood suffrage. Monarchist candidates promised the restoration of peace and political stability. Republican candidates advocated continuation of the war if needed to avoid unacceptable terms for peace. Once again, Paris and the rest of France took different positions at the polls. Most Frenchmen voted for the monarchists and peace. Paris, as always, voted for republican ideals.

The National Assembly chose veteran statesman Adolphe Thiers to head the new government and negotiate peace with Bismarck. The final terms, dictated by a victorious Germany, were as humiliating as republican candidates had predicted. France agreed to surrender the greater part of Alsace and Lorraine, pay an indemnity of 5 billion francs, and support a German army of occupation until the debt was paid. Gambetta and the representatives from Alsace and Lorraine resigned in protest.

Peace concluded, the National Assembly turned its attention to the task of establishing a permanent government. Their first step was to move the seat of government from its temporary quarters in Bordeaux to the traditional royalist capital of Versailles.

With a large monarchical majority in the assembly, it seemed likely that the monarchy would once again be restored. The only question was, which one? With almost 100 years' history of deposing French kings, the Assembly could choose between three different dynasties with claims to the throne. The monarchists in the assembly divided their support almost equally between the Legitimist Bourbon candidate, grandson to Charles X, and the Orleanist candidate, grandson to Louis Philippe. No one supported Bonapartist claims after the recent military debacle.

The Workers' Insurrection

While the monarchists argued over rival dynastic claims to the throne, the mood in Paris was getting ugly. Those who could afford to go left Paris soon after the armistice was signed, leaving behind the working classes and petty bourgeoisie who had suffered the most during the siege. The citizens of Paris who remained were not happy. They had experienced the burden of the war during the four-month siege of the city. They had watched the Germans march through the *Arc de Triumph*, a small humiliation provided for in the peace treaty. They resented the transfer of the government to Versailles rather than to Paris—a symbolic statement in favor of monarchy over republic.

In February, the conservative majority in the assembly passed three laws that did nothing to improve the negative attitude in Paris:

- They ended the wartime moratorium on debt repayment.
- They required the immediate payment of any rent that was not paid during the war.
- They canceled the pay of the National Guard, which was composed of workers who had defended Paris during the siege.

The first two decisions benefited the interests of the landed gentry and financiers who dominated the assembly, but they were disastrous for the lower middle classes. Much of the business of Paris was conducted using bills of exchange. By requiring payment before businesses recovered from the effects of the siege, the assembly forced many small businesses into bankruptcy.

The third decision was intended to demobilize the National Guard, which significantly outnumbered the regular army units then at the government's disposal; it deprived many working-class families of their only income.

The National Guard took the first step of resistance, organizing itself into a governing federation under a central committee with the broad mandate of safeguarding the republic. Within a few days, the Executive Committee of the National Guard federation was the unofficial power. It took no steps toward violent revolution, but took the precaution of securing the city's chief arsenals and seizing 400 cannons that were left behind by the regular army.

Instead of trying to defuse the situation, Thiers sent 6,000 regular army troops into the city early in the morning on March 18 to recapture the cannons from the working-class district of Montmartre and bring the city under control. Thiers's troops easily overran the guard unit and recaptured the cannons. Only then did they realize they had forgotten to bring horses to haul the cannons away. While the army scrambled for horses, an agitated crowd gathered. As usual, when the Parisian mob and the army interacted, things grew violent. Even though the soldiers refused orders to fire on their fellow citizens, two generals were captured and lynched by a mob that included army troops.

What started out as resistance against the effort to disarm the city turned into a full-scale insurrection. As violence spread through the city, Thiers withdrew all troops and government offices out of Paris to Versailles.

The Election of the Communal Council

On March 26, Parisians repudiated the authority of the National Assembly and elected their own government, calling it the Commune of Paris after the revolutionary government of 1793. The leaders of the new government were a mixed group of old-style Jacobins, anti-clericals, Proudhonists, Blanquist socialists, and political opportunists.

Neo-Jacobins

During the last two years of the Second Empire, neo-Jacobinism enjoyed a renaissance among middle-class republicans, many of whom began their political careers in the July Revolution of 1830 and continued to fight for republican values for their entire lives.

Taking their name from the Jacobins of the French Revolution, the neo-Jacobins held the position that the revolution that began in 1789 was never completed. Its motto—Liberty, Fraternity, Equality—was still an unrealized dream. As a group, they came to prominence when they opposed Bonaparte's takeover in 1851. Many of them were imprisoned or exiled as a result.

The best-known member of the neo-Jacobins was journalist Charles Delescluze, whose career was typical of the movement's members. He was a student during the July Revolution of 1830. He was subsequently implicated in a failed attempt to assassinate King Louis-Philippe in 1832 and fled to Brussels, where he lived until 1841. On returning to France, he edited a radical journal, which he used as a forum for attacking Napoleon III and the Second Empire. He was arrested after Napoleon III took power, and held for several years in the prison colony of French Guiana. Delescluze died on the barricades defending the Paris Commune.

Auguste Blanqui

Unlike other socialists of his generation, Auguste Blanqui (1805–1881) was neither an economist nor a philosopher. Instead, he was concerned with the theory of revolution. After participating in student riots during the July Revolution of 1830, he studied the history of the original French Revolution. He concluded that Babeuf and the Conspiracy of Equals were right: Class struggle was inevitable and only a small group of dedicated conspirators could pull off a successful revolution.

ESSENTIAL

Blanqui and other French socialists of the 1830s and 1840s were introduced to Babeuf's egalitarian communism and revolutionary techniques by Filippo Michele Buonarroti. At the age of 69, Buonarroti returned to Paris from his self-imposed exile in Brussels to fight in the July Revolution of 1830.

Blanqui spent the rest of his life organizing secret societies and plotting unsuccessful revolutions on behalf of the working classes of France. He was arrested twice for his activities as a member of the Society of the Friends of the People, which fell apart after a failed revolt of weavers in Lyon in 1834. He then founded the Society of the Seasons, which captured the Hôtel de Ville in Paris with 500 armed revolutionaries in 1839 but was unable to incite the population to revolt. He was one of the leaders of the crowd that stormed the Hôtel de Ville during the demonstration on May 15th during the Revolution of 1848. After each attempt he was arrested, sentenced, and imprisoned. In 1865, he was re-arrested in the interest of public security as soon as his prison term came to an end.

In 1865, Blanqui escaped from prison and fled to Belgium, where he wrote a manual for urban guerilla warfare, *Instructions for Taking Up Arms* (1867–1868). Unable to resist the need to plot, he traveled secretly between Brussels and Paris, where Blanquist groups were being organized among students and workers.

When the first defeats of the Franco-Prussian War began to damage Napoleon III's position, Blanqui returned to Paris, ready to lead the charge to the barricades once more. With the Germans advancing on Paris,

Blanqui formed a revolutionary club and short-lived newspaper, both named *Our Country in Danger.* He urged Parisians to unite against the Germans. Having tried more than once to take over Paris by military means, he now used his experience to point out what measures should be taken for the city's defense. He soon became convinced that the provisional government was not taking adequate defense measures and staged an unsuccessful coup on October 31, 1870.

Blanqui was arrested for his role in the October 31 insurrection on March 17, one day before the Parisians seized control of the city. While still in jail, Blanqui was elected leader of the new Commune. After the defeat of the Commune, Blanqui became a symbol in the struggle over amnesty. Still in prison, he was elected deputy for Bordeaux in 1879.

The "First Dictatorship of the Proletariat"

The leaders of the Paris Commune seemed curiously unaware that controlling Paris was not the same thing as controlling France.

FACT

On March 22, the National Guard battalion at Lyon followed Paris's lead, seizing control of the town government and establishing a provincial commune. Similar uprisings occurred in Saint-Etienne, Marseille, Toulouse, Limoges, Narbonne, and Le Creousot, but they were quickly suppressed. By April 4, the Paris Commune stood alone against the government at Versailles.

The Commune called for a decentralized government, the separation of church and state, and the replacement of the regular army by the citizen controlled National Guard. None of these provisions could be carried out because the authority of the Commune was confined to Paris. The only practical legislation that was passed was a renewal of the wartime moratorium on rents and debts, the institution of a ten-hour workday, and the abolition of night work in bakeries, suggesting that at least one tired baker served in the Commune's legislature.

"The Bloody Week"

While the leaders in Paris spent their time passing impractical legislation, Thiers built up the military strength of the government at Versailles. He was helped in his preparations by a successful appeal to Bismarck. Never a fan of revolution, Bismarck released a large number of French prisoners of war to help Thiers retake the capital.

Thiers's forces laid siege to Paris at the beginning of April. After several weeks of bombarding the city, government troops entered an undefended section of Paris on May 21. The street fighting over the course of what came to be called "the bloody week" was more brutal than anything in the recent war against the Germans. The Communards set up barricades and fought the army's advance street by street. In the last days of fighting, the Commune's soldiers, seeing that their cause was lost, shot their prisoners and hostages, including the archbishop of Paris, and set fire to the public buildings of the city. On March 28, the last organized defenders of the Commune made a final stand at the cemetery of Pére-Lachaise, where, conveniently, they were executed by the National Assembly's troops. All over the city, men suspected of having fought for the Commune were rounded up and shot without trial.

Approximately 20,000 Communards and 750 soldiers died during "the bloody week." Of the roughly 38,000 arrested, some 7,000 were deported to the penal colony of New Caledonia in Melanesia. Others escaped into exile.

The End of One Revolution or the Beginning of Another?

Socialist theorists of all types claimed the Paris Commune for themselves. On May 30, 1871, two days after the Paris Commune died in the cemetery of Pére-Lachaise, Karl Marx read his report on the event to the General Council of the First International, later published as a pamphlet titled *The Civil War in France.* Marx declared the Commune was the "first dictatorship of the proletariat," notable less for its actual accomplishments than for its symbolism. His contemporaries, the anarchists Mikhail Bakunin and Peter Kropotkin, saw the Commune as an effort to replace the centralized state with a decentralized federation of provincial communes.

Later revolutionaries used the example of the Commune for their own purposes, with varying degrees of historical accuracy. Both Vladimir Lenin and Leon Trotsky held the demise of the Commune up as an example of what happens when revolutionaries try to build bridges across class lines. The Soviet Union claimed the Commune as one of its illustrious ancestors.

Kropotkin summed up the appeal of the Paris Commune in the mythology of socialist revolution in his own pamphlet on the subject:

> *Why is the idea represented by the Commune of Paris so attractive to the workers of every land, of every nationality? The answer is easy. The revolution of 1871 was above all a popular one. It was made by the people themselves, it sprang spontaneously from the midst of the mass, and it was among the great masses of the people that it found its defenders, its heroes, its martyrs. It is just because it was so thoroughly "low" that the middle class can never forgive it. And at the same time its moving spirit was the idea of a social revolution; vague certainly, perhaps unconscious, but still the effort to obtain at last, after the struggle of many centuries, true freedom, true equality for all men. It was the revolution of the lowest of the people marching forward to conquer their rights.*

CHAPTER 9

Anarchism and Socialism

Anarchism developed beside, and occasionally intertwined with, socialism. Historically, anarchism was the answer to the question of what went wrong with the French Revolution, which began as a cry for "Equality, Liberty, Fraternity," and ended with the Reign of Terror, a newly rich bourgeoisie, and an emperor in place of a king. Anarchists concluded that the problem lies with government itself. The correct end to social revolution is not a better government, but no government.

What Is Anarchism?

Anarchism, like socialism, covers a broad spectrum of political ideas, all of which share a core belief that central government is both undesirable and unnecessary. For many socialists, the central political question is what type of government will provide the most egalitarian state. Anarchists believe that the state itself is the enemy of equality because the state always protects the interests of the powerful, whether aristocrat, capitalist, or Soviet *apparatchik*, over those of the powerless.

Most versions of anarchism advocate a society right out of the theories of Rousseau and the utopian socialists, with land and the means of production controlled by decentralized, self-governing communities that are based on cooperation rather than on competition or coercion. Local communities are linked in loose federations to meet mutual needs. Some forms of anarchism emphasize the right of an individual or family to control the resources they need to make a living, so long as they do not attempt to control the resources needed by others.

Despite its historical association with violence and assassination, anarchism is fundamentally optimistic about human nature. Anarchist theory assumes that crime is a product of laws and property. Once the state is abolished, society can operate on a moral basis of cooperation and mutual aid.

William Godwin: The Father of Philosophical Anarchism

William Godwin (1756–1836) is generally considered the founder of anarchism. Godwin was a Presbyterian minister who took his first step toward anarchism through the Sandemanian sect of Presbyterianism, which taught that the New Testament did not support the idea of an established church because the Kingdom of Christ is spiritual and not worldly. Over time, he moved from Sandemanianism, to an early form of Unitarianism called *Socianism*.

Godwin's spiritual transformation was paralleled by increasingly radical political beliefs. At first a member of the traditionally monarchist Tory party, he gradually embraced republican views. By 1787, he was, by his own account, a "complete unbeliever" in both spiritual and political matters.

Inspired by both the English tradition of radical nonconformity and the French *philosophes*, Godwin came to the conclusion that men could become virtuous by accepting the supremacy of reason, thereby making government unnecessary. As a community became more enlightened, the institutions of government would lose their authority. He believed that even though the state lacks moral legitimacy, it should be replaced through peaceful evolution rather than revolution, a position known as *philosophical anarchism*.

ALERT

In English history, nonconformists, also called Dissenters, were members of any Protestant church that did not conform to the doctrines of the established Church of England. Perhaps because their members already stood outside the social mainstream, nonconformist groups had a long tradition of political activism.

Godwin laid out the principles of philosophical anarchism in his major work, *An Enquiry Concerning Political Justice and Its Influence on General Virtue and Happiness*. He began with what became the classic anarchist argument against government: Authority is against nature and social ills exist because man is not free to act according to reason. In place of a central government and its institutions, which he contended rule by authority and force, he proposed a decentralized society of small, autonomous communities. Even on this small scale, he avoided the trappings of a democracy because rule by a democratic majority might be dangerous to the rights of minorities.

He also dispensed with anything organized according to rules, including laws, private property, musical concerts, and marriage, which he described as "the worst of laws." He condemned the accumulation of property as a source of power over others and envisioned a loose economic system in which each gives and takes according to ability and need. He argued that in such a society,

> *There would no longer be a handful of rich and a multitude of poor . . . There will be no war, no crime, no administration of justice, as it is called, and no government. Besides this there will be no disease, no anguish, melancholy, or resentment.*

The publication of *Political Justice* brought Godwin instant fame in the 1790s. He became a central figure in radical political and literary circles in London. For a brief time, he enjoyed enthusiastic disciples among the Romantic poets, including his son-in-law Percy Bysshe Shelley, Samuel Taylor Coleridge, Robert Southey, and William Wordsworth. As the French Revolution played out its course and Britain became increasingly conservative, Godwin's views became less popular, but *Political Justice* continued to have an underground life in radical circles.

Pierre-Joseph Proudhon

Pierre-Joseph Proudhon (1809–1865) was the first person to call himself an anarchist. The son of a small brewer and tavern keeper, Proudhon grew up in southwest France near Fourier's home in Besançon. He was always proud of his working class background and suspicious of the role of intellectuals in social movements. A printer and proofreader by trade, he taught himself to read Greek, Latin, and Hebrew. In 1838 he won a scholarship from the Besançon Academy that allowed him to study in Paris, where he built a reputation as a radical journalist.

FACT

Based on the Greek *anarkhia*, meaning contrary to authority or without a ruler, the word "anarchy" had negative connotations long before Proudhon claimed it for his political philosophy. Proudhon's first followers were reluctant to adopt the name and called themselves Mutualists.

Property Is Theft!

Proudhon is best known for the phrase "property is theft," which appeared in his pamphlet *What Is Property?* (1840). He also declared, in the same essay, that "property is freedom." According to Proudhon, property is freedom when it allows a peasant or artisan to control his livelihood through the possession of the land he cultivates or his workshop and the tools of his trade. Property becomes theft when a landowner or capitalist gains control over the homes, land, or livelihood of others by exploiting the labor of others.

ESSENTIAL

Marx attacked Proudhon's statement that "property is theft," saying that by referring to a violation of property rights, Proudhon presupposed that real rights in property existed. In return, Proudhon criticized communism because it destroyed freedom by taking away the individual's control over his livelihood.

Mutualism and Federalism

Proudhon argued that organization without government was not only possible, but preferable. His social and political ideology rested on two basic beliefs:

- Labor should be the basis for social organization
- All systems of government are oppressive

In his view, a perfect society would be made up of independent, self-supporting peasants and artisans. Associations of workers would run the factories and utilities for their mutual benefit. If people worked only for themselves and their families, there would be no exploitation because nothing would be produced for employers. In place of the centralized state, he proposed a loosely knit "federalism" between local communities and industrial societies, which would be bound together by contracts and mutual interests. A system of arbitration would replace courts of law.

The first step to restoring healthy economic relationships between people was to abolish the existing system of credit and exchange. Money and credit would be based on the value of labor rather than the gold standard. By tying money directly to labor, there would be no surplus value and no employer to reduce labor's share of the value it creates. With laborers able to buy the goods they create, there would be no lack of money for capital re-investment, thus no danger of unemployment and social instability.

Direct Action

In his last, posthumously published book, *The Political Capability of the Working Classes* (1865), Proudhon rejects not only representative democracy but also centralized state socialism and communism. He argues that workers are responsible for their own liberation, which can be obtained not through legislative reforms but through organized economic actions. Proudhon's call for direct action by the proletariat became a fundamental tenet of anarchism.

Mikhail Bakunin

Mikhail Bakunin (1814–1876) was born into a conservative noble family in Russia. He served briefly in the Russian army on the Polish frontier before plunging into the intellectual life of Moscow and Premukhino, where he studied romantic Hegelianism and became friends with the novelist Ivan Turgenev.

In 1840, Bakunin traveled to Berlin. Like others before him, he fell in with that nursery school for revolutionaries, the Young Hegelians, who introduced him to another side of Hegel. After brief periods in Berlin and Switzerland, he made his way to Paris. In Paris, he abandoned Hegel in favor of Proudhon and anarchism. He also met a number of Polish émigrés, who interested him in the possibilities of combining the struggle for national liberation with social revolution.

Travels and Escapes

Always more interested in action than in theory, Bakunin was deeply involved in the 1848 revolutions. He followed the uprisings from Paris to Prague to Dresden, traveling on false passports and always one step ahead of the police. The authorities caught up with him after the revolution in Dresden failed. He was arrested and condemned to death. The Dresden authorities happily handed him over to the Austrians, who had a warrant out for his arrest for his revolutionary activity in Prague. The Austrians condemned him to death again, carried him to the border, took back their handcuffs, and handed him over to the Russians. (He complained later that the Russian handcuffs were less comfortable than the Austrian ones.)

After six years in the Peter and Paul Fortress in St. Petersburg, Bakunin was exiled to a Siberian prison that was run by one of his mother's cousins. In 1861, he escaped. Traveling on an American ship by way of Japan, San Francisco, and New York, he made his way to London, a haven of nineteenth-century European refugees from both the left and right.

For several years Bakunin batted around Europe, going anywhere there was a revolution in process. He slowly realized that revolutionaries who were fighting for national liberation usually had no interest in broader social change. Having come to the conclusion that social revolution must be international to succeed, he settled in Italy and began to create a complex network of secret societies—some real, some fictional—that he called the International Social Democratic Alliance.

Anarcho-Communism

Bakunin adapted Proudhon's teachings to create the doctrine later known as anarcho-communism. He shared Marx's vision of communism as a classless society, but rejected the idea of a central Soviet state. Instead, he believed that land, natural resources, and the means of production should be held by local communities, which would form a loose federation with other communities for joint purposes.

Unlike Godwin or Proudhon, Bakunin advocated the use of terror and violence as a weapon to destroy organized government, claiming that "the passion for destruction is also a creative urge." He argued that the state exists to protect private property and private property protects the state. Therefore, the state must be destroyed before property can be communally owned and equally distributed. Paradoxically, the only way to create a free and peaceful society was through violent revolution.

Proletariat or Peasant?

Marx and Engels were convinced that the revolution would begin with the industrial working class in the most advanced capitalist societies, where the conflicts between capital and labor were most acute. Bakunin disagreed. He argued revolutionary change was most likely in the countries that were the least economically developed because their workers were less privileged. Bad as life was for a factory worker in Manchester, it was worse for workers in the countries that were less developed. He made a strong argument that Russian peasants would lead the charge in the revolution. Not only were Russian serfs still legally tied to the land as late as the Emancipation Manifesto of 1864, but they had traditional village communal structures that would form a great foundation for socialism.

"I Am Not a Communist"

In 1864, Marx drew up the founding statement for the International Working Men's Association, also known as the First International. Bakunin immediately challenged the idea of creating a formal organization to win support for communism, asking "How can you expect an egalitarian and free society to emerge from an authoritarian organization?" Four years later, he declared his distaste for the entire idea of communism:

> *I am not a communist because communism concentrates all the powers of society into the state; because it necessarily ends in the centralization of property in the hands of the state, while I want the abolition of the state, which, on the pretext of making men moral and civilized, has up to now enslaved, oppressed, exploited and depraved them.*

The battle between Marx and Bakunin over the control of the First International came to a head in 1872, when Marx and Engels engineered the expulsion of Bakunin and his followers from the First International.

ESSENTIAL

Bakunin accurately predicted the nature of Marxist dictatorships in the twentieth century: "The so-called people's state will be nothing other than the quite despotic administration of the masses by a new and very non-numerous aristocracy of real and supposed learned ones."

The Anarchist Prince

Peter Kropotkin (1842–1921) was the son of a Russian prince. He was educated at an elite military school and served for several years as an officer in Siberia. He resigned his commission in 1867, studied mathematics in St. Petersburg, and became a professional geographer, specializing in the mountain ranges and glaciers of Asia.

In 1872, Kropotkin brought a promising scientific career to a halt. He turned down the secretaryship of the Russian Geographical Society, renounced the title of prince, and joined the revolutionary movement in St. Petersburg. For several years, he worked as part of the Tchaikovsky circle, which distributed revolutionary propaganda to Russian workers and peasants.

Arrested in St. Petersburg in 1876, Kropotkin began a variation of the experience of arrest, expulsion, and escape common to radical reformers of the period. He was held without trial but managed to escape from the prison hospital and make his way to Western Europe. Expelled from Switzerland at the demand of the Russian government in 1881 and arrested in France in 1883, he sought refuge in England, where he made his living as a respected scientific journalist.

Kropotkin was the most widely read of the anarchist theorists. Between 1883 and 1917, when he returned to Russia, he contributed articles on anarchism to leading liberal magazines, radical papers, and the eleventh edition of the *Encyclopedia Britannica.* His anarchistic journalism was translated and published worldwide. Several of his books were published as magazine serials.

Kropotkin tried to give anarchism a scientific basis. The most influential of his works was *Mutual Aid* (1902). In it, he refuted the popular theory of social Darwinism, which justified competition in a free market economy in terms of survival of the fittest. He demonstrated from observation of both animal and human societies that competition within a species is less important than cooperation as a condition for survival.

The Propaganda of the Deed

In the 1870s, French and Italian anarchists began to use a phrase that would become one of the most visible and controversial anarchist doctrines: *the propaganda of the deed.* Essentially a violent form of direct action, the idea was that violent action is the most effective form of propaganda for the revolutionary cause.

FACT

Assassinations of prominent political figures became more common with the ready availability of dynamite, which some revolutionaries welcomed as the "artillery of the proletariat." Patented by Alfred Nobel in 1867, the explosive was widely manufactured by 1875. One anarchist, Johann Most, gave instructions for whipping up a batch at home in *The Science of Revolutionary Warfare*.

At first, the propaganda of the deed referred to rural insurrections intended to rouse the Italian peasantry to revolt. Later, the doctrine became the justification for assassinations and bombings of public places carried out by individual protesters. Sometimes working alone, sometimes as part of a conspiracy, anarchists carried out a series of attacks on prominent political figures, beginning with the attempt to assassinate Kaiser Wilhelm I in 1878 and ending with the deaths of the Archduke Ferdinand and his wife at Sarajevo in 1914.

FACT

The original assassins were members of a revolutionary Shiite sect in eleventh-century Persia, who used the murder of important figures as a way to influence political policies. The object was not to remove a particular leader from power, but to make people believe that the assassins could kill anyone at any time.

Important figures in the anarchist movement repudiated the technique as fundamentally useless. As Kropotkin put it, "A structure based on centuries of history cannot be destroyed with a few kilos of dynamite." Such protests were useless; the lone bomber became the public image of anarchy.

CHAPTER 10

Social Democracy

In the 1860s, Europe was beginning to recover from the first traumas of the industrial revolution. There was no sign that Marx's proletariat revolution was imminent. Capitalism was flourishing. Economic and political injustices remained, but governments began to enact labor laws, lift restrictions on trade unionism, and open the political process, largely as a result of pressure from the socialist and labor movements. Some German socialists began to reconsider the inevitability of the Marxist revolution and look toward the possibility of political action.

What Is Social Democracy?

During the late nineteenth and the early twentieth centuries, a wide range of socialists adopted the term social democrat to distinguish themselves from socialists who advocated violent revolution. The basic tenet of social democracy is the belief that socialist reforms can be achieved democratically through the election of socialist representatives. Social democrats advocate a peaceful, evolutionary transition from capitalism to socialism through the use of the existing political process.

The early proponents of social democracy claimed they were only revising Marxism. Their opponents, the defenders of Marxist orthodoxy, recognized that they were actually replacing Marxism with something entirely different. By the end of the nineteenth century, socialism split into two camps: the social democrats, who believed in the possibility of reform, and the communists, who still believed in revolution.

The Beginnings of Social Democracy in Germany

In the aftermath of the revolutions of 1848, Friedrich Wilhelm IV promulgated a constitution that included a legislature loosely based on the British parliament. Members of the upper house inherited their seats or were appointed by the king. Members of the lower house were elected by a variation on universal manhood suffrage. Voters were divided into three categories according to the amount of taxes they paid, with the votes of the wealthy more heavily weighted than votes of the poor. The intention was to keep conservative landowners in power. The plan backfired. By the end of the 1850s, the vote was weighted in favor of wealthy manufacturers, merchants, bankers, and professionals.

With the rise to power of King Wilhelm I and his chancellor, Otto von Bismarck, Prussia, and by extension the lesser German states under its influence, entered a period of political change in the 1860s. Bismarck and the king, both moderate conservatives, found themselves in conflict with the newly powerful liberals. Since the working classes had at least a nominal vote, they often found themselves allied with the radical wing of the liberal movement.

Working-Class Organizations

The opportunities for working-class organizations were limited. Labor unions were illegal in all the German states and there were heavy restrictions on the formation of political parties.

The primary model was the local worker's educational societies founded by liberals beginning in the 1840s as a way of supplementing low levels of primary education. In the 1860s, workers began to take over these associations from their liberal sponsors and run them on their own behalf. Most associations provided both lecture series and systematic courses designed to teach a specific subject. In 1864 alone, the thirty-three education societies in Prussia sponsored more than 1,000 public lectures. In 1866, many of these societies banded together to form the League of German Workingmen's Associations.

These groups provided the foundation for the first two social democratic workers' parties: the General German Workers' Association, established by Ferdinand Lassalle in 1863, and the German Social Democratic Labor Party, founded by Wilhelm Liebknecht and August Bebel in 1869.

Ferdinand Lassalle

Ferdinand Lassalle (1825–1864) was the son of a wealthy Jewish silk trader in Breslau. After eighteen unhappy months at a commercial school in Leipzig, he convinced his father to send him to the university instead. He spent two years at Breslau, studying philosophy, history, philology, and archeology. After two years, he transferred to Berlin, where he discovered Hegel and the French utopian socialists. Like Marx before him, he intended to pursue a career as a philosopher with the hope of transforming social conditions in Germany. Again like Marx, reality soon derailed his academic career.

FACT

In 1846, Lassalle met Countess Sophie Hatzfeld, who was trying both to divorce her husband and to regain control of her fortune and her children. Over the course of eight years, Lassalle filed thirty-five separate lawsuits in various courts on her behalf. After finally obtaining the divorce in 1854, the countess settled a pension on Lassalle, making him financially independent.

In March 1848, when revolution broke out in the German states, Lassalle was in jail in Düsseldorf as a result of his efforts in the Hatzfeld case. Düsseldorf was an important center of the revolutionary struggle in the industrialized Rhineland. As soon as Lassalle was released from jail in August, he threw himself into the cause. He was not involved for long. The Düsseldorf authorities arrested him in November for an inflammatory speech urging the local military to revolt. He spent six months in jail.

Lassalle Founds a Political Party

Lassalle became a working-class leader almost by accident. From 1849 to 1857, Lassalle lived in Düsseldorf. During this period, he corresponded regularly with Marx, whom he met during the 1848 uprisings; continued his legal battle on behalf of the countess; and wrote on philosophical topics that hovered on the edge of socialism. He came to the conclusion that the battle for democracy had to be fought by the workers through working-class organizations.

In 1859, Lassalle left Düsseldorf for Berlin, where he worked as a political journalist and gave an occasional lecture at one of the educational societies. In 1862, he gave two addresses that fired the imagination of his listeners.

In the first, *On the Special Connection of the Present Historical Period with the Idea of a Working Class*, commonly known as *The Working Man's Program*, Lassalle introduced his audience to Marx's dialectic of social change, in which each society contains within itself the seeds of the next form of social organization. He agreed with Marx that the historical task of the working class is to build a society based on cooperative principles. Unlike Marx, however, Lassalle did not call for revolution. Instead he believed the state can be an instrument for social reform. Therefore, the acquisition of direct universal suffrage must be the first political goal of the proletariat.

Lassalle soon got the chance to speak to a larger audience. Following a visit by German workers to the London International Exhibition of 1862, the educational societies of Berlin and Leipzig called a general congress of German workers. The program committee asked Lassalle to explain his views on the labor problem. They were especially interested in what he had to say about the ideas of Hermann Schulze-Delitzsch regarding cooperative credit unions.

The committee got more than they were expecting. Lassalle responded with an *Open Letter of Reply* in which he declared that universal suffrage was the only means to improve the material situation of the working class. He believed that cooperative credit associations or consumer cooperatives would accomplish little because Ricardo's "iron law of wages" inevitably shaped the workers' place in a capitalist society.

ESSENTIAL

According to Ricardo, the free market will always keep laborers' wages at a subsistence level. Wages will rise and fall in relationship to the cost of food, but capital will never pay more than a cost of living increase because a real wage increase comes directly out of profits.

Lassalle argued that workers would be better off establishing producers' cooperatives than consumer cooperatives. Instead of banding together to buy goods at a wholesale cost, workers should become their own employers through producers' cooperatives, thereby taking a first step toward abolishing the profit system, and ultimately ending the iron law of wages. If workers wanted to make a real change in society, they should create not only small workshops, but also modern factories using capital advanced by the state. None of those changes could occur until workers lobbied for the first, most important, change. Before the state could become an instrument of reform, the working class must have the vote.

In the *Open Letter*, Lassalle laid out a practical program for getting the vote. Workers needed to make their numbers count. He suggested the creation of a mass organization built after the model of the English Anti-Corn Law League. The organization would build a war chest by collecting weekly dues from each member. They would use the money to spread information about the need for direct universal suffrage, found newspapers, and defend members who were arrested on behalf of the cause. He also pointed out that they would get more bang for their Deutsche marks by supporting the Progressive party in any causes in which they shared an interest.

Lassalle's audience received the *Open Letter* as a call to action. Almost without effort on his part, the first working-class political organization, the General German Workers' Association, was founded in May 1863, with Lassalle as its president.

The German Social Democratic Labor Party

Several years after Lassalle's death, August Bebel (1840–1913) and Wilhelm Liebknecht (1826–1900) formed a second working-class political party in Germany, the German Social Democratic Labor Party. Bebel was the son of a noncommissioned officer in the Prussian army. He was orphaned early in life and grew up in poverty. After traveling for several years as a journeyman wood worker, he settled in Leipzig, where he became involved in the local workers' educational society.

Liebknecht was an old-style radical who took refuge in London after the Revolution of 1848. In London, he joined the Communist League, where he worked closely with Marx and Engels and supported himself as a correspondent for the Augsburg Gazette. In 1862, when the Prussian government offered a general amnesty to those who were involved in the 1848 revolutions, he returned to Berlin. Fresh from the fount of Marxist wisdom in London, Liebknecht quickly developed a following among the radical element of working-class Berlin. Just as quickly, Bismarck had him thrown back out of Prussia. This time he only went as far as Leipzig, where he joined Lassalle's General German Workers' Association and met August Bebel.

In 1867, Liebknecht and Bebel were both elected to the constituent assembly for the newly formed North German Confederation. Although both were dedicated Marxists, they held their seats as part of the German People's Party, which was primarily made up of middle-class radicals.

FACT

> The North German Confederation, a union of German states north of the Main River, was formed in 1867 with Berlin as its capital, King Wilhelm I as its president, and Bismarck as its chancellor. In 1871, the North German Confederation became the German Reich.

Bebel and Liebknecht soon came to the conclusion that they would command more respect on the legislative floor if they represented a Marxist organization comparable to the General German Workers' Association. They followed Lassalle's example and turned to the workers' education societies. Bebel had previously served as the chairman of the Leipzig society. In

1868, he was elected president of the Federation of Workingmen's Associations. Under his presidency, the federation passed a resolution committing the federation to the program of the First International. The following year, Bebel and Liebknecht issued an invitation to a German Social Democratic Workers' Congress in Eisenach, out of which the German Social Democratic Labor Party was formed, with Bebel as its chairman.

The German Social Democratic Party (SDP)

The violence of the Paris Commune of 1871 caused a backlash against socialism throughout Europe, especially in the new German Reich, where there were two well established political parties professing socialistic and democratic principles. Fear of socialism on the part of the ruling classes was made worse in 1873, when Europe was hit with another severe economic depression, brought on in part by the financial consequences of the Franco-Prussian War. Once again, businesses failed, domestic prices and wages fell, and unemployment rose. Fearful of a repetition of 1848, the police and the courts began to crack down on socialist organizations.

FACT

The Long Depression began with the fall of the Viennese Stock Exchange on May 9, 1873. The crash set off a period of economic stagnation that continued for two decades. Despite slowed growth and rising unemployment, many members of the working classes actually enjoyed an increased standard of living during this period as a result of a steady fall in the cost of food and manufactured goods.

By 1875, the combination of increasing government persecution and the financial strain of unemployed members were making survival hard for both of Germany's socialist parties. Despite differences in organization and policy, the two organizations agreed to merge. Their leaders met in Gotha, where they created a charter for the new organization, known as the Gotha Program. The new organization, the German Social Democratic Party (SDP), was the largest of the pre-1914 Marxist parties. By 1912, the SDP was the largest single party represented in the Reichstag, holding 110 out of 397 seats.

QUESTION

Evolution or revolution?

The question of whether the proletariat should bring about the socialist state through evolutionary reforms or violent revolution was one of the most debated questions in socialist circles until the Russian Revolution of 1917 created the final split between the Socialist Democratic parties and Communist parties.

Marx bitterly denounced the merger in his *Critique of the Gotha Program*, published posthumously by Engels in 1891. He complained that Lassalle had "conceived of the workers' movement from the narrowest national standpoint," concentrating on converting Germany to socialism. Marx believed that socialism must be an international movement if it was to succeed. Worse, from Marx's perspective, Lassalle and his followers sought to gain control of the state through elections in the hope of transforming capitalism through the establishment of workers' collectives. Marx believed that the only path to socialism was through revolution.

Bismarck's Anti-Socialist Laws

In 1878, Bismarck forced the passage of an anti-socialist law through the Reichstag. Socialist organizations, educational programs, and publications were banned, and arrest warrants were issued for individual socialist leaders.

Bebel told his fellow representatives in the Reichstag that passage of the bill would change nothing: "Your lances will be shattered in this struggle like glass on granite." In the long run he was right. When the law expired in 1890, the SDP won 20 percent of the popular vote, making Bebel the most prominent opponent of the government.

In the short run, the SDP went underground, camouflaged by local clubs of various sorts. Contact between the various clubs was maintained through a magazine, *The Social Democrat.* Published in Switzerland, thousands of copies were smuggled into Germany each week, each copy forming the nucleus for a circle of readers that temporarily replaced the normal party organization.

The Erfurt Program

In 1891, the SDP adopted a new charter, the Erfurt program. The Gotha program was a compromise between the overlapping ideologies of the two original parties. The Erfurt program displayed signs of a more fundamental tension between revisionism and Marxist orthodoxy that had developed within the party.

Karl Kautsky, the defender of Marxist orthodoxy, drafted the first, theoretical, section of the program. In it, he stressed the division of society into two hostile camps and painted a grim picture of a future in which a few large-scale capitalist enterprises expand their control over the economic system.

Eduard Bernstein, the leading theoretician of social democratic revisionism, drafted the second, practical, portion of the program, which consisted of a series of reforms that could be obtained only by working within the system, including that perennial favorite, universal manhood suffrage, secularized schools, compensation for elected officials, and more liberal labor laws.

QUESTION

Why was it important to pay elected officials?
Getting the vote was only the first step in establishing a working-class presence in the legislature. If elected officials don't receive a salary, it is difficult for anyone who has to earn a living to hold office.

The official position was that the Erfurt program was both reformist and revolutionary, combining immediate benefits for the proletariat with the long-term goal of overthrowing capitalism.

Karl Kautsky and Marxist Orthodoxy

Karl Kautsky (1854–1938) was the leader of Marxist orthodoxy in the SDP. He joined the Austrian Social Democrats while a student at Vienna.

Ironically, he became a Marxist in Zurich, where he studied the works of Marx and Engels with revisionist leader Eduard Bernstein.

After Engels death in 1895, Kautsky became the most influential interpreter of Marxist doctrine, not only in the SDP but in the International as a whole. His writings were often the first, and sometimes the only, interpretation of Marx available to an entire generation of socialists in Germany and elsewhere.

Influenced by the European depression of 1873, Kautsky's writings depict a capitalist system spiraling toward its death. He emphasized the inevitability of the eventual triumph of socialism and rejected the fundamental premises of social democracy. He argued that the role of a socialist party was not to create a transition to socialism, but to educate workers about the nature of capitalism and prepare them for the class struggle that would bring about its demise.

Eduard Bernstein and Marxist Revisionism

Social democracy found its theorist in Eduard Bernstein (1850–1932). Called "the father of revisionism," Bernstein built on Lassalle's ideas to produce what would become the basic ideology of social democracy.

e! ALERT

After the Bolshevik revolution, communists began to use the term revisionism to attack what they saw as deviations from the Soviet norm. For instance, Tito's policies in communist Yugoslavia were condemned as "modern revisionism" by the Soviets. (Ironically, Communist China used the same term against Soviet Russia.)

Like Bebel, Bernstein was born into a working-class family and had personal experience of poverty. His father was a railroad engineer who did not make enough to support his ten surviving children. His uncle was the editor of the *Berlin Peoples Times*, a newspaper widely read in progressive working-class circles.

Bernstein attended the local school until he was sixteen, when he took an apprenticeship as a bank clerk. In 1872, he was introduced to socialist ideas by the highly publicized political trial of Bebel and Liebknecht, who were the only two members of the North German Reichstag who refused to vote for war bonds to fund the Franco-Prussian War. The leaders of the German Social Democratic Worker's Party used their defense as an opportunity to preach the socialist gospel and made at least one convert.

From Switzerland to London

In 1878, Bernstein was one of the leaders indicted in Bismarck's anti-socialist laws. With a warrant issued for his arrest, he emigrated to Switzerland, where he became the editor of *The Social Democrat*. Expelled from Switzerland at Bismarck's insistence in 1888, he moved to London, where he became Friedrich Engels's right-hand man—chosen to produce the fourth volume of *Das Kapital* from Marx's badly organized notes and designated the literary executor for Engels's estate.

While in London, Bernstein also met the leaders of the newly formed Fabian Society, Sidney and Beatrice Webb. Under the Webbs' influence, he came to realize that he no longer believed in many of Marx's arguments.

FACT

The London-based Fabian Society was founded in 1884 with the goal of establishing a democratic socialist state in Great Britain. The Fabians advocated a gradualist approach to social change, concentrating on education and participation in Parliamentary politics. Members of the Fabian Society were instrumental in the formation of the British Labour Party.

Evolutionary Socialism

In 1899, faced with a growing gap between the SDP's official ideology of Marxist class struggle and the reality of its parliamentary participation, Bernstein published socialism's most comprehensive theoretical critique of Marxist orthodoxy, *Evolutionary Socialism*. In it, Bernstein rejected two of the key elements of Marxist orthodoxy: historical materialism and class struggle. Instead of waiting for capitalism to collapse, he called on socialists to adapt the tools of parliamentary democracy and participation in government to achieve socialist ends. Instead of class struggle, he urged political cooperation between the working classes, the peasantry, and the dissatisfied members of the middle classes, all of whom suffered from the injustices of capitalism.

After examining Marx's predictions about capitalism and economic development, Bernstein challenged the Marxist orthodoxy that capitalism was doomed. He pointed out that capitalism was overcoming many of its weaknesses, such as unemployment, overproduction, and the uneven distribution of wealth. The number of property owners had increased. Thanks to pressure from the socialist movement, governments tempered the most exploitive inclinations of capitalism with the passage of factory legislation and new laws making trade unions legal.

ESSENTIAL

Bernstein is famous for the comment that "what is termed the final goal of socialism is nothing to me, the movement is everything." He meant that lasting social revolution comes through steady advances, "the ground gained piecemeal by hard, unremitting struggle, rather than through violent upheaval."

Bernstein ended with the conclusion that socialism was not the inevitable product of a revolt against capitalism. It was instead "something that ought to be." The success of socialism didn't depend on the continued and intensifying misery of the working classes but on eliminating that misery. The task for socialism was to develop suggestions for reform that would improve the living conditions of most people. And, as Lassalle argued thirty-five years earlier, the first step was universal suffrage. With the vote, the working classes could create a socialist state by electing socialist representatives to a democratic government, making democracy both the means and the end.

The Second International (1889–1914)

The success of the Social Democrat Party in Germany encouraged the spread of social democracy to other European countries. Between the 1880s and the outbreak of the First World War, there was a massive growth in socialist parties throughout Europe. In 1889, Europe's socialist parties joined together to create the Second International, with the elderly Friedrich Engels as its honorary president.

The Second International was unlike the First International in several ways. Where the First International included representatives from every kind of leftist group, large and small, the Second International limited itself to representatives from national parties and unions. The First International was a highly centralized organization, tightly controlled by Karl Marx, and later Friedrich Engels, from their base in London. The Second International was a loose federation of its member groups. It didn't even have an executive body until 1900.

Possibly the most important way the Second International differed from the first was its relative homogeneity. The First International welcomed members from every branch of the left: radical shoemakers from London, Proudhonists dreaming of cooperative federations, followers of Babeuf caught up in the details of insurrection, orthodox Marxists, and extreme anarchists alike. In the end, it suffered its own version of Marx's dialectic—torn apart by its inherent contradictions. By contrast, the German Social Democrat Party dominated the Second International. In 1886, when the conflict between social democracy and anarchism became too great, the Second International simply expelled the anarchists and continued about its business.

Working-Class Internationalism

The central belief professed by all members of the Second International was the ideal of working-class internationalism. All socialist parties shared the view that the workers had no country because their common enemy was capitalism. They agreed in theory that they would not support their own governments in pursuing a capitalist war. In fact, if war was declared, socialists in belligerent countries would use its hardships to promote socialist revolution.

The First World War proved that working-class internationalism was not as strong as working-class nationalism. Socialists from every country involved chose to support their country rather than their class. The Second International held its last conference in Switzerland in 1915.

CHAPTER 11

Syndicalism

Social democrats weren't the only socialists to reject Marxist orthodoxy. Standing at the intersection between trade unionism and anarchism, syndicalists believed that Marxism simply replaced capitalist factory owners with state bureaucrats. They also rejected social democracy's efforts at working within the system. Caught between state oppression and the futility of politics, syndicalists believed that society could be transformed only through direct action by the working classes themselves, using trade unions and the general strike as their tools.

What Is Syndicalism?

Syndicalism was a militant form of trade unionism that combined the ideas of Marx, Proudhon, and Bakunin with the technique of collective action by workers. Syndicalists advocated workers taking over the means of the production as a first step in abolishing the state. Both the state and the capitalist system would be replaced by a new social order, with the local trade union as its basic unit of organization. The method generally favored for accomplishing this transformation was the general strike.

ALERT

> The word *syndicalism* comes from the French term for labor union: *syndicate* (not to be confused with the English "syndicate," which is something totally different). In France, where the movement was born, *syndicalism* means plain vanilla trade unionism. In France, the union-based socialist movement is called *revolutionary syndicalism* or *anarcho-syndicalism.*

Syndicalists rejected social democracy's policy of reform through parliamentary politics *and* Marxism's reliance on a centralized state after the revolution. Political parties were incapable of producing fundamental change. The state was by its nature a tool of capitalist oppression.

Instead of reform or state socialism, syndicalists looked to revolution by the direct action of the workers. If the unions were not strong enough to risk a strike, their members would attack employers through boycotts and sabotage. The climax of direct action would be the general strike.

After the revolution, a federation of trade unions and labor exchanges would replace the state.

Syndicalism and Trade Unionism

Syndicalism was born in the French trade union movement at the end of the nineteenth century. Industrial trade unions developed alongside socialism. Unlike the earlier craft unions, which represented workers with a shared set of skills, industrial unions were organized to represent large numbers of workers within a specific industry or region—skilled and unskilled, employed or unemployed. Like socialist parties, such unions were motivated by a clear sense of class-consciousness, in the Marxist sense, and the desire to improve the lives of workers.

Despite their similarities, trade unions and socialist parties differed in how they worked for change. The unions' goals were immediate and practical: higher wages, shorter hours, the eight-hour day, better working conditions. Trade unions relied on economic, rather than political, methods. Their primary tools were collective bargaining power, their ability to supply aid to their members, and, as a last recourse, the strike.

ESSENTIAL

The syndicalist idea of the "conscious minority" was related to the socialist idea of "false consciousness." The conscious few must work on behalf of an unconscious majority who support a system that is against their interests. There is an inherent contradiction in syndicalist thought between the idea of the conscious minority and the central role of the general strike.

Syndicalist-run unions, like other trade unionists, used the tactics of collective bargaining and limited strikes to win immediate benefits for their members. Unlike mainstream trade unions, the principal function of the syndicalist trade union was not winning economic gains for its members, but undermining the political order by means of direct action led by a "conscious minority."

Syndicalism and Anarchism

French trade unions were breeding grounds for anarchism from the beginning. Proud of the French revolutionary tradition, workers were suspicious of both government and industry. Many rejected social democracy as corrupt, ineffective—and German. When trade unions were made legal in 1884, the bulk of the members were anarchists in the Proudhon tradition.

In its purest form, anarchism is opposed not only to the state, but also to all types of hierarchy and authority. Anarchists prefer small groups, from revolutionary cells to producers' cooperatives, linked together in a decentralized federation.

The marriage between trade unions and anarchism was uncomfortable. The small groups that anarchists preferred made ineffective trade unions. Some anarchists even feared that the large industrial trade unions would create powerful interest groups in a new society. On the other hand, many union members were uncomfortable with anarchist violence, particularly after the doctrine of the "propaganda of the deed" set off a wave of public bombings beginning in 1882.

Like anarchists, syndicalists rejected organized government and the coercion of the state. They believed power could and should be achieved by the workers themselves, rather than through political parties and the state. Unlike anarchists, syndicalists considered that the basic building block of the ideal society would be trade unions rather than small local communities.

The Federation of Labor Exchanges

Shortly after trade unions were legalized in France in 1884, the government of Leon Gambetta created an institution to help connect employers with laborers seeking work: the labor exchanges (*bourses du travail*). The first exchange opened in Paris in 1887 in a building donated by the local municipal council. Parisian workers demanded the right to run the exchanges themselves. By 1907, there were 150 labor exchanges in cities across France.

Most of the exchanges were founded with the help of local municipalities and began as places where workers could present themselves for hire. In the hands of the trade unions, the labor exchanges developed into much more, combining the function of workers' club, placement service, and mutual aid society. Unions used the exchanges to steer job seekers away from centers of labor disputes, preventing them from becoming strikebreakers. Exchanges served as local labor councils that included all the unions of different trades in a given city. Many exchanges became institutions for working-class education: setting up libraries, museums of labor history, technical colleges, and schools for the education of workers' children.

In 1892, French municipal labor exchanges came together to form the Federation of Labor Exchanges, effectively creating a collective bargaining unit for their organizations. Under the leadership of Fernand Pelloutier, the Federation became an incubator for syndicalism.

Fernand Pelloutier and the Federation of Labor Exchanges

Although syndicalism had no obvious founder, Fernand Pelloutier (1867–1901) was the first person to clearly articulate syndicalist ideals. Pelloutier was involved in the anarchist movement for several years before he became Operating Secretary of the Federation of Labor Exchanges in 1895. Under his leadership, the exchanges took on additional functions, such as providing information on how to find work, how to join unions and cooperatives, and how to go on strike; where possible, exchanges were encouraged to publish their own newspapers and provide information about labor markets to interested proletarian organizations. The membership rose to more than 250,000.

Like Proudhon before him, Pelloutier believed that workers could only be emancipated by their own direct action. He went further than Proudhon by insisting that when the proletariat tried to protect its interests within the framework of the state and socialist political parties, the natural tendency to reach compromises would undermine its moral fiber. Instead, the working class needed to work toward the revolution through its own institutions: the trade unions and labor exchanges.

ESSENTIAL

Pelloutier hoped that workers who were educated in schools created by the labor exchanges would build a new system of values in which technical skill and discipline were valued over wealth, comfort, and leisure. Like Saint-Simon, he believed that the new leaders of the producing class would form a technical elite.

Pelloutier envisioned the labor exchanges as the beginning of a new proletarian civilization centered on trade unions. Once workers gained control of the methods of production, unions and labor exchanges would play different roles in society.

The local trade union would be the basic unit of society, with the job of producing goods and services. Individual unions would coordinate production within a specific sector of the economy, defined either by region or industry. Unions would be linked together in a loose federation of the type visualized earlier by Proudhon.

Unions would send representatives to the labor exchanges, which would be responsible for coordinating efforts between the different sectors of production. The labor exchanges would function as decentralized planning bodies. They would gather and disseminate information on production matters and consumer interests, giving the unions an overarching view of the production process.

After Pelloutier's death in 1901, the Federation of Labor Exchanges merged with the Federation of Trade Unions to create the General Confederation of Labor (CGT), which was dominated by syndicalism until 1921.

General Strikes

The idea of the general strike was based on the belief that the industrial economy cannot survive even a short disruption of basic services. (Anyone who has been in a major city when the garbage collectors go on strike will understand the concept.)

British radical William Benbow first proposed the idea of a month-long general strike in 1831, euphemistically calling it a "Grand National Holiday." Bakunists also considered a "Sacred Month" of collective work stoppage.

In the 1890s, French syndicalists expanded the idea of the general strike. Earlier socialists envisioned the general strike as an act of noncooperation designed to win a concession from government or business. In syndicalist thought, the general strike became a "revolution of folded arms": a tactic for overthrowing the government by bringing the economy to a halt.

Some syndicalists argued that every small strike was a skirmish in the larger class struggle. At least in theory, this meant that it didn't matter whether a "partial" strike for higher wages or an eight-hour day succeeded or failed because the very act of striking was a blow against the capitalist system.

During the heyday of syndicalism, between 1900 and 1914, syndicalist groups attempted general strikes in Italy, Belgium, Holland, and Sweden, usually at the cost of violent response by the governments.

Syndicalism Put to the Test

In 1906, the CGT scheduled a nationwide strike for May 1. Many hoped that it would prove to be the general strike that would bring the government down.

The strike was triggered prematurely on March 10 by a coal mine disaster at Courrières. A gas explosion killed between 1,060 and 1,300 miners. Rescue operations were slow, made more difficult by an unseasonable snowstorm. (The last thirteen survivors were recovered twenty days after the explosion.) More than 15,000 people attended the first funerals, creating an explosion of another sort. By March 13, 61,000 miners were on strike.

The Courrières explosion was one of the first disasters reported in the French popular press. Reporters from across the country competed for news from the mine and published appeals for humanitarian aid for the victims and their families. Newspapers couldn't print photographs, but picture postcards of the disaster and the survivors spread across the country. With public sympathy engaged, the CGT called for the planned strike to begin on March 18; hundreds of thousands of strikers joined the miners' demonstrations in the *departements* of Pais-de-Calais and the Nord.

FACT

Funds collected for the miners became part of an official fund, set up by law within four days after the explosion. Together, the various efforts collected 750,000 francs. (The daily wage for a miner was less than 6 francs.) Mine owners donated more than half the amount raised.

The minister of the interior, Georges Clemenceau, reacted quickly to suppress the strikes, flooding the region with troops and arresting 700 union leaders.

The Charter of Amiens

The ferocity of the government's response left many union members shaken. When the CGT Congress met at Amiens later that year, several argued that the unions should abandon the idea of direct action, follow the lead of the democratic socialists, and lobby for change through the political system. The proposal was rejected. Representatives at the Congress passed a resounding vote of support for syndicalist ideas. The broad resolution known as the Charter of Amiens is perhaps the clearest and most influential statement of syndicalist ideals:

> *In the daily fight, Syndicalism pursues the co-ordination of workers' struggles, and the increase of working-class welfare through the achievement of immediate reforms such as a decrease in the hours of the working day, increased salaries, etc. . . . But this task is only one aspect of Syndicalism, which also prepares the ground for complete emancipation. This can only be realized by the expropriation of the capitalists through the General Strike. The trade union, which today is a defensive institution, will be, in the future, the basis of production, distribution and the re-organization of society.*

Georges Sorel and the Power of Myth

The most well-known and complex discussion of syndicalist theory came from a man who was never a union member and had little direct influence on the ideology or strategies of syndicalist leaders. Political and social philosopher Georges Sorel (1847–1922) was a civil engineer by trade. He retired from business when he was forty-five and spent the rest of his life working as an independent scholar. His writing on syndicalism was only part of a larger critique of European society. His best-known book, *Reflections on Violence* (1908), had a profound, and largely negative, influence on how people outside the socialist community saw the syndicalist movement.

Sorel and Morality

Sorel's primary interest was morality, not politics. He believed that Europe was morally decadent: interested in rewards out of proportion to the effort expended to receive them. He condemned bourgeois democracy as the triumph of mediocrity. He dismissed social democracy, claiming that new civilizations are born through revolutions, not by replacing bourgeois parliamentary representatives with socialist parliamentary representatives.

At first, Sorel thought he found a cure for Europe's moral decline in Marxism. He believed that the dialectical process of history would produce a new morality more appropriate to the industrial age than Christianity. If each system of production carries with it a superstructure of ideas, beliefs, and habits, then the proletarian revolution would be followed by a new society with forms of art, politics, and morality created by the working class.

ESSENTIAL

In *Reflections on Violence* (1908), Sorel argued that direct action, in the form of violence, was the creative power by which the proletariat would accomplish the moral rejuvenation of society. He contrasted violence to force, which he defined as the state's power of coercion.

Over time, Sorel grew more critical of Marx's work. As he saw it, the key problem to social revolution was the moral preparation of the proletariat. The fall of capitalism could lead to a more just society only if the workers who led the "dictatorship of the proletariat" had already attained a high level of moral culture.

Syndicalism Is the Answer

In 1898, in *The Socialist Future of Trade Unions*, Sorel described syndicalism as the best possibility for fostering the moral development of the proletariat. Like Pelloutier, Sorel believed that workers needed to be economically independent of both the state and the capitalist system before they could create a new mode of production and new forms of social organization. The best way to make this happen was to use workers' organizations, such as unions, cooperatives, and credit unions, to create an alternative economy within capitalist society.

ALERT

Flexibility was one of Sorel's virtues. In 1909, he turned away from syndicalism as the source for society's moral renewal and became a monarchist. Following the Russian Revolution of 1917, he made another abrupt change and declared himself a Bolshevik supporter.

Sorel insisted that the working class must abandon “scientific” approaches to socialism, such as Marxism, in favor of a mytho-poetical approach. He argued that since man is moved by his passions rather than reason, it is necessary to use imagery and myth to rouse people to action. Sorel’s preferred myth was the idea of the general strike, which he believed would give the proletariat a sense of power and mission and invigorate it in the class struggle.

CHAPTER 12

The Emergence of Communist Russia

Marx predicted that the end of capitalism would begin in mature industrial societies. The merciless dialectic between capital and labor would bring the internal conflicts of capitalism to the breaking point and outraged labor would revolt against their misery. Instead the first avowedly Marxist revolution took place in Tsarist Russia, where the proletariat formed only a small portion of the population, but there was plenty of misery to go around.

What Was It Like in Russia in 1900?

In 1900, Russia looked disturbingly like France in 1789. Tsar Nicholas II (1894–1917) and the Orthodox Church still believed in the divine right of kings. Nicholas was the last of Europe's absolute monarchs: unfettered by constitutional restraints or parliamentary institutions. The population was largely divided between wealthy aristocrats and struggling peasants, with only a small middle class in the cities. The gulf between rich and poor was enormous. But things were starting to change.

Russia Begins an Industrial Revolution

Russia took its first steps toward industrialization in 1856, after the Crimean War made it clear that modern wars were won with railroads and industrial capacity. The process was slow at first, but by the 1880s Russia was finally in the grip of the Industrial Revolution, with a few peculiarly Russian twists.

In Western Europe, the Industrial Revolution began with small workshops. Enterprises grew larger over time as a new industrial class emerged and accumulated both the capital and the knowledge for economic development.

By the time Russia entered the game, the day of small workshops was long over. Without a homegrown base of capital and expertise, the Industrial Revolution started from the top down. The tsarist government was a large entrepreneur in its own right, responsible for constructing a railroad network across the country and a major player in the development of the coal and iron industries. For the most part, the landowning aristocracy had no interest in investing in industry, so much of the capital came from abroad. By 1900, more than 50 percent of the capital in Russian manufacturing companies was foreign. In crucial industries, like iron, the percentage was even higher.

Peasants and the Proletariat

Russia could only dream of having an urban proletariat in 1900. The tsar's grandfather, Alexander II (1818–1881), emancipated the serfs in 1861, in part to make it possible for peasants to emigrate to the cities and become industrial workers. Emancipation tied former serfs to the land in new ways.

The process by which land was distributed to the peasants required them to "redeem" the land from its former owners over a forty-nine year period. Ownership was further complicated by the traditional village commune, known as the *mir*. The self-governing units held the land in common and allotments were redistributed periodically to ensure economic equality. Before emancipation, the *mir* was responsible for taxes and obligations to the landlord; after emancipation, the *mir* was responsible for taxes and redemption payments to the landlord. A peasant who wanted to move to the city had to give up all claim to the land or return to work the harvest.

FACT

Prior to the Emancipation Manifesto of 1861, Russian peasants were legally tied to the land they were born on: not quite slaves but certainly not free. The Manifesto gave roughly 23 million people the rights of full citizens, including the right to marry without their landlord's consent, to leave the land, and to own property or a business.

The ongoing tie of urban worker to the land changed the way in which the proletariat developed in Russia. In Western Europe, peasants who moved to the cities to work soon lost their connection with the villages they came from. The problems of peasants and proletariat were kept separate. In Russia, many urban workers returned home every fall, where they complained about the conditions they worked under, and heard similar complaints from their relatives back home, creating a revolutionary potential that Lenin was prepared to exploit in 1917.

The proletariat had plenty to complain about. The requirement to return for the harvest meant that many of them were transient workers who took whatever unskilled job was available. Wages were extremely low, even by the standards of other proletariats: in 1880, a factory worker in Moscow earned only a quarter of the wage earned by his British counterpart. With no tradition of personal freedom, many workers were treated like industrial serfs, housed in barracks from which they were marched back and forth to work each day.

Repression and Reform Movements

The brief period of reform during the reign of Alexander II was followed by an absolutist reaction under his successors. The corrupt and inefficient bureaucracy that ruled the empire on a day-to-day basis included a large force of secret police. Suspicion and insecurity were a way of life. The right to association, necessary for any public discussion of reform, was limited.

Political parties and trade unions were illegal. Even professional associations were highly regulated and their meetings were supervised. One of the few legal forms of organization was the *zemstvo*, a type of elected regional council established by Alexander II. Controlled by the nobility, *zemstvos* were legally limited to dealing with local and charitable issues, though some liberally minded aristocrats attempted to extend the councils' scope to include political matters.

Newspapers, magazines, and books, both those published in Russian and those imported from abroad, were rigorously censored. Political literature had to be secretly printed and distributed. It was often published by political émigrés and smuggled into the country.

All opposition parties—reformers and revolutionaries alike—worked underground, shadowed by the threat of imprisonment, exile to Siberia, or execution. With no other outlet for voicing opposition, assassination attempts against members of the royal family and high government officials were common. Secret police infiltrated opposition groups and revolutionaries offered themselves as police spies to find out about police plans.

From Marxism to Bolshevism

The Russian Social-Democratic Workers' Party was founded in 1898, with the intention of bringing Russian Marxists together in a single organization. Unity didn't last long. At the organization's second congress, held in Brussels and London in 1903, party members found themselves divided over two related questions:

- Should party membership be limited to active revolutionaries?
- Could a socialist revolution occur in a country that was still in the initial stages of capitalism?

The debate split the party into two factions: the Bolshevik (majority) party, led by Vladimir Lenin, and the Menshevik (minority) party, led by Leon Trotsky.

ALERT

It is typical of the complicated relationship between the two groups that the Menshevik faction actually represented the majority of the Social-Democratic party. The names came about as a result of a questionable vote at the 1903 Congress that gave Lenin's faction control of the party for a short time. The Mensheviks quickly regained control, but the names stuck.

Although both groups claimed to be Marxist, there were fundamental differences in their approach to revolution. The Mensheviks took an approach halfway between revisionist and orthodox Marxism. They believed that Russia could achieve socialism only after it developed into a bourgeois society with an oppressed proletariat. Until the budding Russian proletariat was fully developed and ready for revolution, they were willing to cooperate with nonsocialist liberals to implement reforms. The Bolsheviks were prepared to adapt Marxism to fit Russian political realities. Unlike the Mensheviks, they recognized that the peasants were as oppressed as any urban proletariat and represented a potential revolutionary force.

The Socialist Revolutionary Party

The Russian Social-Democratic Labor Party wasn't the only game in town for would-be Russian revolutionaries. The Socialist Revolutionary Party, founded in 1901, worked chiefly among the rural population. The Marxist-based Social-Democrats looked forward to a socialist state based on the industrialized working class. The Socialist Revolutionaries hoped that Russia could bypass capitalism, or at least limit its scope. They proposed building a socialist country based on the traditional village *mir.* The land would be nationalized, but would be worked by peasants on the principle of "labor ownership": a cross between squatters' rights and sweat equity.

The First Russian Revolution

At the end of 1904, Russia was buckling under the Japanese. At first glance, the Russo-Japanese conflict looked like a David and Goliath fight, but in fact, the least industrialized of the European powers didn't have a chance against the newly industrialized Japanese.

FACT

> The Russo-Japanese war began with Japan's attack on the Russian naval base at Port Arthur in Manchuria on February 9, 1904, and ended with the destruction of the Russian fleet in the Tsushima Straits on May 27, 1905. Officially, the war was a conflict over who controlled Manchuria and Korea. Unofficially, it was Japan's debut as an international power.

In addition to the sting of national humiliation, the war placed an immense strain on Russia's fragile infrastructure. While the government concentrated on the difficult task of supplying its armed forces in Asia, the systems for provisioning Russia's large cities broke down. The price of essential goods rose so quickly that real wages fell by twenty percent.

Worker Protests

Worker discontent boiled over in December 1904, when the Putilov Iron Works in St. Petersburg began to lay off workers. The Putilov workers went on strike, soon joined by thousands of workers in other parts of the city. The government responded by cutting off electricity to the city, shutting down newspapers, and declaring public areas of the city closed.

"Bloody Sunday"

On January 22, more than 150,000 Russian workers, many of them women and children, marched peacefully on the Winter Palace in St. Petersburg. Calling on their "Little Father" for help in difficult times, the workers tried to present Tsar Nicholas II with a petition demanding the usual political and economic reforms, including a popularly elected assembly, improved working conditions, better wages, reduced hours, universal manhood suffrage—

and the end of the war with Japan. The Imperial Guard blocked the way and fired on the crowd to keep them from moving forward. Between bullets and the panicking crowd, more than 100 people were killed or wounded.

News of what was predictably called "Bloody Sunday" set off insurrections and activism at every level of society. Middle-class professional associations and aristocratically controlled *zemstvos* called for a constituent assembly. Students walked out of universities in protest against the lack of civil liberties. Village *mirs* organized uprisings against landholders. Industrial workers went on strike.

More Insurrection

In June, soon after the Japanese destruction of the Russian fleet, the spirit of insurrection infected the military. Sailors on the battleship *Potemkin* protested against being served rotten meat. When the captain ordered the ringleaders shot, the firing squad refused to carry out his orders and the crew threw their officers overboard. Other units of the army and navy followed the *Potemkin*'s example.

In October, the railway workers went on strike, paralyzing transportation. At the same time, Leon Trotsky and other Mensheviks set up a workers' council (Soviet) in St. Petersburg to coordinate revolutionary activities. Within a matter of weeks, more than fifty Soviets were formed in towns and cities across Russia.

ESSENTIAL

The term *soviet* originally referred to councils of any kind. The workers' Soviets created in the 1905 revolution were made up of elected representatives from each factory or workshop in a town. Soviets became the basic unit of government at the local and regional level in the United Soviet Socialist Republic.

The Tsar's Response

Faced with general unrest, the tsar's chief minister recommended that Nicholas create an elected legislative assembly as a way to appease the public. The tsar reluctantly agreed. He issued the October Manifesto on October 17, which established a limited form of constitutional monarchy in

Russia and guaranteed fundamental civil liberties. The most important provision of the manifesto was the implementation of a new advisory council, the *Duma*, which would be chosen by popular election and would have the authority to approve or reject all legislation.

Radicals found the fact that the *Duma* would only be a consulting body, not a true legislature, hard to swallow. The leaders of the St. Petersburg Soviet denounced the plan and were arrested.

FACT

The October Manifesto resulted in a conservative backlash. Between 1906 and 1914, armed bands known as the Black Hundreds organized pogroms, took punitive action against peasants who were involved in the insurrections, and attacked students and activists. The Black Hundreds were drawn from those invested in the old system: landowners, rich peasants, bureaucrats, merchants, police officers, and Orthodox clergy.

Radical doubts about the proposed *Duma* were well founded. When the *Fundamental Laws* that detailed the structure of the new reforms were released in April 1906, the shape of the *Duma* was radically altered. The right to vote was severely limited. The elected *Duma* was now the lower house of a two-house chamber with only limited control over legislature. Members of the upper house were appointed by the tsar, who retained the right to rule by decree when the *Duma* wasn't in session.

Between 1906 and 1917, four separate *Dumas* were convened. Liberal and socialist groups dominated the first two *Dumas*, which proposed a series of reforms, including universal manhood suffrage, lifting the restrictions on trade unions, and land reform. Each time the *Duma* remained in session for only a few months before Nicholas shut them down.

Vladimir Lenin: Architect of the Bolshevik Revolution

Vladimir Lenin (1870–1924) was born into a middle-class family of educators in a small city near Moscow. When Lenin was a young teenager, his older brother was executed for conspiring to assassinate Tsar Alexander III. After the death of his brother, Lenin began to study revolutionary ideas. By the time he was seventeen, he was already in trouble with the Russian authorities for participating in an illegal student rally. He was expelled from the university system and banished to his grandfather's estate, where his older sister was already under house arrest.

FACT

Lenin's original name was Vladimir Ulyanov. After his return from Siberia, he used a number of aliases as part of his clandestine political work. In 1902, he adopted the pseudonym "Lenin," which was derived from the Lena River in Siberia.

In 1893, after taking his law exams and being admitted to the bar, Lenin moved to St. Petersburg, where he worked as a public defender. He became involved in unifying the city's various Marxist groups into a single organization known as the Union for the Struggle for the Liberation for the Working Classes. The Union issued leaflets pleading the workers' cause, supported strikes, and worked with workers' educational societies.

That sort of thing never went over well with absolutist rulers. In December 1895, the Union's leaders were arrested. Lenin spent fifteen months in jail in St. Petersburg, and then was exiled to Siberia for three years.

At the end of his term in Siberia, Lenin joined the Russian expatriate community, living at various times in Munich, London, and Geneva. During this period, he cofounded the newspaper *Iskra* (*The Spark*), and published books and pamphlets about revolutionary politics.

What Is to Be Done?

Much of the debate at the 1903 congress of the Russian Social-Democrat Workers' Party was based on one of Lenin's most important books: *What Is to Be Done?* (1902). In it, Lenin proposed that the party should be the "vanguard of the proletariat," serving the same purpose in class warfare as the vanguard does in a military war.

ESSENTIAL

Lenin's idea of the "vanguard of the proletariat" is similar to the syndicalist idea of the "conscious minority." Both ideas assume that a more enlightened group must lead the proletariat to revolution. Lenin's "vanguard of the proletariat" would be made up of members of the "bourgeois intelligentsia." The syndicalist "conscious minority" would be members of the labor elite.

Marx and Engels claimed that the working class would emancipate itself; Lenin argued that the working class, left to itself, would develop "trade union consciousness," not "revolutionary consciousness." It was necessary for a vanguard of what Lenin called the "bourgeois intelligentsia" to lead the proletariat in the revolution, and for a hierarchical, strictly disciplined communist party to lead the intelligentsia. No one doubted that Lenin, himself, would lead the party.

The Russian Revolution of 1917

The First World War destroyed whatever faith the Russian people still had in the tsarist government. Ill-equipped and badly led, Russia suffered defeat after defeat, mostly at the hands of Germany. By the end of 1915, 1 million Russian soldiers were killed and another 1 million were captured.

The government was equally inept at organizing the home front. Its greatest failure was an inability to organize food distribution, creating rising prices and artificial food shortages in the cities.

The February Revolution

On February 2, 1917, Petrograd was in the throes of a general strike. The transportation system failed so there was no way to distribute the food that sat in the city's warehouses. The streets were crowded with people standing in food lines in the bitter cold.

When the inevitable bread riot broke out, the police fired on the crowd. Everything was business as usual until the army unit that was sent to reinforce the police instead disarmed them and joined the strikers. Suddenly the bread riot was a full-scale rebellion.

It took several days for the news to reach Tsar Nicholas, who insisted on staying with the army at the front. It apparently took a little longer to make him understand that this was more than just another bread riot. Finally, under pressure from both the *Duma* and his senior military officers, Tsar Nicholas abdicated in favor of his brother, the Archduke Michael. The Archduke, apparently quicker on the uptake than his brother, declined to accept the throne.

QUESTION

Is it Petersburg, Petrograd, or Leningrad?
It depends when you're talking about. Peter the Great founded the city in 1710, claiming he named it after his patron saint. In 1914, the name became Petrograd because many Russians thought St. Petersburg sounded too German. In 1924, the city became Leningrad in Lenin's honor. In 1991, residents voted to change the name back to St. Petersburg.

The *Duma* quickly established a provisional government made up of the leaders of all the bourgeois parties. At the same time, the leaders of the Russian Social-Democratic Workers' Party organized the Petrograd Soviet of Workers' and Soldiers' Deputies: 2,500 elected representatives from factories and military units around the city.

Lenin and the Bolshevik Takeover

Lenin returned from exile on April 3, 1917, a month after the Tsar abdicated, and immediately became a leading voice in the Bolshevik faction of the Social-Democratic Workers' Party. Most Bolsheviks still believed that it was impossible for a socialist revolution to take place in a country that was in the first stages of the Industrial Revolution. Lenin took the position that the revolution did not solve the fundamental problems of the Russian proletariat and the task ahead was to turn the bourgeois revolution into a proletarian revolution.

In May, Lenin gained an ally when Leon Trotsky, leader of the Menshevik faction of the Social Democrats, returned from exile in the United States. By June, Lenin and Trotsky formed an alliance and began to plot the overthrow of the provisional government.

On October 24, 1917, the Bolsheviks staged a relatively bloodless coup, with soldiers from the Soviet taking control of strategic points throughout Petrograd. The following day, the all-Russian Congress of Soviets approved the formation of a revolutionary Bolshevik government with Lenin at its head.

FACT

Leon Trotsky (1879–1940) was a leading figure in the Bolshevik revolution and the early Soviet regime. When Joseph Stalin came to power after Lenin's death, he expelled Trotsky from the Soviet Union. In exile, Trotsky denounced Stalin's betrayal of the revolution and sought to revive the original spirit of Bolshevism. Stalin's agents assassinated Trotsky in Mexico in 1940.

War Communism

The new Bolshevik regime started out well. On October 26, the temporary ruling council passed a series of decrees that addressed popular concerns with land distribution, economic equality, and the shape of the new government. The great estates would be partitioned and distributed to the peasant communes with compensation to the former owners. Workers were given control over factories. Banks were nationalized. Plans were put forward to elect a constituent assembly to replace the temporary council. The long-awaited socialist revolution was on its way.

On October 27, the revolution took a detour when the ruling council passed the Decree of the Press, censoring all Russian publications. In the coming weeks, the temporary council passed further restrictive measures.

In December, the *Cheka* (secret police) was established to discover and suppress any attempts at counter-revolution. When election results for the proposed Constituent Assembly were tallied in January 1918, the Bolsheviks found they won only 21 percent of the vote. Lenin followed the precedent set by Nicholas II and dissolved the assembly, saying that the choices were Bolshevik rule or the return of the extreme right.

QUESTION

Why are socialists described as red?
The identification of socialists as "reds" began with the flag of the Paris Commune of 1871. The Commune chose red in memory of the blood that was shed by French workers during 100 years of revolution. It was also a symbol of equality, based on the idea that all men's blood is red.

Each new extension of power was justified as a temporary measure. After all, Russia was at war. As soon as Lenin signed a treaty with Germany, the Red Army found itself fighting a civil war against the counter-revolutionary Whites, made up of nationalists, aristocrats, and remnants of the tsarist army, financed by Russia's former allies. When a member of the Socialist Revolutionary party nearly succeeded in an attempt to assassinate Lenin in August 1918, the war against counter-revolutionaries was unleashed on the population as a whole in the form of the Red Terror. On Lenin's orders, the *Cheka* executed thousands of "opponents of the state" without trial.

The Third International (1919–1943)

The Russian Revolution tore the socialist community in two. Many European socialists doubted whether the Bolshevik revolution was really socialist. Lenin declared that democratic socialists were traitors and renegades. In January 1918, the Bolshevik party formally acknowledged the break between social democrats and communists by changing its name from the Russian Social-Democratic Labor Party (Bolshevik) to the Russian Communist Party.

In 1919, Lenin pre-empted efforts by moderate socialist leaders to revive the Second International, by creating his own international organization. In May 1919, Russia hosted the first meeting of the Communist International, also known as the *Comintern*, in Moscow. Unlike the First and Second International, the Comintern accepted no variations in socialist philosophy. The organization's stated purpose was to promote the spread of the socialist revolution across the industrialized world. In order to be admitted to the Comintern, socialist parties were required to model themselves on the Bolshevik party pattern and expel moderate socialists and pacifists from their membership rolls.

Stalinist Russia

Joseph Stalin (1879–1953) was the son of an alcoholic cobbler. Stalin enrolled in the Orthodox seminary to please his mother, who wanted him to be a priest. He was soon expelled for revolutionary activity and joined the political underground in the Caucasus, where he served more as an instigator of violent clashes than an organizer. In a party dominated by the self-proclaimed "bourgeois intelligentsia," he soon earned a reputation for a practical approach to revolution. (Lenin thought of him as a useful thug.) Once the Bolsheviks were in power, Stalin was the man who took care of the dull details of party and state administration.

FACT

Stalin wasn't Russian: he was born in the Caucasian province of Georgia. His original name was Joseb Dzhugashuli. Like Lenin, he used several aliases when he was active in the political underground. Stalin is from the Russian word for steel, a good choice for a self-professed hard man.

Having control over the political machine helped Stalin triumph over his rivals in the power struggle that followed Lenin's death in 1924. Within four years, he was the supreme Soviet leader.

Stalinism

The term Stalinism is used to describe a set of policies and a style of government rather than an ideology. Stalin would have been the first to declare that he was not a theory guy. He prided himself on adhering to the tenets of Marxist-Leninist ideology. Despite his protests, Stalin made two contributions to communist political theory that changed the shape of the Soviet state and its satellites: the theory that class struggle continues after the revolution and the idea that socialist revolutions did not have to be international.

"Aggravation of Class Struggle Along with the Development of Socialism"

According to Stalin, class struggle does not end with the revolution. In fact, the closer a society is to attaining a truly socialist state, the more the doomed remnants of the capitalist classes will struggle. Beginning in the 1930s, Stalin used this as the theory to justify the political repression of his political opponents, real and perceived, as counter-revolutionaries.

ALERT

Many people opposed Stalin's methods, including party leader Sergei Kirov, who was assassinated in December 1934. Following Kirov's murder, Stalin launched a purge of alleged spies and counter-revolutionaries from the party, removing anyone who presented a threat to his authority. It is estimated that 500,000 people were executed and 12 million sent to the labor camps.

Socialism in One Country

Lenin took the position that revolution in one country was not enough. In fact, he argued that because Russia was the weakest link in the industrialized world, revolution there would cause the entire capitalist-imperialist structure to fall. When it became clear that the socialist revolution was not going to spread into Western Europe, Stalin stood Lenin's dictum on its head and proclaimed "the proletariat can and must build the socialist society in one country."

The Growth of the Soviet Bloc

The USSR remained the only communist state until the end of World War II, when the Soviet Union installed left-wing governments in the countries of Eastern Europe that the Red Army liberated from the Germans. These governments followed the Soviet pattern of a single-party system, substantial state ownership of the economy, adherence to an official ideology based on Marxism, and the maintenance of power through non-democratic means.

CHAPTER 13

British Socialism Takes a Different Path

Even though Karl Marx spent the most productive years of his career studying in the British Library, he had little influence on the development of British socialism. Unlike their European counterparts, British socialists drew their inspiration from a homegrown radical tradition built on religious nonconformity, the concept of British liberties, and Robert Owens's cooperative movement. Whether based on labor, economics, or an outraged sense of beauty, British socialism leaned toward reform rather than revolution.

Chartism: The First Mass Working-Class Movement

Chartism was a movement for Parliamentary reform that grew out of working-class protests against the economic injustices caused by the Industrial Revolution. In 1815, the passage of the Corn Laws made it clear to working-class radicals that the people who controlled Parliament made laws that primarily benefited themselves. It was a classic Catch-22. The only way the working classes could improve the conditions under which they worked was to get the vote so they could send their own representatives to Parliament. In order to get the vote, they had to change the laws.

The Chartist movement was named after the People's Charter, drafted by London radical William Lovett in May 1838. The charter contained six demands for political change:

- Universal manhood suffrage
- Equally populated electoral districts
- Vote by secret ballot
- Annually elected Parliaments
- Payment of stipends to members of Parliament
- Abolition of property qualifications for Members of Parliament

When the Charter was first distributed to popular groups for discussion, many radicals dismissed it as too moderate, but it clearly fired the popular imagination. All over the country, local working-class institutions of all types—trade unions, educational societies, and radical associations—transformed themselves into Chartist centers.

QUESTION

Why did equal populations in electoral districts matter?
Population growth, internal migration, and new industrial cities meant parliamentary representation no longer reflected population distribution. Growing cities like Manchester had no representatives while boroughs with declining populations had two. The most notorious of the "rotten boroughs" was Old Sarum, which had a representative but no town.

Taking the slogan "Political power our means, social happiness our end," the first Chartist convention met in London in February 1839, to prepare a petition to present to Parliament. When the convention moved to Birmingham in May, riots led to the arrest of the "moral force" leaders, Lovett and John Collins. The remaining members returned to London, where Thomas Attwood, a Member of Parliament with reformist leanings, presented the petition to the House of Commons in July. Parliament refused to even hear the petition, voting it down 237 to 48.

With Lovett and Collins in jail, leadership shifted to the more radical element of the movement. In November, a group of "physical force" Chartists staged an armed uprising at Newport. It was quickly suppressed. While the majority of the Chartists concentrated on petitioning for the Newport leaders to be released from jail, others led small uprisings in Sheffield, East London, and Bradford. The principal leaders were transported to the penal colony in Australia. Other Chartist leaders were arrested and served short jail sentences.

FACT

The original leaders of the Chartist movement had no interest in violence, preferring to rely on "moral force" to persuade Parliament to accept the Charter. Others, known as "physical force" Chartists, reserved the possibility of force as an alternative means of persuasion.

The first stage of the Chartist movement was a loose federation of working-class organizations held together by a common goal. With many of the original leaders in jail, a second generation came forward who had a new emphasis on efficient organization and moderate tactics. Using skills learned in the trade union movement, they formed the National Charter Association of Great Britain, complete with constitution, quarterly dues, and membership cards. Under their leadership, Chartists collected more than 3 million signatures on a second petition, which they presented in 1842. Parliament paid no more attention to the second petition than it had to the first.

The last great burst of Chartism appeared in 1848: Britain's response to the "Hungry '40s." On April 10, a new Chartist convention convened a mass meeting in Kensington Commons in preparation for a march to present yet another petition to Parliament. The army refused to allow the procession to cross the Thames, forcing the leaders to deliver the document in a hansom cab. The petition itself had only 1.9 million signatures, including presumed forgeries from Queen Victoria and Mr. Punch of Punch and Judy. Even the Queen's signature wasn't enough; Parliament ignored the Charter for a third time.

e! ALERT

The Chartist movement died, but the ideas behind it did not. Between 1858 and 1918, Parliament adopted five of the six points of the Charter. The only point that was never adopted was the annual election of Parliament; presumably members of Parliament couldn't face the idea of annual campaigning.

William Lovett

William Lovett (1800–1877) was a prime example of a British working-class radical. A cabinetmaker by trade, he was self-educated in politics and economics. In addition to Parliamentary reform, he believed in self-help, education, and the cooperative movement. Over the course of his life, he was involved in a variety of working-class causes and organizations, including:

- The British Association for the Promotion of Cooperative Knowledge
- The London Workingmen's Association (not to be confused with the International Working Men's Association, also known as the First International)
- The National Association for Promoting the Political and Social Improvement of the People

With fellow Chartist leader John Collins, Lovett wrote *Chartism: A New Organization for the People*. He also wrote several textbooks for working-class students. His autobiography was published in 1876.

Christian Socialism

The Christian socialism movement began shortly after the failure of the final Chartist effort in April 1848. In many ways, Christian socialism was the flip-side of Chartism: a largely middle-class movement that attempted to ameliorate the problems caused by the Industrial Revolution by applying the social principles of Christianity to modern industrial life.

The main force behind the movement was Anglican theologian Frederick Denison Maurice (1805–1872). In 1838, Maurice laid out the central principals of Christian socialism in *Kingdom of Christ*, proclaiming "socialism's true character as the great Christian revolution of the nineteenth century." He argued that the competition that lies at the heart of capitalism is fundamentally un-Christian and the source of society's ills. The answer was to replace competition with cooperation.

ALERT

Christian socialists occasionally took positions that upset more conservative Christians. Four years after Marx declared religion was the opiate of the people, the most well known Christian socialist, novelist Charles Kingsley, warned readers in *Politics for the People* that the Bible was used as an "opium dose for keeping beasts of burden quiet while they are being unloaded."

In practical terms, Christian socialism meant the creation of Owenite cooperative societies, which Maurice saw as a modern application of the communal tradition of early Christianity. Christian socialists joined forces with the cooperative movement and founded several small cooperative societies that promoted co-partnerships and profit sharing in industry. The longest lasting of the movement's social experiments was the formation of the Working Men's College in London in 1854.

The original adherents of Christian socialism drifted away from the movement in the late 1850s. The 1880s saw a more formal revival of the movement, with different denominations founding officially sanctioned Christian socialist groups.

William Morris

Poet and craftsman William Morris (1834–1896) is best known today for his wallpaper designs and his often quoted dictum that a person should have nothing in his home that he does "not know to be useful or believe to be beautiful." Long before he made his way to socialism, Morris began what he described as a "campaign against the age," rejecting the commercial, industrial, and scientific society of his time for its visual squalor and social complacency. Part of the Pre-Raphaelite Brotherhood, with its romantic yearnings for the medieval, Morris designed wallpaper, textiles, rugs, and furniture. Morris's design company, known as The Firm, was originally an artistic cooperative with seven members who led the international design revival known as the Arts and Crafts movement. The Firm served as a pattern for Morris's vision of small artisanal studios as the economic base for society.

Morris came to socialism through his belief that without dignified, creative work, people become disconnected from life. Building on Thomas Carlyle's *Past and Present* (1843) and John Ruskin's *The Stones of Venice* (1851–1853), Morris looked at bleak industrial cities and an impoverished proletariat and questioned whether either constituted real progress.

As a socialist, Morris rejected industrialism and capitalism because they degraded human beings and undervalued craftsmanship. The transition from workshop to factory meant that men were put to work making shoddy goods and needless gadgets. Morris wanted mankind to find fulfillment in the production of beautiful objects. His version of socialism was intended to liberate the average man from drudgery and restore beauty to his life.

Morris envisioned an alternative society in which everyone had equal opportunities for education. The division of labor that stands at the heart of factory work would be restricted so that the work of artists and craftsmen would be valued. He emphasized the importance of returning to small artisanal production and the right of all members of society to find joy and self-expression in work.

Morris and Organized Socialism

Morris came to organized socialism late. In the 1870s he became increasingly disturbed by what he believed were the related issues of Britain's class divisions and apathy toward art. He tackled the question of art first, founding an early conservation group, the Society for the Protection of Ancient Buildings, and giving hundreds of public lectures on the relationship between a country's aesthetic standards and its social conditions.

In 1883, at the age of forty-nine, Morris joined the Social Democratic Federation, a revolutionary socialist party with Marxist roots. The Federation soon divided over the question of involvement in parliamentary politics. In 1884, Morris found himself the unwilling leader of the Socialist League, a breakaway group that stood against political action.

Morris remained active in the socialist movement until the 1890s, when his health began to fail and internal dissentions divided the Socialist League.

New Age

Morris's work profoundly influenced a group of architects, artists, and intellectuals associated with the progressive newspaper *New Age*, between 1907 and 1920. Under the leadership of Alfred Richard Orage, *New Age* was the early twentieth-century paper of record for alternative thinkers. Dissatisfied with Fabian socialism, Orage searched instead for a basic "re-evaluation of values." Demanding political and economic rights for man was only the first step. As far as Orage himself was concerned, the search for new values meant an "ethical and spiritual rejection of capitalism and its vision of progress," based on his reading of Carlyle, Ruskin, Morris, and Marx.

Seeking a third path between capitalism and socialism, the paper published attacks on modern industrial society from both the right and the left: anarchists, Jacobites, medieval revivalists, and land reformers. The magazine's most well-known contributors were Hilaire Belloc, G. K. Chesterton, and Ezra Pound.

Guild Socialism

A combination of trade unionism and nineteenth-century medievalism, guild socialism flourished briefly in Great Britain during the first two decades of the twentieth century. The doctrine had its roots in *The Restoration of the Gild System* (1906) by architect A. J. Penty (1875–1937). An architect and devotee of the Arts and Crafts Movement, Penty spent his early adult life searching for a solution to his moral and aesthetic dissatisfaction with industrial society. He began as a member of Annie Besant's Theosophical Society. In the late 1890s, he moved from theosophy to socialism, joining both the Independent Labour Party and the Fabian Society.

Penty believed that a society's morality is reflected in its buildings. Over time, his fusion of politics with aesthetics led him to reject mainstream socialism and create a new political theory that took into account the individual's spiritual relationship to work and art.

Built on a combination of Marxism, trade unionism, the cooperative movement, and the Arts and Crafts aesthetic, guild socialism bears a resemblance to syndicalism, without the anarchism. It begins with the premise that man is a worker for most of his life, and therefore, society must be designed in such a way that man is not alienated from his work.

ESSENTIAL

Marx's theory of alienation holds that when a worker loses control over the conditions under which he works, he also loses control over his life, until "he feels at home when he is not working, and when he is working he does not feel at home."

According to Penty, the worker is not free. When a worker accepts a wage from an employer, he gives up all control over the conditions of his labor and what happens to the product he creates. Under these conditions, labor is no more than a commodity. In order for labor to be freed, the capitalist wage system must be abolished. In its place, Penty urged the return to a simpler economic system that revived the spirit and structure of the medieval guilds, which controlled the price and quality of the goods they produced, trained apprentices in the practice of a trade, and regulated the conditions of individual workshops. Since the obvious body to replicate the guild system was the trade unions, the organization and control of industry should be placed in their hands.

Guild socialism, as presented in *The Restoration of the Gild System*, was exactly what Orage of *New Age* was looking for. The magazine became the theoretical journal for the guild socialism movement.

Guild Socialism Reaches a Wider Audience

In the hands of Penty and *New Age*, guild socialism remained a utopian blueprint for an ideal society. G. D. H. Cole (1889–1959) attempted to turn it into a practical program for transforming society.

As a student at Oxford, Cole became heavily involved in political activities. He joined the Fabian Society and the Independent Labour Party, was an activist for the Workers' Educational Association, and edited the *Oxford Reformer*. For his thesis, he wrote a comparative account of the development of trade unionism in Europe and North America. Published when he was twenty-four as *The World of Labor* (1913), the thesis was more than a survey of existing trade unions. Cole turned Penty's guild socialism into an indictment of Fabian-style social democracy.

Like the syndicalists, Cole urged British socialists to abandon the hope of instituting change through Parliamentary politics and look to direct action on the part of the trade unions. Still under the Fabian Society's influence, Cole called for gradual change rather than revolution: unions would use strikes to gain "encroaching control" over industry. The end result would be a society run by a loose federation of unions, organized on the democratic principles of the medieval guilds. The state would be no more than another association, charged with protecting the interests of consumers just as the guilds would protect the interest of their members.

After a failed attempt to stage a coup at the Fabian Society in 1914, Cole founded an alternative political organization, the National Guilds League, which published a series of magazines devoted to guild socialism. Always attractive to socialist intellectuals, guild socialism enjoyed a brief period of working-class influence during World War I. The doctrine was embraced by the shop stewards' movement, which called for worker control of war industries. After the war, a group of construction workers founded building guilds with government support. The shop stewards' movement ended with the war. The building guilds did not survive the economic slump of 1921. The National Guilds League dissolved in 1925, leaving behind ideas about worker control of industry that became part of mainstream trade union, socialist, and Labour Party programs in Britain.

The Fabian Society

Economist and historian Sidney Webb coined the phrase "the inevitability of gradualness" to describe the Fabian Society's approach to socialism. Founded in 1884, the Fabian Society believed that the transformation of British society from capitalism to socialism could be best achieved through what Sidney Webb described as "permeation of the nation's intellectual and political life." Although they agreed with Marx that this transformation was inevitable, they disagreed about the process. The Fabians believed that the transformation of society would be gradual and experimental, the result of parliamentary reforms rather than revolution.

FACT

The Fabian Society took its name from Roman general Quintus Fabius Maximus Cuncator, who earned the nickname "Fabius the Delayer" during the Punic wars, when his tactics of avoiding pitched battles allowed him to wear down, and ultimately defeat, the stronger Carthaginian forces.

The ultimate goal for society, outlined by Beatrice Webb in the *Minority Report to the Royal Commission into the Operation of the Poor Laws* (1909), was a democratically elected, centralized socialist state which would guarantee its citizens a "national minimum standard of civilized life." The Fabians envisioned the establishment of public enterprises at the local, regional, and state level, which would be financed by taxes on rent, as defined by David Ricardo. Since these public enterprises would be funded through taxes, they would not be burdened with some of the expenses common to private enterprises and could therefore offer better wages and working conditions. The Fabians also proposed that public utilities, common carriers, and businesses that were already under the control of private monopolies should be nationalized.

For the most part, the Fabians were middle-class intellectuals, led by Sidney and Beatrice Webb and playwright George Bernard Shaw. The society's membership was never large: only 8,400 at its height in 1946.

The main activities of the society were intended to educate the public about socialist issues. The Fabians sponsored public lectures, discussion groups, and summer schools. They carried out research into political, economic, and social problems, producing studies that moved the discussion of economic and social problems from abstract ideology to facts. Lots and lots of facts. They published a flood of books, pamphlets, and periodicals. Even Shaw's enormously popular plays were at some level socialist tracts.

FACT

The London School of Economics and Political Studies was founded in 1895 by the Fabian Society for the purpose of creating a better society through the study of poverty issues. In the early twentieth century, the school became a training ground for third-world leaders.

Rather than founding a political party, the Fabians preferred to influence existing parties. In 1900, the Fabians helped organize the Labour Representative Committee, which became the Labour Party in 1906.

Keir Hardie: "The Man in the Cloth Cap"

Scottish socialist Keir Hardie (1856–1915) became a symbol of the working class in Victorian England, his famous cloth cap the antithesis of the top hat worn by members of the privileged classes. Born James Kerr, Hardie was the illegitimate son of a farm maidservant and a ship's carpenter. His father was an early trade unionist.

Hardie went to work when he was seven or eight. When he was eleven, he took a job in the local mines as a trapper, working the airshaft traps that ventilate the mines. He worked as a coal miner for the next eleven years.

FACT

Like many working-class radicals, Hardie was largely self-taught. With little formal education, he was widely read in history and literature. Later in life, he claimed he was particularly influenced by Thomas Carlyle's satirical novel *Sartor Resartus* (1833–1834). In addition to reading widely, he taught himself to write Pittman's shorthand.

In 1878, Hardie left the mines to become active in the trade union movement. At first he opened a small shop in Glasgow and wrote articles for a Glasgow paper. Beginning in 1881, he was involved in the effort to organize a miners' union, moving from county to county as he established local chapters. For several years, he cobbled together a living, supplementing his salary as corresponding secretary for different union chapters with various part-time jobs.

In 1886, with the Ayrshire Union stable enough to pay Hardie a full time salary, he began to shift his interest to politics and socialism. He threw himself into politics with the same fervor he showed as a union organizer. He founded two monthly journals, the short-lived *The Miner*, which advocated a Scottish miner's federation, and the more widely based *Labor Leader*; served as Operating Secretary for the short-lived Glasgow Labour Party; and attended the inaugural congress of the Second International in Paris in 1889, educating himself by attending both Marxist and non-Marxist sessions.

In 1888, Hardie ran for Parliament for the first time as an independent labor candidate. He received only 617 votes, but caught the attention of the Liberal political machine. In 1891, the Liberal Party offered him the candidacy for West Ham South in London, a working-class neighborhood with a heavy union presence.

Hardie's first term in Parliament was not a success. He lost his seat in the 1895 elections. He ran again, without success, in 1896 and 1900.

e! ALERT

In Great Britain, Parliamentary elections are not held on a fixed cycle. Sessions of Parliament cannot last more than five years, but the sovereign may dissolve a session of Parliament at any time after consulting with the Prime Minister. Sessions are dissolved for a variety of reasons, including the inability to maintain a working coalition in the House of Commons.

Even though he was losing at the polls, Hardie was building a strong political foundation for the future. Rather than relying on loose alliances with the Liberal Party, he founded the Independent Labour Party (ILP) in 1893, with the basic strategy of creating an alliance between the trade unions and the socialist societies. In 1894, he began to publish *Labor Leader* every week rather than once a month, giving himself a platform for his positions.

The British Labour Party

In February 1900, Hardie's Independent Labour Party joined with other labor and socialist groups, including the Trades Union Congress and the Fabian Society, to form the Labour Representation Committee (LRC). A forerunner of the Labour Party, the LRC was organized to promote the election of working-class candidates to Parliament. In 1906, the LRC turned itself into the Labour Party and won twenty-nine seats in Parliament in the general election. Hardie was elected Member of Parliament for Merthyr in South Wales, which remained his political base for the rest of his life.

By the end of World War I, the Labour Party had a solid membership base, thanks to two important changes in the political climate:

- A substantial growth in the number of trade union members.
- The Representation of the People Act of 1918, which extended the vote to all men over twenty-one and gave the vote for the first time to women over thirty.

In 1918, the Labour Party officially proclaimed itself a socialist party and unveiled a new reform program, *Labour and the New Social Order*, drafted by Fabian Society leaders Sidney and Beatrice Webb. The party's new goals included full employment with a minimum wage and a maximum workweek, public ownership of industry, progressive taxation, and the expansion of education and social service.

By 1922, the Labour Party replaced the Liberals as the official opposition party. In 1924, Britain elected its first Labour government.

CHAPTER 14

Socialism in America, Part I: Socialism of the Working Class

Two of the basic issues that drove Europe's socialist movement did not exist in America. All adult, white, male citizens had the vote. And, while there were enormous discrepancies in wealth, there was no *ancien régime* with hereditary privileges. Social mobility was possible for those blessed with talent and luck. Nonetheless, America still suffered the problems of industrialization, especially in the cities of the Northeast. Social mobility and access to western land were balanced by social disillusionment and crowded cities.

The Roots of American Radicalism

America had a strong radical tradition long before European immigrants packed socialism in their trunks along with their boots. American radicalism had two clear roots: Enlightenment ideas about the social contract and the rights of man, filtered through the experience of the American Revolution, and the strong dissenting and evangelical religious tradition.

The Second Great Awakening

In the early nineteenth century, these two traditions came together in a spasm of religious revivalism known at the Second Great Awakening. From New York to as far west as St. Louis, Missouri, and as far south as Knoxville, Tennessee, thousands flocked to revivalist camp meetings, and went home to put the doctrine of perfectionism to the test. *Perfectionism* held that grace gave man the power to conquer sin and remake himself. Since society was a collection of sinful individuals, society could also be remade.

eFACT

Evangelical minister Charles Grandison Finney (1792–1895) was the theologian credited with the creation of Perfectionism and the driving force behind the Second Great Awakening. When the newly converted asked Finney what they should do next, he had two pieces of advice: Join a church and become an active member of a reform movement.

The result was what believers called the "benevolent empire" of voluntary reform associations. Most were local and noncontroversial. Some advocated changes in personal and social behavior that ranged from vegetarianism to polygamy. A handful of large issues stood at the center of the reform movement: temperance, asylum and penal reform, women's rights, education, and, largest of all, abolition.

At the end of the Civil War, with abolition no longer an issue, the impulse to reform extended to solving the evils of industrial society. Reformers who previously were active in the abolition movement created Labor Reform Leagues and Eight-Hour Associations.

Yankee Utopias and Bible Communists

Owenites, Fourierists, and Icarians were not the only groups to establish utopian communities in the United States. The great religious revival of the early nineteenth century inspired utopian communities as well as reform societies. In the first half of the nineteenth century, there are records of at least 178 communities organized under some form of socialism, both religious and secular. They ranged in size from fifteen to 900 members. There were some groups like the Shakers that practiced complete chastity and others like the John Humphrey Noyes's Oneida community that preached "free love." Some shared communal property; others were organized as joint stock companies. Some lived entirely by barter with the outside world; others, like the Amana Colonies in Iowa and the Oneida Community in New York, built thriving industries that outlived their ideological foundations.

A few of these communities lasted for more than a decade, but most lasted for less than two years. They were torn apart by internal dissensions; external pressures; the lack of business ability, manual skills, supplies, or funding; and occasionally by legal difficulties, including lawsuits brought by members against the association.

Socialism Comes to America

Thousands of radical European refugees, mostly from the German states, arrived in American cities in the last half of 1848, fleeing the repercussions of the failed revolutions. Known as the "Forty-Eighters," most of them settled in the Midwest, where they were active in education, journalism, and politics. (A substantial minority settled in the Texas hill country.) The majority of them were moderate reformers, who gravitated in 1854 toward the new Republican Party, with its slogan "free labor, free land, free men." The remainder included a mixture of socialists of every kind, including a few genuine Marxists.

The radical element of the Forty-Eighters was very visible. They formed political organizations, gave public lectures, and published radical papers. They formed cooperatives, workers' halls, and mutual-aid societies.

The First International in America

Despite warnings from Marx that "the available Germans who are worth anything become easily Americanized" and that America had no real proletariat in the European sense, a handful of German Marxists founded an American branch of the International Workingmen's Association in 1864, just in time to catch the attention of post–Civil War reformers who were interested in the labor question. Marx and his German-American cohorts envisioned the American branch of the First International as a coalition of German and Irish workers who would radicalize the American proletariat. Instead, what Marx dismissively called "Yankee radicals" flooded the organization. By 1870, the American reformer element outnumbered the German socialists, turning the organization into an umbrella for broad-based egalitarian reforms.

The mixture was not a success. In 1871, the German faction expelled their English-speaking fellow travelers from the party, unwittingly cutting themselves off from all access to an American political base. With no local base, the American branch of the First International did not survive the death of the larger organization in 1876.

Industrialization, Labor, and Socialism

In the late nineteenth century, American socialism became virtually synonymous with the labor movement. In 1860, manufacturing generated only 12 percent of America's gross national product, while agriculture was responsible for 31 percent. By the 1894 depression, industrial production had tripled, bypassing agriculture as the main source of America's wealth, and the United States was the world's leading industrial power.

The growth in manufacturing was accompanied by growth in urban labor, fed by both displaced agricultural workers and immigration. Between 1870 and 1900, the labor population in America's three largest cities, New York, Philadelphia, and Chicago, increased by 245 percent. Inner city neighborhoods were crowded and dirty. Few had paved streets, street lighting, or sewer and water lines, "public improvements" that were paid for by special tax assessments on local property owners.

Forty percent of America's working class lived in actual poverty, making less than the $500 needed to feed a family of five an adequate diet for a year. The top 15 percent of the working class, mostly highly skilled tradesmen, lived lives similar to the lower middle class. The balance of the working class earned enough to get by as long as they were employed.

ALERT

Freedom of association wasn't enough to protect the growing trade union movement from attack. Business owners maintained black lists of union members, hired private security firms to break strikes, and required employees to live in company-owned towns. Municipal police, state militias, and federal troops were regularly used to protect strikebreakers.

In Europe, laws often prohibited the creation of working-class organizations. In the United States, the Bill of Rights guarantees the freedom of association. The new working class, including immigrant Europeans with socialist roots, took full advantage of that freedom, forming mutual aid societies and trade associations.

The Knights of Labor

The Knights of Labor was founded in 1869 by Uriah Stephens (1821–1882) as a secret fraternal society, complete with rituals and vows borrowed from the Freemasons. When family financial problems put studying for the ministry out of his reach, Stephens apprenticed himself to a tailor. After several years of traveling through the West Indies, Central America, and Mexico, Stephens settled in Philadelphia in 1858, where he became involved in antebellum reform movements, including abolitionism and utopian socialism.

In 1862, Stephens added union organizing to the reform causes he espoused. His first effort was the formation of the Garment Cutters' Association of Philadelphia. When the Garment Cutters' Association collapsed in 1869, Stephens and other Garment Cutters founded the Noble Order of the Knights of Labor, with Stephens serving as the union's first Grand Master Workman.

The Knights of Labor was the first important national labor organization in the United States. Unlike later labor organizations, the Knights had an open membership policy. The organization not only welcomed both skilled and unskilled labor, it actively recruited women, African Americans, and immigrants. (At its height, the Knights had 95,000 African American members.) The only classes of society that were not welcome were bankers, lawyers, stockbrokers, gamblers, doctors, and purveyors of alcohol.

ALERT

The Knights of Labor's otherwise excellent record of inclusiveness was marred by their position on Chinese immigration. Fearful that unskilled American workers would not be able to compete with Chinese labor brought in on work contracts, the Knights joined other workers' organizations in lobbying for the Chinese Exclusion Act of 1882, which "suspended" Chinese immigration for ten years.

The organization's original program was based on the belief that the small producers of society—shopkeepers, farmers, and laborers—shared basic goals. Like other utopian socialists, Stephens's ultimate goal was to replace capitalism with a system of workers' cooperatives to replace capitalism.

Over time, Stephens's vision for the Knights no longer fit with that of its members. In 1878, he resigned as leader in favor of Terrence V. Powderly (1849–1924). Under Powderly's leadership, the Knights worked for improvements in the living conditions of their workers rather than a radical transformation of society. In addition to campaigning for better wages, hours, and working conditions, the Knights also fought for child labor laws, an end to convict labor, and equal opportunities and pay for women. (Powderly's mother didn't like the fact that she couldn't vote and made sure her family knew it.) Membership grew from a base of less than 10,000 in 1879 to 750,000 in 1886.

The Knights' influence fell sharply after 1886, when Samuel Gompers and other members left to form the American Federation of Labor.

Samuel Gompers and the American Federation of Labor

Samuel Gompers (1850–1924) was born in East London. His family immigrated to America when he was thirteen, settling in the Jewish community on Manhattan's Lower East Side. For eighteen months, Gompers and his father rolled cigars in their small apartment before finding better jobs in cigar workshops.

In the evenings, Gompers attended free lectures and classes at Cooper Union. He received an education on the floor of the cigar workshop as well. Unlike many other skilled trades, cigar rolling was quiet work and talking was allowed. Sometimes one of the men in the shop would read to the others. Political discussion on the floor was dominated by a group of immigrants who belonged to the American branch of the First International. One of the men in Gompers's workshop, Ferdinand Laurrell, was a member of First International's executive committee and introduced Gompers to the *Communist Manifesto*.

From the Cigar Makers' International Union to the American Federation of Labor (AFL)

Gompers and his father soon joined a branch of the United Cigar Makers' Union. Gompers was not very active in union business until the early 1870s when the position of skilled cigar makers was threatened by the proposed introduction of a cigar mold that simplified an important step in the cigar-making process. He joined other union members in a series of strikes protesting the use of the mold, with its threat of making skilled workers less necessary.

During this period, Gompers also attended socialist meetings and demonstrations. He was drawn to Marx's critique of capitalism, but came to the conclusion that socialist goals of long-term transformation were in conflict with the desire of most workers for immediate change.

After the failure of a 107-day strike, Gompers and fellow union member Adolph Strasser decided to reorganize the Cigar Makers' Union on the model of English trade unions. The new Cigar Makers' International Union charged relatively high dues, which allowed them to build a strike fund and offer a benefits program. The idea was to build a sense of identity among union members based on their shared skill and bind them to the union through an extensive benefit system.

In 1881, Gompers was instrumental in creating another level of union strength in the form of a national federation of trade unions, the Federation of Organized Trade and Labor Unions, which became the American Federation of Labor (AFL) in 1886. By 1900, the AFL had roughly 1 million members.

Bread and Butter Unionism

Gompers shifted the primary goal of American unionism away from political action. When political action was needed, Gompers urged union members to vote for those supporting a labor agenda rather than directly competing in politics.

ESSENTIAL

"... a struggle is going on in all the civilized world between oppressors and oppressed of all countries, between capitalist and laborer, which grows in intensity from year to year ... It therefore behooves the Representatives of the Trade and Labor Unions of America ... [to] disseminate such principles among the mechanics and laborers of our country as will permanently unite them." (Preamble, *AFL Constitution*)

The AFL focused on improving workers' lives through collective bargaining with employers over wages, benefits, and working conditions. He called his labor philosophy "bread and butter" unionism or "pure and simple" unionism.

Many saw "bread and butter unionism" as the antithesis of revolutionary ideology. Gompers argued that it was the logical extension of the teachings of Marx and Engels. He believed that their central message was the self-liberation of the working class. Building on the Marxist concept of class struggle, he said that workers have different interests from either the middle class or the wealthy. Since the working classes don't have the power to control the state, and consequently decide which laws should be passed, they cannot rely on the state to protect them. The trade union was the only organization that was purely proletarian.

Daniel De Leon and the Socialist Labor Party

Daniel De Leon (1852–1914) was born in Curacao in the Dutch Antilles. After being educated in England and Germany, he came to America in 1874. While a student and later a teacher at Columbia University, he was converted to socialism through the writings of Edward Bellamy.

In 1890, De Leon joined the Socialist Labor Party, which replaced the First International in 1877. He wrote the party's first formal platform, calling for the replacement of the capitalist state with a workers' democracy and a socialist reorganization of the economy. In 1891, he ran as the Socialist Labor Party's candidate for governor of New York, winning only 13,000 votes.

De Leon was one of the chief propagandists for socialism in the American labor movement. He argued for the revolutionary overthrow of capitalism in the United States, claiming that since America was the most developed country it was "ripe for the execution of Marxian revolutionary tactics." The only thing missing was a fully developed proletariat class-consciousness.

Since American society was ready for revolution, reform was not only unnecessary, it was counterproductive. Instead the socialist party should concentrate on transforming American labor into a class capable of its own liberation by providing them with "the proper knowledge." Since forming trade unions was an instinctive act on the part of the worker, a result of the small amount of class-consciousness already present in the proletariat, the natural vehicle for working-class education was the trade unions. Once the socialists won control of the state, the party would dissolve, leaving the administration of production in the hands of the industrial unions.

In 1895, De Leon founded the Socialist Trade and Labor Alliance as an alternative to Samuel Gompers's AFL. The organization's founding documents declared "the methods and spirit of labor organizations are absolutely impotent to resist the aggressions of organized capital." American labor apparently disagreed. De Leon's alliance had only 13,000 members at its height compared to more than 1 million members in the AFL at the same time.

Eugene V. Debs: Socialist for President

Born in Terre Haute, Indiana, labor organizer Eugene V. Debs (1855–1926) left home when he was fourteen to work for the railroad. In 1875, he helped organize a local lodge of the Brotherhood of Locomotive Firemen. He rose rapidly in the organization, becoming its national secretary and treasurer in 1880. In 1893, he became president of the newly established American Railway Union, which successfully united railway workers from different crafts into the first industrial union in the United States.

Debs was dubbed "King" Debs in the national press after his union successfully struck for higher wages from the Great Northern Railway in April 1894.

The Pullman Strike

During the panic of 1893, the Pullman Palace Car Company cut its wages by 25 percent. It did not cut rents for workers' housing in Pullman, Illinois, its company town near Chicago. Local members of the American Railway Union sent a delegation to talk to Pullman's president, George M. Pullman. He refused to meet with them. In response, the union's national council called for a nationwide boycott of trains carrying Pullman cars. Within four days union locals in twenty-seven states went out on sympathy strikes, affecting twenty-nine railroads.

Illinois Governor John P. Altgeld sympathized with the strikers and refused to call out the militia, so the railroads' management called on the federal government for help. On July 2, U.S. Attorney General Richard Olney got an injunction against the strike from local judges on the grounds that the union was impeding mail service and interstate commerce. Union leaders ignored the injunction. On July 4, President Grover Cleveland ordered 2,500 federal troops to Chicago. The strike ended within a week and troops were recalled on July 20. Debs was sentenced to six months in jail for contempt of court and conspiring against interstate commerce.

Debs Converts to Socialism

During his prison term at Woodstock, Illinois, Debs read broadly. Introduced for the first time to the work of Karl Marx, he came to see the labor movement as a struggle between classes.

After announcing his conversion to socialism in 1897, Debs joined forces with journalist Victor Berger to found the Social Democratic Party, renamed the Socialist Party in 1901. Debs ran as the Socialist Party candidate for President five times between 1900 and 1920. His highest popular vote came in 1920, when he received about 915,000 votes. Debs was in prison at the time, serving a sentence for criticizing the federal government's use of the 1917 Sabotage and Espionage Act.

Anarchism in America

Two different strains of anarchism were active in America in the nineteenth century: an immigrant tradition of insurrectionary anarchism, of the type promoted by Bakunin and Kropotkin, and an indigenous tradition of individual anarchism, sometimes known as Boston anarchism.

Rooted in the American tradition of extreme individualism, practitioners of individual anarchism on both the right and the left condemned the state's restriction of individual freedoms. The most well-known proponent of individual anarchism is Henry David Thoreau, whose technique of nonviolent noncooperation later inspired Mohandas Gandhi, Dr. Martin Luther King, Jr., and Nelson Mandela.

ESSENTIAL

Emma Goldman (1869–1940), known in the press as "Red Emma," was the best-known anarchist in America in the years before World War I. Born in Lithuania, she was already an anarchist when she immigrated to the United States in 1885. A follower of Kropotkin, Goldman spent much of her life giving lectures on anarchism and related causes.

The immigrant tradition was far more visible, linked with acts of terrorism thanks to the actions of anarchists such as Alexander Berkman, who attempted to assassinate steel magnate Henry Clay Frick in 1892, and Leon Czolgosz, who assassinated President William McKinley in 1901. In 1903, Congress passed a law barring all foreign anarchists from entering or remaining in the country.

The Haymarket Square Riot

The image of the bomb-throwing anarchist entered the American imagination as a result of the Haymarket Square Riot. The Knights of Labor, then the largest and most successful union in America, called for a general strike on May 1, 1886, as part of a campaign for an eight-hour work day. On May 3, fighting broke out on the picket line at the McCormick Harvesting Machine Company in Chicago. When the police intervened, several picketers were killed. Union leaders called for a protest meeting at Haymarket Square the next day.

Mayor Carter Harrison, who attended the meeting as an observer, commented on what a peaceful demonstration it was. After Harrison and most of the demonstrators left, a group of anarchists began to make inflammatory speeches. When the police arrived and demanded that the crowd disperse, a bomb exploded and killed one of the policemen. The police responded with gunfire. Not surprisingly, the remaining crowd panicked. Several people were killed, including six policemen. Many more were injured.

The bomb thrower was never identified, but eight anarchist leaders were arrested and charged with murder and conspiracy. Four members of the "Chicago Eight" were hanged on November 11, 1887. One committed suicide in his cell. The remaining three were given long jail sentences and later pardoned by Governor John P. Altgeld, who believed the atmosphere surrounding the trials made a fair trial impossible. The Haymarket Square Riot linked the labor movement with anarchism in the minds of many Americans at the time.

The "Wobblies"

The Industrial Workers of the World (IWW), popularly known as "the Wobblies," was founded in 1905 by representatives of forty-three different labor groups who were opposed to the "pure and simple" unionism of Samuel Gompers's American Federation of Labor. The most extreme of America's pre–World War I labor groups, the IWW rejected political action, arbitration, and binding contracts. Instead they put their faith in the strike and nothing but the strike. Inspired by European syndicalism, the IWW wanted to organize all workers into "One Big Union," with the ultimate goal of a revolutionary general strike that would overthrow capitalism and create a workers' society.

The principal founders of the IWW were Daniel De Leon of the Socialist Labor Party, Eugene V. Debs of the Socialist Party, and William D. ("Big

Bill") Haywood of the Western Federation of Miners. De Leon and Debs came out of the social democratic tradition of the socialist left. Haywood's ideological base was the militant unionism of the Western Federation of Miners, which spent a decade fighting mine owners and the government in its efforts to unionize hard rock miners and smelter workers.

ESSENTIAL

"The working class and the employing class have nothing in common . . . Between these two classes a struggle must go on until the workers of the world organize as a class, take possession of the means of production, abolish the wage system, and live in harmony with the Earth." (Preamble, *IWW Constitution*)

In 1908, the Wobblies split into two factions. One faction, led by De Leon and Debs, argued for creating change through political action by socialist parties and labor unions. The other faction, led by Haywood, came down in favor of syndicalist-style direct action: general strikes, boycotts, and sabotage. The syndicalists won and expelled the socialists from the organization.

Under Haywood's leadership, the Wobblies adopted an American version of syndicalism: class warfare based on direct industrial action. The IWW's actions often led to arrests and sensational publicity. Haywood himself was arrested and acquitted on a labor-related murder charge in 1906–1907. The group led a number of important strikes in the east between 1907 and 1913, but its main area of operation was among western workers in mining, lumber, transportation, and agriculture

The Effect of World War I on Socialism in America

The United States' entry into World War I in 1917 created a permanent break between socialists and the labor movement. When the war began, labor leaders and socialists alike called for neutrality. As soon as the United States entered the war in 1917, labor unions gave the government their wholehearted support. Socialists continued to oppose the war. Many were arrested under the 1917 Sabotage and Espionage Act, which made it illegal to undermine the war effort.

FACT

The IWW was the only labor organization to oppose U.S. involvement in the war. They protested by attempting to limit copper production in the western states. The government responded by prosecuting IWW leaders under the newly enacted Sabotage and Espionage Acts.

The Bolshevik Revolution in October 1917 split the socialist party. Reform-minded moderates abhorred the Bolshevik takeover. More radical members applauded it. The moderates, who controlled the party, expelled those who supported the revolution. The radicals subsequently founded the American Communist Party.

The First Red Scare

After the war, Attorney General A. Mitchell Palmer became convinced that communists and socialists were planning to overthrow the government, in part because an Italian anarchist blew himself up outside Palmer's home in Washington. On the second anniversary of the Russian Revolution, more than 10,000 suspected socialists, communists, and anarchists were arrested in what became known as the "Palmer Raids." Charged with advocating force, violence, and unlawful means to overthrow the government, the suspected revolutionaries were held without trial for an extended period. The courts ultimately found no evidence of a proposed revolution, and most were released. A small number, including Emma Goldman, were declared to be subversive aliens and deported to the Soviet Union.

CHAPTER 15

Fascism and Socialism

Nationalism was in the air at the beginning of the twentieth century. Ethnic minorities in the Russian and Austrian empires called out for national independence. The newly unified states of Germany and Italy looked with covetous eyes at German and Italian speaking regions under Austrian control. A gun-wielding Serbian nationalist pushed Europe into the First World War. Four years later, the Treaty of Versailles was shaped by the idea of national self-determination. A new political philosophy based on extreme nationalism was born from Versailles' failed policies: fascism.

What Is Fascism?

Scholars find it difficult to define fascism. Not only did the fascist states of the 1920s and 1930s differ from each other in significant ways, but fascist leaders had a habit of welding together ideas from disparate sources to create a Rube Goldberg ideology that fit the needs of the moment. Spanish philosopher José Ortega y Gasset (1883–1955), writing on fascism in 1927, when the movement was at it height, described the problem well:

> *Fascism has an enigmatic countenance because in it appears the most counterpoised contents. It asserts authoritarianism and organizes rebellion. It fights against contemporary democracy and, on the other hand, does not believe in the restoration of any past rule. It seems to pose itself as the force of a strong State, and uses means most conducive to its dissolution, as if it were a destructive faction of a secret society. Whichever way we approach fascism, we find that it is simultaneously one thing and the contrary. It is A and not A . . .*

The common thread that holds fascism together as a political philosophy is extreme nationalism. All of fascism's borrowed ideological trimmings combine to elevate the nation into the primary focus of loyalty. The ideal is to unite all classes into a nation that is permanently mobilized against its enemies, internal and external alike.

FACT

The difficulty of defining fascism is increased by the term's popular usage as a negative epithet, applied equally to an authoritarian ruler or someone who thrusts his personal preferences on others. This is not a new phenomenon. In 1944, George Orwell, in his essay "What Is Fascism?", complained "almost any English person would accept 'bully' as a synonym for 'Fascist.'"

Fascist states define the nation in different ways. The Nazis defined the nation in biological terms; other fascist groups defined it historically or culturally. However the nation is defined, it is embodied by a single, militarized, mass party whose sovereignty is expressed through a charismatic leader.

Fascist parties are difficult to place on the political continuum between right and left. They typically reject the conventional sources of conservative authority and traditional leaders. Instead, a new elite draws its authority directly from the nation-party. At the same time, fascism condemns other "isms" on the grounds that they place another value above the nation: class, gender, or religion.

ESSENTIAL

Italian journalist Giovanni Amendola (1882–1926) coined the term *totalitarian* (*totalitario*) to describe the fascist state. Although the term was intended as an insult, Mussolini embraced it, summing up the ideal state as "All within the state, none outside the state, none against the state."

Fascism positioned itself as a "third way" between capitalism and socialism, sometimes described as "extremism of the center." Fascists blamed capitalism for creating class conflict and socialism for fanning class conflict into class struggle. Although they never advocated abolishing capitalism, they believed it was necessary to control private enterprise for the good of the state.

Mussolini: The Original "Red Diaper Baby"

Benito Amilcare Andrea Mussolini (1883–1945) grew up socialist the way some people grow up Baptist. Mussolini's father, Alessandro, was a member of the First International, who read *Das Kapital* aloud to his family at night. Like many Italian socialists, Alessandro leaned toward Bakunin's brand of anarchism. According to Mussolini, his father's "heart and mind were always filled and pulsing with socialistic theories . . . He discussed them in the evening with his friends and his eyes filled with light." Alessandro named Mussolini after three leftist revolutionary heroes: Benito Juarez, who fought against the French occupation of Mexico, and the Italian anarchists Amilcare Cipriani and Andrea Costa.

By the time he was eighteen, Mussolini was already an active socialist. After a year of teaching school and working as the secretary of a local socialist organization, he left Italy for Switzerland to avoid being conscripted into the military. In Switzerland, Mussolini became involved in the world of international socialism in the form of Angelica Balabanoff, a close disciple of Lenin who was involved in socialist agitation among the Italians in Switzerland. Under her tutelage, Mussolini translated Kautsky into Italian, published articles and poems in socialist publications, and made anticlerical stump speeches.

In 1905, the twenty-two-year-old Mussolini took advantage of a general amnesty for draft dodgers to return to Italy. For several years he did his military service, drank, chased girls, and read the political philosophy of Marx, Nietzsche, and Sorel.

In 1909, Mussolini accepted a job as the editor of a socialist weekly paper in Trentino, an Italian region under Austrian rule. Before the Austrian authorities expelled him, he accumulated several libel convictions for articles accusing various clergy members of moral turpitude. (He also published a pulp novel on the topic, titled *Claudia Particella, the Cardinal's Mistress*.)

Back in Italy, Mussolini became the secretary of the Socialist Federation of Forli and editor of its paper, *The Class Struggle*. He quickly established himself as a leading proponent of proletarian internationalism, taking the position that "The national flag is for us a rag to be planted on a dunghill."

Mussolini Moves Toward the Left

In 1911, Italy invaded Tripoli and Cyrenaica in an effort to take Libya from the Ottomans. The leaders of the socialist party's large moderate faction supported the action against the Ottomans. Mussolini emerged as a vocal opponent of the invasion and was arrested for urging his followers to blow up Italian railway lines as a way to stop troop movements.

Mussolini was on his way up in the party. At the 1912 Socialist Party congress, he became a member of the party executive and editor of the party's national paper *Avanti!* At the same time, Mussolini launched a monthly theoretical journal, *Utopia*, in which he considered some of the problems he saw in classical Marxism. The most troubling of these was the familiar issue of false consciousness: the tendency of the average worker to focus on immediate improvements to his own life to the exclusion of class struggle.

ESSENTIAL

Antonio Gramsci (1891–1937) is best known for *Prison Notebooks*, an analysis of communism, society, and revolution written while he was imprisoned under Mussolini's rule. The central element of his analysis is the idea that society is controlled by a shared cultural consensus, which he calls hegemony. To establish a new social order, the revolutionary must establish a new hegemony.

Over the next two years, a growing number of Socialist Party members began calling themselves "Mussoliniani," including Antonio Gramsci and Amedeo Bordiga, who later founded the Italian Communist Party. By the time of the 1914 party congress, Mussolini was the dominant leader of the party.

Mussolini Joins the Fascists

At the start of the First World War, Mussolini held to his previous anti-war stance. In every issue of *Avanti!* he denounced the conflict as an "unpardonable crime" and advocated that Italy remain neutral.

Over the course of two months, Mussolini's position began to change. Instead of denouncing the war in the pages of *Avanti!*, he advocated entering the conflict on the side of the Triple Entente (Britain, France, and Russia). The change in position led to an angry disagreement about policy with *Avanti!*'s editorial board and Mussolini's resignation.

Mussolini quickly founded a pro-war alternative paper, *Popolo d'Italia*, in which he encouraged Italy's involvement in the war on the grounds that it would kindle revolution. A month later, in an open party meeting in Milan, Mussolini was expelled from the Socialist Party for "political and moral unworthiness." As he left, he shook his fist at his accusers and shouted:

> *You think you can turn me out, but you will find I shall come back again. I am and shall remain a socialist and my convictions will never change. They are bred in my very bones.*

Instead of returning to the Socialist Party, Mussolini found a new political home with a group of pro-war revolutionary syndicalists, the *Fascio*

Autonomo d'Azione Rivoluzionaria. Like Mussolini, the members argued for Italy's entrance into the war as a step toward the socialist revolution. They described Germany as an entrenched bastion of reactionary thought. Defeating the Hohenzollern and Hapsburg empires would liberate the Italians who still remained under Austrian rule, thus completing the process of national unification and creating the necessary framework for Italy's transition to socialism.

FACT

The literal translation of *fascio* is "bundle," derived from the bundle of rods (*fasces*) that were the insignia of magistrates in ancient Rome. By the mid-nineteenth century, *fascio* was used by revolutionary groups to mean "league." The symbolism is that while each rod can easily be broken on its own, the bundle as a whole cannot.

In 1914, the Second International tore itself apart over the relative value of nationalism and internationalism. Mussolini began to question whether a socialist state could transcend "the old barriers of race and historical intention." Previously he believed the socialist truism that class bonds were more important than national bonds. Now he was less sure: "I have asked myself if internationalism is an absolutely necessary constituent of the notion of socialism. A future socialism might well concern itself with finding an equilibrium between nation and class." He came to the conclusion, shared in the pages of *Il Popolo d'Italia*, that "It is necessary to assassinate the Party in order to save Socialism." Having decided in favor of nationalism, Mussolini called on his readers to take part in mass demonstrations for entry into the war.

Mussolini in World War I

A few months after Italy entered the war in 1915, Mussolini was called into service. In February 1917, he suffered severe shrapnel wounds and was discharged from service after several months in the hospital. He returned from the front with a new awareness of the power of nationalism. In 1912, he declared that he was a socialist in his bones; now he realized that he was "desperately Italian."

From the time he was discharged from the army until the armistice in 1918, Mussolini agitated for total commitment to the war effort. More important for the future, Mussolini developed the idea of what he called *trincerocrazia*: rule by those who had served in the trenches. Marxist theory claimed that members of the proletariat were bound together into a political class by their experience as workers. Mussolini argued that the experience of shared combat would bind men together even more tightly. Socialist parties championed the cause of the industrial worker; fascism would champion the cause of veterans.

Mussolini: Socialist "Heretic"

Shortly after the end of the war, Mussolini called together the various fascist groups to create a national organization, the *Fasci italiani di combattimento*. The party was small at first, made up primarily of revolutionary syndicalists, Futurists, and war veterans who were proud of their service and indignant over the repudiation of the victory by socialists and liberals.

FACT

Futurism was an art movement that began in Milan about 1909. Futurists rejected the classical standards of beauty as irrelevant to the modern world. Instead, they revered speed, movement, and change. Their work has been described as the "cult of the machine" and the "cult of the modern." Italian Futurists were drawn to fascism's revolutionary rhetoric.

In its early years, fascism owed as much to socialism as it did to radical nationalism. Its political platform called for land for the peasants and worker representation in management, a progressive tax on capital, higher inheritance taxes, nationalization of the armaments industry, a fixed minimum wage, abolition of the senate, female suffrage, and a decentralized government.

In reconciling socialism and nationalism, fascism embraced the thinking of nationalist intellectual Enrico Corradini, who argued that Italy was a "proletarian nation," exploited by its richer, more powerful European neighbors. Therefore, its struggle against richer nations paralleled the struggle of workers against capitalists.

In the 1919 parliamentary elections, fascist candidates presented themselves as part of the Left not only in their beliefs, but also in their willingness to ally with other leftist parties. The combination of nationalism and left-wing politics did not prove popular with the voters. All the fascist candidates, including Mussolini, were defeated. The socialists, on the other hand, won one-third of the total vote and 150 seats in the legislature.

The Heretics

Mussolini began to reposition the party, announcing, "Two religions are today contending . . . for sway over the world—the black and the red. We declare ourselves the heretics."

He found a ready audience of other heretics. Many of the syndicalists who helped found fascism argued that there were sound Marxist grounds for postponing the revolution. Italy wasn't a fully industrialized country and did not yet have a fully radicalized proletariat. The Bolsheviks had tried to make the leap directly to socialism without waiting to experience full capitalist development. Lenin himself acknowledged that his New Economic Proposal of 1920 was a retreat to capitalism. If Lenin couldn't successfully skip the capitalist phase, there was no reason to believe that Italy could.

Mussolini Rises to Power

Italy was on the winning side of World War I, but it felt like they had lost. The Treaty of Versailles brought Italy less territory than the nationalists thought they deserved. Inflation was high: the lira was worth only one-sixth of its prewar value. Grain harvests and manufacturing wages were low. Unemployment rose as soldiers returned home looking for work.

The "Red Years": 1918–1920

Unlike most of their European counterparts, the Italian Socialist Party never supported the government in its war effort. With peace at hand, the socialists sponsored a wave of strikes intended to overthrow constitutional monarchy, paralyzing railroad, telegraph, and mail service. In the countryside, landless laborers seized land and agricultural workers went on strike during the harvest. Socialist deputies walked out of parliament to protest the presence of King Victor Emmanuel II. An anarchist detonated a bomb in Milan's Diana Theater during a performance, killing eighteen.

In regions where the socialists gained control of the government, they removed the Italian flag from government buildings and replaced it with the red flag. A few municipalities under socialist control declared Monday the day of rest instead of Sunday as a gesture against "clerical superstitions." Revolution seemed to be imminent.

The "two red years" ended with the seizure of factories across northern Italy in August and September. For three weeks, worker groups continued to operate the factories on their own, with the intention of proving they could replace the "owning class."

The "Black Years": 1921–1922

In 1919, fascist squads, known as Blackshirts, began to break up strikes. They soon moved on to attack the offices of trade unions, peasant cooperatives, and employment bureaus. They killed labor leaders and burned the homes of agitators. In April, they made a symbolic strike against the offices of *Avanti!* By 1920, Blackshirt violence was more of a problem than socialist direct action.

FACT

The fascist squads were made up of young unemployed war veterans who distinguished themselves by wearing black shirts, like those worn by army shock troops during the war. The shirts quickly became fascism's symbol, a visible rejection of socialist red. The Blackshirts were organized into paramilitary legions commanded by "consuls." Each legion was sub-divided into cohorts, *centurie*, and squads.

Unable to stop the disintegration of civil order, the government called for new elections in May 1921. This time, Mussolini's newly renamed National Fascist Party stood squarely with the right and won thirty-five of the 247 seats in the parliament.

By 1922, violent street confrontations between the Fascists and the parties on the left were a regular event. The Socialists and Communists called a general strike on July 31 to protest the government's failure to suppress Fascist violence. Without waiting for the government to take action, Mussolini dispatched groups of Blackshirts to act as strikebreakers and threaten anyone who tried to stop them. The strike was over within a day.

Mussolini's "March on Rome"

In October 1922, Mussolini organized a "March on Rome" by his supporters. The Fascist Party had 250,000 members. On October 27, roughly 25,000 of them marched on the capital from four directions and occupied railroad stations and government offices. The prime minister urged the king to declare martial law. The king refused, fearful that the army and police would refuse to fight the Fascists. Instead, on October 29, the king asked Mussolini to take the office of prime minister and form a new government.

For eighteen months, Mussolini ruled through normal government channels, gradually concentrating power in his own hands and altering the laws to ensure the Fascist Party won a majority of seats in the 1924 elections. The Blackshirt squads were transformed into an official militia. Beginning in 1923, he began to demolish Italy's constitutional safeguards. By 1926, his control was secure enough to ban all other political parties and arrest their leaders.

Corporatism

Under Mussolini's rule, the Italian government set up state-run holding companies to bail out failing banks and provide capital for new industrial investments, becoming a powerful shareholder in vital sectors of the economy without actually nationalizing them. At the same time, Mussolini inaugurated a major welfare and public works program, boasting, "There is little which social welfare research has adjudged practical to national economy or wise for social happiness which has not already been advanced by me."

Mussolini's ultimate goal was to organize the state using the principles of "corporatism," which he claimed moved beyond both capitalism and socialism to create a new synthesis. In fact, corporatism borrows heavily from Georges Sorel's theories of revolutionary syndicalism. Each of the major sectors of the economy, including industry, agriculture, the professions, and the arts, would be organized in government-controlled trade unions and employer associations called *corporations*. Each corporation would be run by a committee that included representatives of employers, employees, and the government. The committees' decisions regarding wages, hours, and working conditions would be binding. Strikes would be illegal. Representatives of each corporation would represent its interests in a corporatist parliament.

Fascist Parties Across Europe

Despite Mussolini's often-quoted statement that "fascism is not for export," fascist movements sprang up in more than a dozen European countries during the 1920s and 1930s. Like Mussolini, the leaders of many of these groups began as members of leftist groups.

The ideologies of these parties were not uniform, but they all shared two defining beliefs:

- Extreme nationalism
- Anti-Bolshevism

Most of them were anti-democratic and anti-Semitic. The fact that they were opposed to Bolshevism did not mean they supported capitalism. More often they did not.

Socialism and National Socialism

Despite the name, the link between fascism and socialists was less direct in the case of the National Socialist German Workers' Party.

Munich locksmith and toolmaker Anton Drexler spent several years bouncing between political parties, like Goldilocks in search of a chair that was just right. The German Social Democrat Party wasn't nationalist enough. The Fatherland Party didn't have enough concern for workers. In 1919, Drexler stopped searching and founded the German Workers' Party, which reconciled conservative nationalism with radical socialism.

Hitler joined the party several months later. At his suggestion, Drexler added the words "National Socialist" to the name to emphasize the blending of nationalism with socialism. The point was reinforced by the party's flag, which Hitler explained in *Mein Kampf*: "In red we see the social idea of the movement, in white the nationalistic idea, in the swastika the mission of the struggle for the victory of the Aryan man."

All elements of radical socialism were stripped out of the party rhetoric after Hitler came to power in 1933, leaving extreme nationalism as its sole ideological base.

CHAPTER 16

Communism in China

Mao Zedong's idea of a peasant-based socialist revolution was an innovation in Marxist thinking, which held that the revolution would come from the urban poor. The idea of a peasant-based revolution was less startling in China where dynasties often rose or fell as a result of peasant uprisings. In fact, it was a political truism that peasants are like water: They can float the boat or they can sink the boat.

Maoism

According to the Chinese constitution, *Maoism* (called "Mao Zedong thought" in China) is simply "Marxism-Leninism defined in a Chinese context." Mao's most original contribution to Marxism was his recognition of Chinese peasants as the main force of revolution in China. As early as 1925, in his *Report on the Hunan Peasant Movement*, he urged the Chinese Communist Party to turn its attention to the countryside. He argued that proletarianism was a mindset as much as an economic condition and that the Chinese peasants would be the "vanguard of the revolution."

Mao's Little Red Book

Very few people have read Marx's *Das Kapital*, but millions of people have read a simplified version of Mao's political philosophy. *Quotations from Chairman Mao*, known in the West as *Mao's Little Red Book*, was commissioned by General Lin Biao in 1964. Made up of selections from Mao's writings, the book was intended to simplify Maoist thought for the relatively uneducated soldiers of the People's Liberation Army. Lin issued a free copy of the book to every soldier. It quickly became a vehicle for spreading both Maoist ideology and for increasing literacy.

During the infamous Cultural Revolution in the 1960s and 1970s, the book was made available to the public for the first time. Everyone in China soon owned a copy and it became a talisman for members of the Red Guard.

The Chinese Revolution Begins

In 1912, Dr. Sun Yat-sen's nationalist Revolutionary Alliance overthrew the Qing dynasty, which had ruled China since 1644. Sun became the provisional president of the Republic of China.

The Republic didn't last long. In 1916, China's second president, Yuan Shikai, dissolved the new parliament and tried to make himself emperor. He was met with immediate opposition, both political protests and military revolts in the provinces. Yuan died before he could consolidate his power. He left behind a conservative government seated in Beijing that claimed to rule all of China. In fact, the country was a mess of semi-independent warlords and armed political parties, most notably Sun Yat-sen's Kuomintang (Nationalist) Party.

e! ALERT

Both the People's Republic of China and Taiwan claim revolutionary leader Sun Yat-sen (1886–1925) as their founding father. Trained as a doctor in Hawaii, Sun returned to China to battle against the Qing dynasty, which he saw as the source of Chinese "backwardness." At first he envisioned establishing a constitutional monarchy, but soon changed his goal to full democracy.

The Beginnings of Chinese Communism

A new intelligentsia began to emerge at the end of the Qing dynasty as a result of educational reforms and the end of the centuries-old civil service examination system, which was based on history, poetry, and calligraphy. Thousands of young Chinese went to Japan, Europe, and the United States to study subjects that were not included in the classic Chinese curriculum: science, engineering, medicine, economics, law, and military science. They came to China with new academic knowledge and revolutionary ideas.

The New Culture Movement

The student leaders of the New Culture Movement, sometimes called the Chinese Renaissance, called for "new thought" and "new literature" as they questioned Confucian values and institutions in the light of Western ideas. As a group, they were interested in national independence, individual liberties, and recreating Chinese society and culture on modern terms.

One outcome of their rejection of Chinese tradition was the movement to use a version of the spoken vernacular for literary purposes rather than the esoteric classical Chinese associated with the traditional governing classes. The movement toward a vernacular literary language resulted in experimental literature inspired by Western forms and a wave of new literary journals.

The most important of these was *New Youth*, which was founded by Chen Duxiu (1879–1942) in 1915 in opposition to Yuan Shikai's imperial ambitions. With Yuan's death, Chen broadened his scope, calling for an intellectual and cultural revolution that would regenerate the nation. Many of the contributors to *New Youth* went on to become important members of the Chinese Communist Party, including Mao Zedong.

The May Fourth Movement

On May 4, 1919, the news reached Beijing that the peacemakers at Versailles decided to transfer the former German concessions in Shandong province to Japan instead of returning them to Chinese control. More than 3,000 students demonstrated against the treaty provisions in Beijing's Tiananmen Square. Over the following weeks, demonstrations against the Shandong provision spread beyond the students to the general population. Merchants closed their shops, workers went on strike, and banks suspended business.

QUESTION

What were *treaty ports*?
In the nineteenth century, the so-called *Unequal Treaties* between the Qing dynasty and various European governments opened "treaty ports" to foreign trade and habitation. Foreigners who lived in their own compounds in the treaty ports, called *concessions*, did not have to pay Chinese taxes, and were exempt from Chinese laws.

Faced with widespread demonstrations of anti-Japanese feeling, the Chinese government refused to sign the peace treaty.

Chinese Communist Party

The Chinese Communist Party grew directly out of the May Fourth Movement. The party's early leaders were professors and students who believed that China needed a social revolution.

Prior to 1905, the few Chinese socialists were students who discovered Proudhon, Bakunin, and Kropotkin while they studied in Paris and Tokyo.

The attempted Russian revolution in 1905 excited interest among reform-minded Chinese, who saw parallels between the Qing dynasty and the Russian tsars. A translation of the *Communist Manifesto* into Chinese appeared in 1906, ending with a somewhat muted rendition of the original call to arms: "Then the world will be for the common people, and the sounds of happiness will reach the deepest springs. Ah! Come! People of every land, how can you not be roused?"

ESSENTIAL

The Chinese translator anticipated Mao's placement of peasants at the center of the Chinese revolution. In a note he explains that he used the phrase *common people* as the translation for *proletariat* since the Chinese word for worker did not include peasants.

After the initial flurry of excitement, Chinese radicals put Marxism to one side. After all, Marx himself claimed that his cycle of historical development didn't apply to China.

The Russian Revolution of 1917 induced some Chinese intellectuals to look at Marx more closely. The most prominent among them was Li Dazhao (1889–1927), the head librarian of Beijing University. Excited by the possibilities of following the Russian example, Li created an informal study group that met at his office to discuss political developments and discuss *Das Kapital*. Six months later, Chen Duxiu, now dean of Beijing University, ran a special issue of *New Youth* devoted to Marxism, with Li Dazhao as the general editor. Soon radical study groups were meeting in half a dozen cities.

In May 1920, Chen Duxiu and Li Dazhao moved from studying Marxism to organizing. With the help of two agents from the Comintern, they founded a Soviet Youth League, laid plans for the creation of a communist party, and began recruiting. They soon had fifty members located throughout China and Japan.

Chen and Li held the founding meeting of the Chinese Communist Party (CCP) in July 1921, in Shanghai. Thirteen Chinese communists, including Mao Zedong, and two Comintern agents, attended it. Chen was elected to be the party's first secretary-general.

The CCP spent the next two years recruiting new members, publicizing Marxist ideology, campaigning for the need for a national revolution directed against foreign imperialism, and attempting to organize China's handful of railway and industrial workers into unions.

By 1923, the party had almost 300 members, and it became dangerous to be a known communist. With some arm-twisting on the part of the Comintern, the CCP became part of the Kuomintang.

Karl Marx Bad-Mouths China

Marxist theory posed a problem for aspiring Chinese revolutionaries because Marx didn't believe a socialist revolution was possible in China. In Marx's assessment, China stood outside history, trapped in what he termed the "Asiatic mode of production." The Asiatic mode of production was marked by a despotic centralized state that had a monopoly on land ownership and control over public services, particularly irrigation systems. Since the state itself controlled the mode of production, it formed an economic Mobius strip: both superstructure and the underlying economic determinant of superstructure. The result was stagnant economic and social relations.

ESSENTIAL

In his assessment of Marxism, Li Dazhao played down the doctrine of a proletarian struggle. Instead, he envisioned a Chinese socialist revolution in terms of a populist uprising against the exploitation of foreign imperialists. The CCP adopted Li's version of revolution rather than Marx's.

In Marx's view, the solution was what he called the "regenerative role of imperialism," in which Western imperialists would introduce capitalist relationships into the Chinese economy and set it back on the path of history.

Mao Zedong Discovers Marxism

Mao Zedong (1893–1976) was the son of a wealthy peasant in Hunan province. His father wanted him to be a farmer and took him out of the local school when he was thirteen. Mao wanted more. Four years later he left home to study at the teacher's college in Hunan's provincial capital, where he became caught up in the revolution against the Qing dynasty in 1911.

In 1918, Mao finally graduated with his teaching certificate and went to Beijing to attend the university there. Like other graduate students, he had little money. He took a job as a library assistant to Li Dazhao, who introduced him to Marxism. Although Mao was one of the original members of the Chinese Communist Party, he did not become a party leader until the 1930s.

Civil War

After Sun Yat-sen's death in 1925, Chiang Kai-shek became the head of the Kuomintang. He immediately mobilized a massive campaign against the warlords in Northern China. His intentions were to consolidate his power within the party and unify the country under his own leadership. In 1927, concerned about the rising influence of the Chinese Communist Party within the ranks of the Kuomintang, he ordered the arrest and execution of hundreds of communists and other leftists.

FACT

Unlike most of the Chinese revolutionaries, Chiang Kai-shek (1887–1975) trained as a career military officer. He served with the Japanese army from 1909 to 1911. While in Tokyo, he met young Chinese revolutionaries who converted him to republicanism. He fought in the revolt against the Qing dynasty and joined the Kuomintang in 1918.

The international community formally recognized Chiang's government after he conquered Beijing in 1928, but his hold on the country remained precarious. Northern warlords still challenged his authority. The Japanese invaded Manchuria in 1931, and showed signs of taking a large bite out of China's northern border. Closer to home, the communists who survived the 1927 purge created a Soviet-style republic in Jiangxi Province, with its own army and government. Aided by a popular program of land redistribution, the Jiangxi Soviet controlled several million people by 1930.

Chiang decided to deal with the communist threat first. Between 1930 and 1934, he launched five campaigns against the Jiangxi Soviet. The communists successfully fought off the first four attacks using guerilla techniques that Mao designed.

Chiang brought in more forces for the fifth attack. In 1934, he built a series of concrete blockhouses around the communist positions manned with 700,000 troops. The communists might have succeeded in fending off the fifth attack if they continued to use Mao's guerilla tactics. Unfortunately for them, the CCP's Central Committee took over the command of the communist forces when it moved to Jiangxi earlier that year. Instead of fighting a guerilla campaign, they met the larger and better-armed Kuomintang forces using more conventional military tactics.

The Long March

In October 1934, faced with defeat by Chiang's forces, the Red Army had only two options, surrender or retreat. They chose to retreat.

On October 16, the remaining 86,000 members of the Red Army, including administrative personnel and thirty women, broke through the Kuomintang line and began a 6,000 mile march from their base in southern China to the northwest province of Shanxi. The Long March took 368 days. For the first three months, they suffered repeated Kuomintang attacks from the air and on the ground. They quickly ran out of rice and were reduced to eating first their horses and then their leather belts. Finally they marched with empty stomachs. Only 8,000 survived the march.

By the time they reached Shanxi, Mao was the undisputed leader of the CCP. Other communist units in search of a leader soon joined them, raising their strength to 30,000.

The United Front

In 1937, Japan invaded China. Like squabbling siblings who quickly resolve their differences when an outsider picks on one of them, the Communist Party and the Kuomintang suspended hostilities and fought together against the Japanese.

The Sino-Japanese War gave the CCP a chance to revitalize itself. Operating out of their base in Shanxi, the communists used guerilla warfare tactics to harass the Japanese, often sending small units behind the enemy lines to provide a nucleus for local resistance. In rural areas, the communist fighters were often the only organized opposition to Japanese brutality. At the same time that they organized a willing population to supply food and hiding places for guerilla units, they also recruited new party members.

By the time Japan surrendered in 1945, popular opinion shifted in favor of the communists. Disaffected Kuomintang troops joined Mao's army in large numbers, armed with captured Japanese weapons.

The People's Republic of China

American efforts to build a coalition government between the two sides failed. Full-scale civil war broke out again in June 1946.

Despite American aid, Chiang's forces were on the run by late 1948. Beijing fell without a fight on January 31, 1949. The communist army took the Kuomintang capital of Nanking on April 23. Chiang Kai-shek and his supporters retreated to the island of Taiwan. On October 1, Chairman Mao announced the formation of the People's Republic of China, which he declared to be a "people's democratic dictatorship."

The CCP faced an enormous challenge. China had been torn by civil war for more than thirty years. With the brief exception of the Jiangxi Soviet, they had no experience in government. At first, communist policies were based on what Mao later described as "copying from the Soviets." Ignoring his own policy of "encircling the cities from the countryside," Mao instituted a five-year plan focused on urban industrialization with Soviet technical assistance.

The Hundred Flowers Campaign

In 1956, Mao ignored the advice of key party members and initiated a campaign of "letting a hundred flowers bloom." Intellectuals were encouraged to speak out against abuses within the party.

To Mao's dismay, they did. For five weeks, from May 1 to June 7, people spoke out in closed party meetings and public rallies, in the official press and posters on city walls. They complained about harsh campaigns against counter-revolutionaries, the low standard of living, Soviet development models, censorship of foreign literature, and special privileges for CCP members. Students at the university in Beijing created a "Democratic Wall" covered with posters criticizing the CCP. Students began protest riots in cities across the country.

The backlash against the educated elite began in June. By the end of the year, more than 300,000 intellectuals were branded "anti-communist, counter-revolutionary rightists." Many were sent to labor camps, imprisoned, or exiled to the countryside to experience life on the land.

The Great Leap Forward

In 1958, Mao introduced a three-year program, known as the Great Leap Forward, which was designed to increase production using labor rather than machines and capital expenditures. The capitalist model of industrialization was unacceptable for ideological reasons. The Soviet model of converting capital gained by the sale of agricultural products into heavy machinery was not viable: China's already large population meant there was no agricultural surplus to sell. Instead of slowly accumulating capital, Mao decided to leap forward by combining industrialization with collectivization.

The peasants were organized into large communes. Communal kitchens were established so women could be freed for agricultural work. Small "backyard furnaces" were set up in every village and urban neighborhood. Communes were given unreasonable goals for production and little guidance on how to achieve them. Productive agriculture ended almost overnight as farm labor was diverted into small-scale industry.

Errors in implementing the program were made worse by a series of natural disasters, creating a large-scale famine. An estimated 20 million people died of starvation between 1959 and 1961, when the program was abandoned.

The Cultural Revolution

Following the failure of the Great Leap Forward, Mao began to denounce the development of "new bourgeois elements" among the party and technical elites in both the Soviet Union and China. Adapting the Marxist-Leninist theory of "permanent revolution," he proclaimed that "protracted, complex, and sometimes even violent class struggle" would be constant elements of the revolution until the final stage of socialism was achieved.

In 1966, Mao announced a program that was officially intended to reaffirm the core values of Chinese communism and attack creeping bourgeois tendencies in the party bureaucracy: the Great Proletarian Cultural Revolution. Its unofficial purpose was to purge the party leadership of anyone who opposed him.

Mao closed schools and invited student groups to join paramilitary Red Guard units. Working under the slogan "fight selfishness, criticize revisionism," the Red Guard burned books, destroyed Confucian and Buddhist temples, and hunted down "counter-revolutionaries." Revisionists, intellectuals, and anyone suspected of "ideological weakness" (code for disagreeing with Mao) were all fair targets. Some were punished with nothing worse than wearing a dunce cap and publicly confessing their errors. Others were beaten, tortured, killed, or driven to commit suicide. Urban residents, intellectuals, and government officials were relocated to the country to "learn from the peasants." The worst of the Cultural Revolution ended with Mao's death in 1976.

CHAPTER 17

The Creation of Welfare Socialism

The one-two punch of the Great Depression and World War II left Western Europe ready for a change. Economies and societies needed to be rebuilt. In an overwhelming rejection of the free-market economy and the parties that supported it, Western Europe voted Left. Britain, Norway, and Sweden elected socialist governments. Socialist parties helped form coalition governments in Holland, Denmark, Switzerland, Austria, Belgium, Italy, and France. For the first time, socialist parties were in power in virtually all of Western Europe.

The Roots of the Welfare State

The Russian Revolution left a clear divide between parties that described themselves as socialist and those that described themselves as communist. In 1945, Western Europe's socialist parties were the heirs of Eduard Bernstein and the Fabians, not those of Marx and Lenin. Although they retained an ideological commitment to the creation of a socialist state, they abandoned revolution in favor of reform before they took power. Elected to office with a clear mandate for change, Europe's socialist parties developed variations of "welfare socialism": all of which included a range of social welfare programs and a reformed capitalist structure regulated by the state.

FACT

The German Social Democratic Party, reconstructed after its demise at the hands of the Nazis, dropped its commitment to Marxism in its 1959 Bad Godesberg program. The party replaced Marxism with the pursuit of a "social market economy" that would include "as much competition as possible—as much planning as necessary."

In fact, post-war socialist parties weren't the first to set up social welfare programs. In a move intended to win the allegiance of the working classes away from the socialists, Chancellor Otto van Bismarck set up the first compulsory national social insurance programs in Germany, including a health insurance plan in 1893, workers' compensation in 1894, and general pensions for the elderly and the disabled in 1889. Austria and Hungary soon followed Germany's example. Conscious of the new Labour Party breathing down its neck, Herbert Asquith's Liberal government instituted a similar series of reforms in Britain in 1911, including Britain's first health and unemployment insurance plans, old-age pensions, a national network of labor exchanges, and trade boards with the power to set minimum wages for their industries.

The Swedish Model for the Welfare State

The Swedish Social Democratic Labor Party (SAP) pioneered the creation of "mixed economies," which combined largely private ownership of the means of production with government direction of the economy and substantial welfare programs. Other nations' socialist parties followed their lead.

Hjalmar Branting

Hjalmar Branting (1860–1925) was the driving force behind the formation of the Swedish Social Democratic Labor Party in 1889. The son of one of the developers of the Swedish school of gymnastics, Branting was educated in the exclusive Beskow School in Stockholm and studied mathematics at the University of Uppsala. After graduating, he took a position as the assistant to the director of the Stockholm Observatory in 1882.

Traveling across Europe the following year, he stumbled across socialist doctrines everywhere. He attended lectures in Paris by revolutionary Marxist Paul Lafargue. He learned about social democracy from Eduard Bernstein in Zurich. He discussed revolution in Russia.

In 1884, Branting gave up his scientific career to become the foreign editor of a radical Stockholm paper, *The Times*. When *The Times* failed in 1886, he became the editor of another socialist paper, *Social Democrat*, a position he held for the next thirty-one years. Branting believed that socialism was an applied theory of democratic development and that it could only be achieved by the active involvement of workingmen.

In 1889, Branting and trade union leader August Palm (1849–1922) formed the Swedish Social Democratic Labor Party, taking the German Social Democratic party as their model. At its initial congress, the party passed a resolution disclaiming any intention of violent revolution.

Branting was elected to the Lower Chamber of the Riksdag in 1896. He remained the only socialist in the parliament until 1902, when the Social Democrats won four of the 230 seats in the Lower Chamber. At the next election, they won thirteen. By 1917, the Social Democrats controlled enough seats to unbalance the two-party system. They formed a short-lived coalition government with the Liberals, with Branting as minister of finance.

The Great Depression and Sweden's First Social Democratic Government

The full impact of the Great Depression reached Sweden in March 1932, when the collapse of "match king" Ivar Kreuger's business empire nearly brought down the Swedish banking system. During World War I Kreuger succeeded in bringing Sweden's match production into a single firm. After the war, he tried to expand his monopoly worldwide, often using short-term credit from Swedish banks to make long-term loans to countries that were short of foreign currency in exchange for agreements giving him a monopoly. By 1928, Kreuger controlled more than half of the match production in the world. With the onset of the global depression, Kreuger's ability to juggle his debt burden failed. He killed himself on March 12, 1932.

A number of Swedish banks that loaned Kreuger money had to be bailed out by the Swedish government. Kreuger's failure affected more than the banking system. He had extensive holdings in other Swedish companies. When his shares were dumped on the market, stock prices spiraled down. Personal fortunes evaporated and export sales fell. Production dropped 34 percent in the export industries and 13 percent in domestic industries. The number of unemployed workers rose from a predepression low of 10,000 to 189,225 in 1933.

Wigforss and Hansson Tame Unemployment

In 1931, months before the collapse of Kreuger's matchstick empire, economist Ernst Wigforss (1881–1977) developed a radical program of massive government intervention to fight unemployment and stimulate economic recovery. His program rested on two basic ideas:

- The systematic use of government-financed public works to provide employment and stimulate the economy
- An effort to increase purchasing power using deficit government financing and redistribution of income in the form of social services and subsidies to the industrial working classes and farmers

SAP took Wigforss's program to the polls in the 1932 elections, winning more than 40 percent of the vote.

FACT

Between 1932 and 1976, the Swedish Social Democratic Labor Party ruled Sweden without interruption. Since 1976, SAP has been removed from office four times: in 1976, 1991, 2006, and 2010. The first three changes in government brought no major changes in Sweden's social welfare programs. It is too soon to tell what changes the 2010 government will bring.

Under the leadership of Per Albin Hansson (1885–1946), who served as premier four times between 1932 and 1946, SAP implemented a reform plan based on Wigforss's program. With the informal support of the Agrarian Party, the SAP government transformed an existing system of relief work into a dynamic public works program. They began work immediately on any state and municipal public works that were already on the planning board for the future: schools, hospitals, railways, roads, harbor construction, and improvements in forestry and agriculture. The old relief system paid workers 15 percent less than the minimum wage an unskilled worker could earn in the open market. Men employed on the new public works program were paid a full market wage. The government borrowed money to fund the public works projects rather than raising the money through taxes, which would have neutralized the stimulus to the economy.

At the same time, the government introduced new social security measures, which were designed both to provide an economic safety net for the poor and to increase their purchasing power: unemployment insurance, increased old-age pensions, and housing loans for large families. They also implemented guaranteed prices for agricultural goods, special grants for rebuilding farm buildings, and easier access to agricultural credit. (The same banks that were willing to lend Ivar Kreuger millions were less welcoming to small farmers.) Sweden paid for these services through a progressive income tax. All together, the Wigforss program reduced unemployment from 189,225 in 1933 to 9,600 in 1937.

Folkhemmet

The key idea in Swedish social democracy is *folkhemmet*: the concept that the society and state are the people's home. Per Albin Hansson described the concept of *folkhemmet* in an often-quoted statement:

> *The basis of the home is togetherness and common feeling. The good house does not consider anyone either as privileged or unappreciated; it knows no special favorites or stepchildren. There no one looks down upon anyone else, there no one tries to gain advantage at another's expense, and the stronger do not suppress and plunder the weaker. In the good home, equality, consideration, co-operation, and helpfulness prevail. Applied to the great people's and citizen's home this would mean the breaking down of all the social and economic barriers that now divide citizens into the privileged and the unfortunate, the rulers and subjects.*

Clement Attlee and the British Labour Party

At the end of World War II, the British people were eager for a change. The Conservative Party had been in power since 1931. During his years as Prime Minister, Sir Winston Churchill had led Britain to victory, but Britain no longer felt the need for war leadership.

The Conservative Party's prewar record did not match its wartime success. The Conservatives were slow to enact measures to overcome the miseries of the Great Depression. Chamberlain's appeasement policy was not only a failure but a disgrace. The Conservative Party's further failure to begin rearmament left Britain scrambling to catch up in the face of Nazi aggression.

The Labour Party, by contrast, had no embarrassing prewar record to overcome. Moreover, Labour was a highly visible and effective coalition partner in Churchill's wartime government. In fact, Labour MP Clement Attlee served as Churchill's deputy prime minister.

Clement Attlee

Clement Attlee (1883–1967) was an unlikely labor leader. He was small, painfully shy, and handicapped by family money. After three years at Oxford, he became a lawyer, but took very few cases. Instead he lived on an annual allowance from his father and spent what he later described as "a good deal of time practicing billiards."

In 1905, his brother Lawrence convinced him to visit a boy's club in the Limehouse district of East London. He soon became a regular volunteer. In 1907, he became the club's resident manager.

Attlee had found his purpose in life. The poverty that he saw every day outraged him. The "abundant instances of kindness and much quiet heroism in these mean streets" inspired him to embrace socialism.

His first stop was the Fabian Society, where he was intimidated and uncomfortable. He found his home in Keir Hardie's Independent Labour Party, where he worked his way up through the ranks, doing the odd jobs that no one else had the time or inclination to do.

Churchill and Attlee on the Campaign Trail

When the election was announced in 1944, Attlee and Churchill hit the campaign trail. Churchill traveled in a motorcade. Attlee traveled in his own car, driven erratically by his wife. Churchill preached on the dangers of socialism. Attlee's mild-mannered presence refuted Churchill's rhetoric.

Attlee's platform was simple:

> *If in war, despite the diversions of most of our energies to making instruments of destruction, and despite the shortage of supply imposed by war conditions, we were able to provide food, clothing and employment for all our people, it is not impossible to do the same in peace, provided the government has the will and the power to act.*

There was little doubt in the minds of the British public that they could expect more social reform from Labor than from the Conservatives. In July 1945, a month before Japan's surrender, the British electorate celebrated the end of the war by voting out Winston Churchill's war government.

A Mandate for Change

The Labour Party was elected with a mandate for change. With a majority of 146 seats in the House of Commons, Clement Attlee formed a Labour government that became known for the scope of its reforms.

The Beveridge Report

In 1941, Winston Churchill commissioned William Beveridge (1879–1963) to create a report on how Britain should be rebuilt after the war. The resulting *Social Insurance and Allied Services* (1942), also known as The Beveridge Report, was adopted by Clement Attlee's Labour government as a blueprint for Britain's post–World War II welfare state.

Beveridge was an obvious choice to write the report. A protégée of Beatrice Webb, his lifelong interest in solutions for unemployment began in 1908 when he served as the sub-warden of a London settlement house. His first book, *Unemployment: A Problem of Industry* (1909), led to him being asked to advise Asquith's Liberal government on the formation of their national insurance and pension legislation.

FACT

The settlement movement, popular from the 1880s to the 1920s, held that poverty could be alleviated if the rich and poor lived together in interdependent communities. The movement built settlement houses in poor urban areas, where middle-class, volunteer "settlement workers" lived and provided education and services to their neighbors. The best-known settlement house in America was Chicago's Hull House.

In *Social Insurance and Allied Services*, Beveridge laid out three guiding principles for the government to follow in combating what he called the "five giants on the road to reconstruction," want, disease, ignorance, squalor, and idleness:

- "Sectional interests" formed in the past should not limit proposals for the future: "A revolutionary moment in the world's history is a time for revolution, not for patching."

- Social insurance should be only part of a "comprehensive package of social progress."
- Policies of social security should be achieved through cooperation between the state and the individual. The state "should not stifle incentive, opportunity, responsibility; in establishing a national minimum, it should leave room and encouragement for voluntary action by each individual to provide more than that minimum for himself and his family."

The proposals that followed included a free National Health Service that would prevent medical bills from becoming a source of poverty and a commitment to full employment to ensure that wages were there to help fund benefits.

Beveridge opposed means-tested benefits, arguing that they created a poverty-trap for their recipients, making them unable to afford to make small improvements to their situations for fear of losing their safety nets. Instead he proposed a flat-rate contribution from everyone and a flat-rate benefit for everyone. This principle of universality became one of the defining characteristics of welfare socialism.

ESSENTIAL

British economist John Maynard Keynes (1883–1946) provided the theoretical basis for government full-employment policies in his revolutionary *General Theory of Employment, Interest and Money* (1936). Keynes argued unemployment results from insufficient demand for goods and services. Government can directly influence the demand for goods and services through its tax policies and public expenditures, indirectly increasing the level of employment.

The Beveridge Report was an unexpected bestseller. Eager to get a copy, people lined up outside the Stationary Office the night before it was released, as excited as if it were the latest volume of *Harry Potter*. More than 100,000 copies were sold the first month; 800,000 copies were sold in total. It was translated into twenty-two languages, distributed to the British troops, and airdropped over Nazi Germany. Beveridge became an unlikely popular hero, known as "The People's William."

The British Welfare State

Between 1945 and 1951, Attlee's government built the British welfare system using the Beveridge report as its guide. The National Insurance Act provided retirement pensions, unemployment benefits, sick pay, maternity benefits, and funeral benefits. The Industrial Injuries Act paid for occupational disabilities. The National Health Service Act, passed in spite of the hostility of Britain's medical community, made complete medical care available to all residents of Britain.

Nationalization

During the same period, the Labor government nationalized the Bank of England, railways, long-distance hauling, telecommunications, coal mines, civil aviation, canals and docks, electricity, gas, and the iron and steel industries. All were basic to the economy or public utilities. None of them were flourishing prior to nationalization, with the exception of long-distance hauling.

The idea of introducing industrial democracy or worker control over the nationalized industries was never considered. Government appointed boards managed the nationalized industries. Unlike the seizure of major industries in Russia, former owners were compensated for their property.

The only serious opposition to Attlee's program of nationalization came over the iron and steel industries, which were stable and had good relationships with their unions. The act of nationalizing these industries was the only measure proposed during Labour's term in office that the House of Lords delayed. The act became law in 1949, and took affect in 1951.

Soon after the law took affect, Labour lost the general election. The Conservative Party reprivatized iron and steel as soon as they took office in 1951. Iron and steel were the only industries to be returned to the private sector prior to the 1980s.

CHAPTER 18

Socialism in Developing Nations

Socialism in developing nations was tightly interwoven with nationalism. As European colonies in Asia, Africa, and the Middle East won their independence in the years after World War II, many of them created socialist governments. Some combined aspects of indigenous traditions with the Marxist-Leninist model of one-party rule. Others followed the gradualist policies of the social democrats or the Fabian Society. Most received aid from the Soviet Union and/or the People's Republic of China, which saw the newly formed socialist regimes as chess pieces in the Cold War.

The Kibbutz Movement in Israel

The kibbutz movement was an outgrowth of Zionism. Although Jews had longed dreamed of returning to Israel, the political movement known as Zionism took shape at the end of the nineteenth century in Central and Eastern Europe. Zionism was nationalism with a twist: instead of reclaiming their nation from a colonial power, members of the Jewish diaspora wanted to build a homeland for their nation.

The Zionist ideology first found expression in Moses Hess's influential book *Rome and Jerusalem: A Study in Jewish Nationalism* (1862). Hess argued that the Jewish people could never be fully accepted by others until they had a homeland.

Zionism's most important proponent was Austrian journalist Theodor Herzl (1860–1904). Herzl always claimed that the Dreyfus affair made him a Zionist. Herzl was accustomed to dealing with anti-Semitism in Austria. When a leading Viennese newspaper hired him to be their Paris correspondent, Herzl was shocked to find that anti-Semitism was equally strong in France, the home of "Equality, Fraternity, and Liberty."

Herzl previously believed that Jews could overcome anti-Semitism through assimilation; now he believed that anti-Semitism made assimilation impossible. In 1896, Herzl published *The Jewish State* in which he argued that Jews were forced to exist as a separate nation by those around them, but were unable to function as a nation as long as they were dispersed across Europe. They could lead a true national existence only if they joined together in one territory.

FACT

In 1894, Alfred Dreyfus, a French army officer of Jewish descent, was falsely accused of providing military secrets to Germany. His trial became a battleground between the French right and left. Right-wing papers declared his trial proved Jews were disloyal. Leftist papers revealed a trial smirched with fabricated evidence. Dreyfus was exonerated in 1906 and given the Legion of Honor.

Herzl believed that the "Jewish question" was neither a religious nor a social issue. It was a political problem that should be settled by a world council of nations. With that in mind, he convened the First International Zionist Congress. More than 200 delegates from around the world, representing a variety of social classes and strains of Judaism, met in Basel, Switzerland, in 1897 to discuss the goal of a Jewish homeland. The delegates created a new organization, the World Zionist Organization, with the goal of creating "for the Jewish people a home in Palestine secured by public law."

ALERT

In 1903, the British government offered the World Zionist Organization 6,000 square miles of "uninhabited" land in Uganda for Jewish settlement. Herzl recommended that the organization accept the offer, but was voted down. As far as most of the Zionists were concerned, Palestine was the only acceptable location.

In 1901, the World Zionist Organization established the Jewish National Fund with the purpose of purchasing land in Palestine, which was then controlled by the Ottoman Empire. The fund purchased its first land in 1903: 50 acres in Hadera.

Emigration to Palestine

The Zionist movement accelerated after the failed Russian Revolution of 1905. A wave of pogroms inspired an increase in emigration among Russian Jews. Many went to America. Others decided to try the Zionist dream and go to Palestine as pioneer settlers.

The first kibbutz was founded at Deganya in 1909 on land owned by the Jewish National Fund. Others were created in the following years. By 1914, there were roughly 90,000 Jews in Palestine, 13,000 of them living in agricultural settlements. By the early twenty-first century, there were more than 250 kibbutzim in Israel, with a total population of more than 100,000.

What Is a Kibbutz?

There are two different types of cooperative settlements in Israel: the moshav and the kibbutz. In a moshav, each family is an economic and social unit that lives in its own house and works its own fields. Although each farm family is independent, the village cooperative purchases supplies and markets produce. The cooperative also provides the farmer with credit and other services. The first settlements of this type were founded in Jezreel Valley in 1921.

A kibbutz is a true collective that holds all wealth in common and pools both labor and income. Most kibbutzim are agricultural, but a few have expanded into industrial production. Most members work on the kibbutz itself. Kibbutz members receive no salary or wages because the kibbutz provides all the members' needs.

At first the kibbutz community took precedence over the family. Adults had private quarters and children were housed and cared for as a group. Today most children sleep in their parents' house but spend their days with their peer group. Cooking and dining are in common. Profits are reinvested in the settlement after members have been provided with food, clothing, shelter, and social and medical services. Some of the early kibbutzim carried the objection to personal property so far that when a man sent a shirt to the laundry he received back any shirt that fit, not a particular shirt. Over time, some settlements have adopted more tolerance for personal property and privacy.

Nehru's India

Before he met Mohandas Gandhi, Jawaharlal Nehru (1889–1964) was an Englishman in Indian clothing. After studying at home under a series of English governesses and tutors, he was sent to school in England at the age of fifteen. Known to his English friends as "Joe Nehru," he attended Harrow and Cambridge, where he took a degree in natural sciences, with a minor in actresses and social life, and then read for the bar at the Inns of Court in London. He spent his vacations traveling in Europe. In 1912, Nehru returned to India, with little enthusiasm, to practice law with his father, the prominent barrister Motilal Nehru.

Motilal Nehru was already active in the Indian nationalist movement and a leader in the Indian National Congress, which at the time was fighting for dominion status within the British Empire. Jawaharlal Nehru joined his father as a Congress member in 1918, with the same lack of enthusiasm that he brought to the practice of law.

Involvement in the Independence Movement

In 1919, Nehru overheard General R. H. Dyer boasting about the recent massacre of Indian protestors at Jallianwalla Bagh, in which Dyer ordered Gurkha soldiers to fire on thousands of Indians gathered for a religious observance in a public park. Outraged, Nehru became seriously involved in the independence movement: touring rural India, organizing nationalist volunteers, and making public speeches. Under Gandhi's influence, Nehru abandoned his Westernized lifestyle and began wearing clothes made from *khadi* (homespun), studying the *Baghavat Gita*, and practicing yoga.

Traveling through India, Nehru was exposed for the first time to what he described as "this vast multitude of semi-naked sons and daughters of India." He began to grope for a systematic solution for India's problems. While touring Europe for his wife's health in 1926 and 1927, he attended the Congress of the League of Oppressed Peoples in Brussels and came to the conclusion that India's struggle against the British was part of a larger struggle between capitalist imperialism and anti-capitalist socialism.

Indian Independence

When India achieved independence from Great Britain in 1947, Nehru became the first prime minister and minister for external affairs, a dual position he held until his death in 1964.

ALERT

> Nehru's daughter, Indira, became prime minister two years after her father's death, using her married name, Gandhi. (Her husband was no relation to the Mahatma.) Between them, Indira, and her son, Rajiv, held the position of prime minister for twenty years between 1966 and 1989.

Nehru believed that the answers to India's problems lay in socialist economic theory, but he didn't let his socialist convictions affect his foreign policy decisions. Instead of picking sides in the Cold War, he chose "positive neutrality," and served as a key spokesperson for the unaligned countries of Asia and Africa. On the domestic front, he committed India to a policy of industrialization, reorganization of its states on a linguistic basis, and the development of a casteless, secular state.

ESSENTIAL

The professed goals of the Indian Constitution, which became law in 1950, are "to secure to all its citizens . . . JUSTICE social, economic and political; LIBERTY of thought, expression, belief, faith and worship; EQUALITY of status and opportunity; and to promote among them all FRATERNITY assuring the dignity of the individual and the unity of the Nation."

Nehru and Gandhi agreed that poverty was India's greatest challenge after independence, but they disagreed on the solution. Gandhi, like many of the utopian socialists of the nineteenth century, believed the solution was self-sufficiency at the level of the village commune: shared labor and wealth, and a spinning wheel in every hut. Nehru looked for national self-sufficiency, based on "tractors and big machinery."

Under Nehru's leadership, India adopted a mixture of Fabian-style central planning and free enterprise to rebuild the country's ravaged economy. The government instituted a series of five-year plans intended to build India's production capabilities and improve agricultural yields. At the same time, it launched several major campaigns against rural poverty.

A year before he died, Nehru stated his basic policies clearly:

> *Obviously, everybody will agree, almost everybody, that we have to provide a good life to all our citizens . . . a good life means certain basic material things that everybody should have, like enough food and clothing, a house to live in, education, health services and work . . . How do we do that?*

Nasser's Egypt

The son of a village post office clerk, Gamal Abdel Nasser (1918–1970) led his first demonstrations protesting British influence over Egypt's government and economy when he was sixteen. After graduating from secondary school,

Nasser spent several months as a law student before he gave in and took the easiest path to upward mobility—the army. He entered the Egyptian Royal Military Academy in 1936, graduating as a second lieutenant.

Egypt's defeat at the hands of the new state of Israel in 1948, and the country's continued occupation by the British, reinforced Nasser's opinion that the Egyptian government of King Faruq was inefficient and corrupt. With three fellow officers, he formed the revolutionary Free Officers movement with the objective of seizing control of Egypt from the British and the Egyptian royal family.

Revolution and Reform

On July 23, 1952, following a breakdown of law and order in Cairo, Nasser and eighty-nine other Free Officers carried out a bloodless coup against King Faruq, who spent the rest of his life in exile in Monaco. A year later, Nasser emerged as the unquestioned leader of Egypt.

The Free Officers were held together by the belief that the interests of Egypt as a whole were more important than those of any faction or party. Nasser found himself at the head of a successful revolution with no doctrine and no political organization in place.

Under Nasser's leadership, the new regime replaced the monarchy with a one-party state based on a new political elite of army officers and middle-class bureaucrats. Egyptian nationalism developed into a vision of pan-Arabic nationalism, with Egypt as the natural leader of the Arab world.

With his new government in place, Nasser began a program of reforms based on what he described as "Arab socialism," which was derived from a rejection of imperialism rather than class struggle. He believed that state ownership or control of the means of production and redistribution of income were necessary to make Egypt strong.

ALERT

> Nasser's "Arab socialism" drew complaints from devout Muslims and Marxists alike. The extremist Muslim Brotherhood accused Nasser of camouflaging a secular policy with Islamic language. Marxists claimed that since "Arab socialism" wasn't based on the concept of class struggle it wasn't socialism at all.

Agrarian Reforms

Nasser's first major reforms were agrarian. Beginning with King Faruq's extensive personal holdings, large estates were broken up and distributed to peasant families. The law in 1953 limited land ownership to 200 *feddans* per family. Subsequent legislation further limited ownership to first 100 and later 50 *feddans*. Along with land redistribution, Nasser's government introduced state-controlled agricultural cooperatives to provide farmers with credit, fertilizer, and seeds, began a program to reclaim land from the desert, and extended labor laws to cover agricultural workers.

The controversial nationalization of the Suez Canal in 1956 was only the first step in a program designed to bring the economy under centralized government control. In 1960 and 1961, banks and major industries were nationalized and direct government control was imposed over important sectors of the economy, including insurance and transportation. Only retail businesses and housing were left in private hands.

FACT

The Suez Canal provided the shortest route for shipping between Asia and Europe. It also turned out to be the shortest route for European occupation of Egypt—debts incurred in its construction allowed the British and French to take "dual control" of Egypt's finances in 1876. In 1956, a large portion of the canal was still owned by Britain and France.

The creation of a centralized economy was accompanied by the implementation of social reforms. Nasser's government introduced new protections for labor, and extended public health services and a system of industrial profit sharing that funded insurance and welfare services.

The National Charter

In 1962, Nasser submitted a document called *The National Charter* to the National Congress of the short-lived United Arab Republic. In ten short chapters, he outlined the ideological foundation of Arab socialism. The charter begins with a list of the six principles that led to the 1952 revolution:

- To end imperialism
- To end the system of feudal landlords
- To end the domination of capital over the government
- To establish a basis of social justice
- To build a powerful national army
- To establish a sound democratic system

It ends with a call for Arab unity.

Ho Chi Minh's Vietnam

Ho Chi Minh (1890–1969), born Nguyen Sinh Cung, grew up in the French possession of Indochina. Formed in 1887, French Indochina originally included Cambodia and the Vietnamese regions of Annam, Tonkin, and Cochinchina. Laos was added in 1893. Ho's father was a scholar who lost his position due to his political views. He scraped together a meager living writing and reading letters for illiterate peasants.

Ho received a French education and spent several years as a schoolteacher. In 1911, at the age of twenty-one, he decided to join the navy and see the world. He spent three years working as a cook on a French steamer. After living in London for several years, he moved to France, where he became an active socialist and anti-colonial activist. Working under the name Nguyen Ai Quoc (Nguyen the Patriot), he organized a group of expatriate Vietnamese and was one of the founders of the French Communist Party. In 1919, he addressed a petition to the Versailles Peace Conference calling on the French to give their Indochinese subjects equal rights. The members of the peace conference ignored him, but he caught the attention of politically conscious Vietnamese as someone to watch.

FACT

Like Lenin and Stalin before him, Ho Chi Minh spent much of his life traveling and working under assumed names to avoid official scrutiny. In 1940, he adopted the name Ho Chi Minh (He Who Enlightens). North Vietnamese nationalists often referred to him as "Uncle Ho."

Ho left France in 1923. He spent the next ten years traveling between communist strongholds and organizing expatriate Vietnamese nationalists. In 1924, he played an active role in the Fifth Congress of the Communist International, taking the French Communist Party to task for not opposing colonialism more vigorously. Later that year, he traveled to Canton under the assumed name of Ly Thuy, where he organized Vietnamese nationalists who had been exiled from Indochina for their political beliefs into the Vietnam Thanh Nien Cach Menh Dong (Vietnamese Revolutionary Youth Association), better known as Thanh Nien. When Chiang Kai-Shek expelled the communists from Canton in 1927, Ho went on the road again, traveling to Moscow, Brussels, and Paris before settling in Siam (now Thailand) as the Comintern's representative in Southeast Asia.

In 1930, Ho Chi Minh returned to Vietnam to preside over the formation of the Indochinese Communist Party (PCI), which was organized by members of the Thanh Nien and activists in Hanoi, Hue, and Saigon.

World War II and the Formation of Vietnam

In 1940, France signed an armistice with Germany, establishing the rule of the Vichy government, and Japan invaded Indochina for the first time. Seeing an opportunity, Ho Chi Minh returned secretly to Indochina in January 1941, then returned to South China, where he organized the Viet Nam Doc Lap Dongh Minh Hoi (League for the Independence of Vietnam), popularly known as the Viet Minh.

FACT

Imprisoned by Chiang Kai-Shek for eighteen months in 1941–1942, Ho wrote *Notebook from Prison*, a collection of short poems written in classical Chinese using a traditional Vietnamese verse form. Beginning with the line "It is your body which is in prison/Not your mind," the collection describes prison life and calls out for revolution.

In 1945, the Japanese overran Indochina and imprisoned or executed all the French officials. Ho contacted the United States forces and began to collaborate with the Operation of Strategic Services against the Japanese.

At the same time, Viet Minh guerrillas fought the Japanese in the mountains of South China while groups of commandos began to move toward the Vietnamese capital of Hanoi.

Japan surrendered to the Allies on August 14, 1945. The Viet Minh entered Hanoi on August 19. Two weeks later, Ho Chi Minh declared Vietnamese independence to an enormous crowd in Ba Dinh Square.

QUESTION

Was Ho Chi Minh familiar with the Declaration of Independence?
Very likely. The words Ho used to announce Vietnam's independence sound very similar to Thomas Jefferson's: "All men are born equal: the Creator has given us inviolable rights: life, liberty and happiness."

Independence wasn't that simple. An Allied treaty with Chiang Kai-Shek gave the Chinese Nationalists the right to replace the Japanese north of the Sixteen Parallel. Not surprisingly, liberated France, under the leadership of General Charles de Gaulle, had no intention of giving up Indochina without a fight.

The French quickly recaptured South Vietnam and began negotiations with Ho Chi Minh. Neither side was satisfied with the final agreement, which recognized Vietnam as an independent state with its own government, army, and finances, integrated into a French Union controlled by Paris.

The uneasy peace flared into war in November 1946, when a French cruiser opened fire on the town of Haiphong after a clash between French and Vietnamese soldiers. By the end of 1953, most of the countryside was under Viet Minh control and the country's larger cities were under siege. The French defeat at Dien Bien Phu in 1954 ended France's Southeast Asian empire.

Vietnam Divided

The Geneva Accords, signed on July 21, 1954, divided Vietnam at the Seventeenth Parallel, creating a communist state in the north led by Ho Chi Minh and an anti-communist state in the south led by Ngo Dinh Diem. The division of Vietnam created a Cold War battlefront, with the United States supporting Ngo Dinh Diem and the Soviet Union and the People's Republic of China providing aid to Ho Chi Minh.

The Accords called for a 1956 election that would re-establish a unified Vietnam. When the time came for the elections, South Vietnam refused to play, setting the stage for the United States' entry into the Vietnam War.

Castro's Cuba

In 1895, Cuba rebelled against Spanish rule. Revolts and rebellions had been a way of life in Cuba for almost 400 years, but this time things were different. Spanish efforts to repress the rebellion aroused popular sympathy in Cuba's big neighbor to the north. When the U.S. battleship *Maine* mysteriously blew up in Havana's harbor on February 15, 1898, America declared war on Spain. Cuban hopes that American involvement meant independence were soon dashed. When the Spanish American War ended, the United States continued to occupy Cuba. It began to look like Cuba had exchanged one colonial ruler for another.

When the Cuban Constitutional Convention met in July 1900, its members discovered that the United States intended to attach an amendment to their constitution. Written by American Secretary of State Elihu Root, the Platt Amendment allowed the United States to intervene in Cuban affairs whenever order was threatened, forbade the Cuban government to borrow money without American permission, and forced Cuba to lease land to the United States for naval bases. Cuba reluctantly accepted the Platt Amendment and became "independent" in May 1902.

FACT

Franklin Roosevelt annulled the Platt Amendment in 1934 as part of his "Good Neighbor Policy" toward Latin America. Revoking the amendment made little practical difference. America still maintained a naval base at Guantanamo Bay. As Cuba's biggest trade partner, the United States continued to meddle in Cuban affairs.

For the next fifty years, Cuban politics were shaped by economic dependence on sugar, frequent military coups, and regular interference in its internal affairs by the United States.

Beginning in 1933, successive Cuban governments depended on the support of military strongman Fulgencio Batista (1901–1973). In 1940, Batista was elected president in his own right. After completing a four-year term of office, he stepped down after he was defeated in a democratic election. In 1952, Batista ran for president again. Defeated for a second time, he overthrew the constitutional government and established a regime even more corrupt and repressive than those of his predecessors.

Fidel Castro

The son of a prosperous sugar cane farmer, Fidel Castro (1926–) was a committed political activist before he was twenty. While studying law at the University of Havana, Castro joined an abortive attempt to overthrow General Rafael Trujillo in the Dominican Republic and took part in street riots in Colombia. After he received his degree in 1950, he seemed to settle down. He opened a law practice in Havana and became a member of a moderate reform party, the Cuban People's Party, also known as the *Ortodoxos*. He ran as that party's candidate for a seat in the House of Representatives in the 1952 elections.

Castro reverted to revolutionary type after Batista's 1952 coup. When legal means to overturn Batista failed, Castro attempted to start a revolution by attacking the Moncado military barracks with a group of 160 men on July 26, 1953. The attempt was a total failure. Most of the attackers were killed. Castro and his brother Raul were arrested and sentenced to fifteen years in prison. Released two years later as part of a general amnesty, the brothers went into self-imposed exile in Mexico, where they trained a small revolutionary force.

In late 1956, a small yacht landed Castro, Raul, and a rebel force of eighty-one men on the southeast coast of Cuba. The so-called 26th of July Movement was routed and almost destroyed by Batista's security forces. A dozen survivors retreated to the Sierra Maestra mountains and began a guerilla war against the Batista dictatorship. Over the next year, they recruited more insurgents and built alliances with other revolutionary groups, including disaffected liberal politicians. By 1958, Batista's regime was in trouble. Several of his military leaders joined the revolutionaries. The United States government withdrew its support, hoping to reach an agreement with the revolutionary forces similar to the one it had with Batista and his predecessors. After all, political coups were nothing new in Cuba.

In December 1958, Batista fled the country, leaving Castro in power as the undisputed leader of the revolution.

Castro Rebuilds Cuba

Over the next few years, Castro and the 26th of July Movement created the first socialist country in the Americas. Castro's initial program wasn't explicitly socialist. Its major features were land reforms and progressive tax policies aimed at foreign investors, the sugar industry, large businesses, and the tourist industries of Havana. Not surprisingly, he quickly gained a following of peasants, urban workers, and leftists of all varieties. The propertied classes were less enthusiastic. Many of them left Cuba for the United States.

Over the course of 1959 and 1960, Castro nationalized foreign businesses, established a centrally planned economy, and brought basic social services to poor and rural areas. In February 1960, he signed a trade deal with the Soviet Union. Already angry about the loss of nationalized property, the United States retaliated for Castro's new relationship with Russia by imposing a trade embargo, plotting to assassinate Castro, and supporting an unsuccessful invasion attempt by Cuban exiles at the Bay of Pigs. America's hard-line attitude only made Castro more popular in Cuba and forced him to become increasingly dependent on Soviet trade policies.

Nyerere's Tanzania

Julius Nyerere (1922–1999) was the first president of independent Tanzania. The son of a chief of the small Zanaki ethnic group, Nyerere had a traditional tribal upbringing. He received a Western education almost by chance. Two of his older brothers already went to school and his father thought that was plenty. When he was twelve, the British commissioner selected the adopted son of one of Nyerere's older brothers to study at a mission school thirty miles away. Nyerere was sent with him to keep him company.

Nyerere proved to be a good student. He was accepted at Tabora Secondary School, which was run by the colonial administration. After six years at Tabora, he received a scholarship to Makerere College in Uganda.

In 1945, degree in hand, Nyerere returned to Tabora, where he taught biology and history and discussed the end of imperial rule with other members of the Western-educated elite.

In 1949, Nyerere applied to Edinburgh University under the pretext of studying biology. As soon as he arrived, he changed his course of study, determined to give himself the knowledge that would prepare him for the coming struggle for independence. He read history, philosophy, economics, and political science. He found another kind of education among the local members of the Labour Party and the Fabian Society. Reading socialist descriptions of an ideal society, Nyerere was struck by the resemblance to traditional Zanaki tribal life, which included communal ownership of property, collective decision-making, and relative social and economic equality among the male members of the tribe.

In 1952, Nyerere completed his degree and went home. He took a job teaching school and became part of the nascent independence movement. He joined the Tanganyika African Association, quickly becoming its president in 1953. In 1954, he helped convert the stuffy social club into an unequivocally political organization, changing its name to the Tanganyika African National Union (TANU).

Britain was in the mood to divest itself of colonial baggage, so Tanganyika did not have to fight long or hard to obtain its independence. The country gained responsible self-government in 1960 and became independent in 1961, with Nyerere as its first prime minister.

Ujamaa

Nyerere served as the president of Tanganyika, and its successor state, the United Republic of Tanzania, from 1962 to 1985. During this period, he also headed Tanzania's only political party, Chama Cha Mapinduzi (CCM).

FACT

Jawaharlal Nehru was affectionately known to Indians as "Pandit ji." Tanzanians called Julius Nyerere "Mwalimu." Both sobriquets mean *teacher* and are used as a title of respect, similar to the way *professor* is used as a title in Western colleges.

Nyerere outlined his political principles in the speech known as the Arusha Declaration. Nyerere's goal was the creation of an egalitarian socialist society in the indigenous tradition of *ujamaa*: a form of socialism based on the traditional African institution of the extended family. He completely rejected the idea of class struggle, as he described it in the Arusha Declaration:

> *Ujamaa, then, or "family hood," describes our Socialism. It is opposed to capitalism, which seeks to build a happy society on the basis of the exploitation of man by man. And it is equally opposed to doctrinaire Socialism, which seeks to build its happy society on a philosophy of the inevitable conflict between man and man.*

In practical terms, Nyerere's attempts to create a self-sufficient socialist state depended on two programs: nationalized industry and the creation of collective agricultural villages. Both programs were an economic failure. Nyerere himself admitted that he left the country in a worse financial condition than he found it. His regime was not an entire failure. Unlike many of the independent African states founded by his contemporaries, Tanzania was politically stable and firmly egalitarian. He left behind a population with one of the highest literacy rates in Africa.

CHAPTER 19

Socialism in America, Part II: The Socialism of Compassion

At the same time that socialism became a political force in Europe, it became increasingly marginalized in the United States. Before World War I, the American left was based in the labor movement and the traditions of American populism. America's entrance into World War I separated socialists from liberals and the labor movement. Severed from its working-class roots, American socialism changed from a movement devoted to revolution by the proletariat into one driven by the compassion of the privileged.

Norman Thomas: The Conscience of America

Pacifist and social reformer Norman Thomas (1884–1968) was often called the "conscience of America." For forty years, he was the Socialist Party's unofficial popular spokesman, offering America a brand of socialism that was an alternative to both communism and twentieth-century capitalism.

The son of a Presbyterian minister, Thomas was born in Marion, Ohio. He followed his father into the ministry. After graduating from New York's Union Theological Seminary in 1911, Thomas accepted the pastorate of the East Harlem Church and the chairmanship of the American Parish, a settlement house in one of the poorest sections of New York City.

Thomas and the Social Gospel Movement

Confronted on a daily basis with the problems of poverty, Thomas became involved in the Social Gospel movement. The movement was a Protestant response to the combined effects of industrialization and immigration in urban areas at the end of the nineteenth century. Like Christian Socialism, the Social Gospel movement attempted to apply Christian principles to industrial life, with a particular emphasis on charity and justice. Social Gospelers encouraged cooperation between classes on the grounds that everyone suffered in some way from the materialism and cruelty of the machine age. They tied salvation to good works, primarily by opening settlement houses and working for labor reform laws, including the abolition of child labor, the forty-hour workweek, and factory safety. Aspects of Social Gospel thought shaped Thomas's later socialism, particularly his belief that ethical concerns could and should overcome class interests.

FACT

Founded in 1905 as the Intercollegiate Socialist Society, the League for Industrial Democracy focused on educating college students about the labor movement and socialism. For many years, the League functioned as an intake point for membership in the Socialist Party. The militant group Students for a Democratic Society (SDS) was originally founded as a student auxiliary of the League.

Thomas moved from the Social Gospel movement to socialism through his work as a pacifist during the First World War. In 1918, Thomas joined the Socialist Party and resigned from his East Harlem ministry to devote himself to socialist and pacifist activism. He worked at various times as the secretary of the Fellowship of Reconciliation, an international pacifist organization, the assistant editor of the influential liberal weekly, *The Nation*, and the executive director of the League for Industrial Democracy. He was one of the founders of the American Civil Liberties Union.

Involvement in Politics

Thomas was a frequent candidate for political office. He ran for governor of New York in 1924, mayor of New York in 1925 and 1929, and for the United States presidency in six successive elections, beginning in 1928. His most successful campaign was the 1932 presidential election, which he lost twenty-five to one to Franklin Roosevelt. He was never elected, but he used political campaigns as a way of keeping socialist issues in the public eye.

ALERT

Thomas rejected Marxism as a useful myth for controlling the working classes. He described the Soviet Union's version of socialism as "totalitarianism practically indistinguishable in its burdens upon citizens from Hitler's." His views on Marxism and Soviet Russia led him to support the expulsion of "Reds" from teaching and key government jobs during the McCarthy era.

Thomas's socialism was at heart an ethical rejection of capitalism's inequalities, which he believed were rooted in selfishness and resulted in both human and economic waste. Capitalism wrongly perceived the selfish desires of the individual as the primary starting point, creating a society that "suffers not only from economic waste . . . but from the poison of false standards of value."

Thomas advocated a central, planned economy, but believed that central planning outside of socialism would only benefit the wealthy few. The question was not "how shall we plan, but for whom and for what shall we plan." Like most socialists of his period, he believed public ownership of the means of production was an essential element of socialism. He supported a combination of industrial democracy and the "intelligent application of the merit system," meaning that labor should be allowed to vote for the directors of the companies in which they work, but not for their foremen or immediate managers. He believed that for most workers work is secondary to their other interests. Therefore abundance would lead to "increasing and enriching leisure," but would not end the average worker's alienation from his job.

Thomas was generally critical of Franklin Roosevelt's New Deal, which he believed stressed the solution of economic emergencies and neglected the moral issues that resulted in social inequalities. He spoke out against America's entrance into World War II on pacifist grounds. After World War II, as chairman of the Postwar World Council, he devoted himself to the problem of international peace and was an early opponent of the Vietnam War.

The Great Depression, the New Deal, and American Socialism

In 1932, America was in the depths of the Great Depression. The newly elected president, Franklin D. Roosevelt, promised a "new deal" for everyone. In his first 100 days in office, Roosevelt pushed through fifteen major pieces of legislation, including programs designed to get Americans working again. These programs took three basic forms:

- Short-term relief programs designed to alleviate suffering
- Long-term programs designed to help the economy recover
- Permanent reform programs designed to prevent, or reduce the impact of, future depressions

Many of the programs instituted between 1933 and 1935 aimed at restoring the economy from the top down. The Agricultural Recovery Act sought to stimulate farm prices by paying farmers to produce less. The National Industrial Recovery Act stabilized both prices and wages. Both programs failed to address the basic problem of weak consumer demand as a result of falling wages and rising unemployment.

FACT

Father Charles E. Coughlin (1891–1979) reached tens of millions of listeners with his weekly radio broadcasts. He supported Roosevelt against Herbert Hoover in the 1932 election. Over time, he turned against the New Deal. His attacks against Communists, Jews, and Wall Street became increasingly shrill. In 1942, the Roman Catholic Church ordered Coughlin off the air.

Beginning in 1935, Roosevelt's reforms moved further left, driven in part by pressure from the socialist and populist left. Socialist Party presidential candidate Norman Thomas won three times as many votes in the 1932 election as he had in 1929. More than 5 million elderly Americans joined Townsend Clubs, supporting Dr. Francis Townsend's proposal of a federally funded old-age pension as a way to solve the problem of weak consumer demand. Louisiana senator Huey P. Long rose to national prominence with his "Share the Wealth" plan, which proposed a guaranteed household income for every American family, to be paid for by taxes on the wealthiest Americans. Father Charles E. Coughlin appealed to the urban poor with his call for nationalized industries and currency inflation.

ESSENTIAL

The central idea of Keynesian economic theory is "counter-cyclical demand management": using the government's financial power of taxing and spending to stabilize the economy. According to this theory, the best way to recover from a depression is to use government spending to turn nonconsumers back into consumers.

New Deal programs introduced after 1935 were based on John Maynard Keynes's theory that depressions should be attacked by increasing the spending ability of the people at the bottom of the income pyramid.

The Works Progress Administration employed over 8 million Americans between 1935 and 1943. The Social Security Act set up a worker-funded, government-guaranteed pension system, similar to that called for by the Townsend Clubs. The National Labor Relations Act, often called the Wagner Act, guaranteed the right of collective bargaining for workers.

ALERT

The WPA hired 8.5 million men to build roads, public buildings, bridges, airports, and parks across America. The WPA also hired artists, writers, and actors for cultural programs that included creating art for public buildings, writing state guidebooks, collecting folklore in rural America, and organizing community theaters.

Assessments of Roosevelt's New Deal

Roosevelt's contemporaries at either end of the political spectrum condemned Roosevelt's policies. Right-wing groups denounced the New Deal as the first step toward a communist dictatorship. American communists branded the New Deal as a step toward fascism.

Scholarly assessments of the impact of the New Deal also break down along ideological lines:

- Conservative historians describe the Depression as an extreme market correction and the New Deal as the beginnings of a socialist welfare state, which they believe is an inherently bad thing, resulting in regulation and loss of freedom.
- Liberal historians describe the Depression as the failure of *laissez faire* economics and the New Deal as the beginnings of a democratic welfare state, which they believe is an inherently good thing, as government responds to the needs of the people.
- Leftist historians describe the Depression as the failure of capitalism and the New Deal as reformed capitalism.

The Impact of the New Deal on American Socialism

The Socialist Party lost much of its support when the New Deal came into effect. Roosevelt implemented many programs that were a part of the socialist program. More important, New Deal programs benefited the sections of society that had traditionally supported socialism. The "Roosevelt Coalition" of farmers, union members, working-class people, northern blacks, and liberals turned instead to the Democratic Party.

Dorothy Day and the Catholic Worker Movement

Catholic reformer, anarchist, and pacifist Dorothy Day (1897–1980) discovered socialism while she was a scholarship student at the University of Illinois. She was unenthusiastic about her studies, but read widely in radical writings of all varieties. She was particularly taken with the anarchist writings of Peter Kropotkin. By the end of her first year, she was a member of the Socialist Party.

In 1916, Day moved to New York, where she joined the Industrial Workers of the World, worked on a succession of socialist newspapers, and participated in anti-war and women's suffrage protests. She tried nursing school for a year, but soon returned to radical journalism, working in Chicago and New Orleans.

Day and Catholicism

Day moved to New York in 1924, where she became involved with British anarchist Forster Batterham. Day and Batterham lived together in a common-law marriage for four years. During this period, Day began to struggle with her growing interest in Catholicism. Both her relationship to Batterham and her religious journey came to a head in 1927, when Day gave birth to their daughter. Batterham left them and Day joined the Roman Catholic Church.

Day's conversion estranged her from many of her radical associates. She found a new outlet for her reform instincts in 1932, when she met Peter Maurin, a self-described peasant philosopher and Christian radical.

FACT

Peter Maurin (1877–1949) was born in France, the oldest of twenty-one children. He spent several years as a member of the Christian Brothers. He left them for the LeSillon movement—a group of Catholic activists interested in working-class issues. In 1909, he immigrated to Canada in order to avoid the draft, becoming an itinerant worker and preacher.

When they met, Maurin was speaking on street corners and trying to get the Catholic press to publish his essays on the need for Catholics to incorporate the social teachings of Christianity into their daily lives. Maurin gave Day the means with which to reconcile her new Catholic faith with her socialist convictions. He developed a three-part program designed to reinvent society on the basis of Christian ethics:

- Bring different segments of the population together in round table discussions to wrestle with the problems confronting society
- Establish "houses of hospitality" in response to the gospel command to feed the hungry, clothe the naked, and shelter the homeless
- Create farm communes where people could free themselves from dependence on the wage system

Day was particularly excited about Maurin's proposal for a Catholic labor paper to popularize "the teachings of the Church in regard to social matters, bringing to the man in the street a Christian solution for unemployment and a way of rebuilding the social order."

On May 1, 1933, Day and Maurin sold copies of the first issue of the *Catholic Worker* for one penny to socialists and communists who gathered in Union Square to celebrate May Day. They printed only 2,400 copies of the first issue. In only eight months, the paper's circulation grew to 100,000. That winter, they opened the first house of hospitality: an apartment with space to house ten women. By 1936, there were thirty-five houses of hospitality across the country.

Today there are more than 150 Catholic Worker communities. Day is regarded as one of the great Catholic lay leaders of the twentieth century.

Senator Joseph McCarthy and the Red Scare

During the early 1950s, communist advances into Eastern Europe and China frightened many Americans. Wisconsin Senator Joseph McCarthy (1908–1957) took those fears and turned them into an official witch-hunt.

Born to a farm family near Appleton, Wisconsin, McCarthy left school at fourteen. He worked as a chicken farmer and managed a grocery store before he went back to high school at the age of twenty. He went on to take a law degree from Marquette University.

FACT

During the Cold War, United States foreign policy was dominated by the "domino theory": the idea that if a noncommunist state "fell" to communism, it would lead to the fall of the noncommunist states around that country. The domino theory was first used by President Harry Truman to justify sending military aid to Greece and Turkey in the 1940s.

In 1948, Joseph McCarthy was elected to the United States Senate in an upset victory over incumbent Senator Robert La Follette, Jr. McCarthy ran a dirty campaign. He lied about his war record, claiming to have flown thirty-two missions during World War II when he actually worked a desk job and only flew in training exercises. La Follette was too old for service when Pearl Harbor was bombed, but McCarthy attacked him for not enlisting and accused him of war profiteering.

On his first day as a senator, McCarthy called a little-noticed press conference that was a tune-up for his later performance as a demagogue. He had a modest proposal for ending a coal strike that was in progress: draft union leader John L. Lewis and the striking miners into the army. If they still continued to strike, they should be court-martialed for insubordination and then shot.

By 1950, McCarthy's senate career was in trouble. The story of how he lied about his war record during the election campaign became public. He was under investigation for tax offenses and for accepting bribes from the Pepsi-Cola Co. to support removing wartime controls on sugar.

ALERT

Don't confuse Joseph McCarthy with Minnesota senator Eugene McCarthy (1916–2005). An outspoken critic of the Vietnam War, the later Senator McCarthy's 1968 presidential campaign drew the enthusiastic support of large numbers of college students and members of the New Left.

Attacks on the American Communist Party

McCarthy deliberately directed attention away from his own failings. On February 9, 1950, speaking to a group of Republican women in Wheeling, West Virginia, McCarthy announced that he had a list of 205 State Department employees who were "card-carrying" members of the American Communist Party, some of whom were passing classified information to the Soviet Union. Suddenly McCarthy was in the headlines. When the Senate Committee on Foreign Relations asked McCarthy to testify, he was unable to provide the name of a single "card-carrying communist" in any government department.

Undeterred by the absence of facts, McCarthy began an anti-communist crusade in the national media. Playing on real popular fears, McCarthy used scare tactics to discredit his opponents. He began by claiming that communist subversives had infiltrated President Truman's administration. When the Democrats accused McCarthy of smear tactics, he responded that their accusations were part of the communist conspiracy. As a result of his tactics, the Republicans swept the 1950 elections. The remaining Democrats in Congress were reluctant to criticize him. McCarthy, once voted "the worst U.S. senator" by the Senate press corps, was now one of the most influential men in the Senate.

McCarthyism

Following the 1952 election, McCarthy became the chairman of the Committee on Government Operations of the Senate and of its permanent investigation subcommittee. In an ironic mirror image of Stalin's trials of alleged counter-revolutionaries, McCarthy held hearings against individuals he accused of being communists, and government agencies suspected of harboring them. He attacked journalists who criticized his hearings. He campaigned to have "anti-American" books removed from libraries. When Republican Dwight Eisenhower was elected in 1952, McCarthy attacked him for not being tough enough on communism.

McCarthy ran into trouble when he attempted to discredit the Secretary of the Army. The Army leaked information to journalists who were known to oppose him. As a result, America saw McCarthy's bullying tactics first hand in a televised thirty-six-day hearing in which the Army accused McCarthy of attempting to subvert military officers and civilian officials.

The Republicans lost control of the Senate in the mid-term elections of 1954, in part because of the public's loss of confidence in McCarthy. With a vote of sixty-seven to twenty-two, the Senate subsequently censured McCarthy for conduct "contrary to Senate traditions."

Michael Harrington and *The Other America*

Michael Harrington (1928–1989) is sometimes described as "the man who discovered poverty." Born in St. Louis, Missouri, to a middle-class Irish Catholic family, Harrington started high school when he was twelve. After going to a Jesuit high school and college, he spent a year at Yale Law School and another year doing graduate work at the University of Chicago.

Harrington claimed he was converted to socialism during a summer job working for the St. Louis public school system's Pupil Welfare Department:

> *One rainy day I went into an old decaying building. The cooking smells and the stench from the broken, stopped up toilets and the murmurous cranking sound of the people were a revelation. It was my moment on the road to Damascus. Suddenly the abstract and statistical and aesthetic outrages I had reacted to at Yale and Chicago became real and personal and insistent. A few hours later, riding the Grand Avenue streetcar, I realized that somehow I must spend the rest of my life trying to obliterate that kind of house and to work with the people who lived there.*

In 1951, Harrington moved to New York with the intention of becoming a socialist poet and found his way to Dorothy Day's Catholic Worker House of Hospitality in the Bowery. He quickly took over publication of the *Catholic Worker*.

Harrington stayed with Day for two years, but found her combination of anarchism and Catholicism uncomfortable in face of his growing religious doubts. In 1953, he discovered secular radicalism in the form of the Young People's Socialist League (YPSL), then affiliated with the Socialist Party of America.

The Other America

Harrington is best known for his first book, *The Other America* (1962), which was an influential force in the development of Lyndon Johnson's war on poverty. In it, he argued that there were 40 to 50 million Americans living in poverty who were "not simply neglected and forgotten as in the old rhetoric of reform; what's much worse, they are not seen." American poverty was invisible to the country's middle class because it existed in rural isolation and crowded urban slums. Harrington revealed a culture of poverty that was a product of social neglect, created by generations of inadequate education, nutrition, housing, and medical care. As a result of this "monstrous example of needless suffering in the most advanced society in the world," America's poor lacked both the ambition and ability to help themselves.

FACT

Harrington began his research for *The Other America* in response to another influential work of the period, John Kenneth Galbraith's *The Affluent Society* (1958). Galbraith called for spending less on consumer goods and more on government programs in order to end the gap that he described as "private affluence versus public squalor."

The Other America was not a rallying cry for the proletariat to rise up in revolt, but a call for the more affluent to help the suffering poor. Writing at the end of the McCarthy era, Harrington consciously chose not to mention socialism, fearing the word would divert attention from the plight of the poor: "Proposing a specifically socialist solution would make it more difficult for the millions of trade unionist, liberals and men and women of good will to see the reality of poverty."

Harrington's approach was not political, but his book was politically significant. It shocked important segments of American society out of complacency, becoming required reading for social scientists, government officials, and student activists.

ESSENTIAL

The Other America made Harrington the best-known socialist in America, an honor William F. Buckley once described as similar to being the tallest building in Kansas. He wrote eleven more books after *The Other America*, none of which had the same impact on public awareness.

Lyndon Johnson's Great Society

The Great Society was the most ambitious domestic reform program since Franklin Roosevelt's New Deal. In 1964, campaigning to retain the office of president that he inherited from John F. Kennedy, Lyndon Johnson (1908–1973) called for a war on poverty and the creation of a Great Society, resting on "abundance and liberty for all." He won the presidential election with an overwhelming majority, carrying forty-four out of fifty states. The Democrats gained thirty-eight seats in the House of Representatives. With a clear voter mandate, Johnson outlined his program for sharing American prosperity with everyone in his 1965 State of the Union Address.

Johnson submitted eighty-seven bills to the first session of the eighty-ninth Congress. Eighty-four of the bills passed. Fourteen task forces created a blizzard of new programs intended to transform American society, including federal scholarships for college students, affordable housing programs, a minimum wage increase, funding for schools serving needy children, Medicare, and Medicaid.

The New Left of the 1960s

Socialism enjoyed a brief resurgence in America in the 1960s. A New Left emerged from the interaction between the civil rights movement and the socialist movement of the 1930s (which became known as the Old Left). Composed largely of college students, the New Left refused to be drawn into the communist–anti-communist dichotomy that characterized the Old Left. Their initial concerns were racism and poverty, but these quickly took a back seat to protests against the Vietnam War. The movement peaked in the mid-1960s and had virtually disappeared by the early 1970s.

The most well-known New Left organization was Students for a Democratic Society (SDS). Founded in 1960 as a student affiliate of the League for Industrial Democracy, SDS quickly broke away from the Marxist dogmatism of its founding organization.

In 1962, the SDS held a national convention in Port Huron, Michigan, to create its own operating manifesto. After several days of discussion, the society adopted the Port Huron Statement, written for the most part by University of Michigan student newspaper editor Tom Hayden, who later rose to national prominence as one of the seven young men charged with inciting riots around the Chicago Democratic Convention of 1968. The manifesto drew on a range of socialist and political traditions, from the town hall meeting to Marx. The statement began with a critique of American society that dealt with race relations, the persistence of poverty, and America's role in the Cold War. It then outlined the organization's vision of reform based on a loosely defined concept of "participatory democracy." Along the way, it criticized the Socialist Party for both its anti-communism and its connection to the Democratic Party establishment.

ESSENTIAL

The SDS idea of "participatory democracy" grew out of the writings of John Dewey, as elaborated by University of Michigan professor Arnold Kauffman. The basic idea, as expressed by Dewey, is that "All those who are affected by social institutions must have a share in producing and managing them."

The SDS grew slowly until 1965, when the United States' involvement in the Vietnam War escalated. In 1962, the party had roughly 300 members; estimates of the organization's membership at its highest point range from 30,000 to 100,000. After the party organized a mass anti-war march on Washington in April 1965, the organization grew more militant: staging student strikes and occupying university administration buildings.

At its 1969 convention, the organization disintegrated as the result of a power struggle between the Radical Youth Movement and the Progressive Labor Coalition. Members of the Radical Youth Movement expelled the more moderate faction out of the party. A number of members unaffiliated with either faction resigned in disgust, leaving the party in the hands of its most radical element. Soon thereafter, the remaining members transformed themselves into the violent revolutionary group, the Weathermen.

Micro-Parties: Socialism in America Today

The New Left effectively ended with the close of the Vietnam War, though many student activists, socialist and otherwise, continued to work for change in small grassroots organizations that exemplified the SDS value of participatory democracy.

Today America has no substantial socialist organization and no prominent public figure on the scale of Debs, Thomas, or Harrington. The Communist Party never recovered from the devastation of the McCarthy era. In 1973, the long-standing Socialist Party of America succumbed to the internal factionalism that has plagued American socialism from the beginning. Its three successors have themselves splintered into even smaller parties. These socialist microparties have had some success at the local or even state level, but have had little political impact on national politics.

CHAPTER 20

Socialism in Crisis

The world watched in amazement as crowds tore down the Berlin Wall in November 1989. For twenty-eight years the wall was the symbol of the economic and political divide between the communist countries of Eastern Europe and the noncommunist countries of the West, themselves a political mishmash of democracy, republicanism, social democracy, and constitutional monarchy. Proclaimed as the end of communism, the fall of the Berlin Wall was the most dramatic scene in a worldwide reaction against the rise of socialism in the years after World War II.

Neoliberalism

In the early 1970s, neoliberalist thought rose in response to persistent recessions that Keynesian economics seemed to be unable to resolve. Typified by the work of Milton Friedman and the Chicago School, neoliberalism argued that over-involvement of the state in the economy was the primary constraint on the efficient operation of the market.

Neoliberals insisted that the market was superior to any form of government intervention in ensuring the best use of resources for the well-being of humanity as a whole. Therefore, the role of the state should be limited to providing an environment in which the market can operate effectively by protecting property rights; enforcing contractual obligations; allowing resources, including labor, to move easily; and providing basic safety and security for its people.

Israel Swings to the Right

In 1977, the right-wing Likud party (in English the Unity-National Liberals), led by Menachem Begin, was voted into power in Israel. The Israel Labor Party, and its predecessor, Mapai, had ruled Israel since its founding in 1948.

ESSENTIAL

The kibbutzim played an important part in Israel's Labor governments. Prime Ministers David Ben-Gurion, Levi Eshkol, Golda Meier, Shimon Peres, and Ehud Barak all spent time as kibbutz members. The kibbutzim were an obvious target for Begin, who called the kibbutzniks "millionaires with swimming pools."

The pioneers of Zionist immigration brought with them the ideology of socialist and communist parties of Eastern Europe. Once in Palestine, they formed small political parties that ranged from social democracy to Leninism. In 1930, Israel's two largest labor parties—Unity of Workers, which was founded in 1919, and Young Worker, which was founded in 1905—merged to form "a Zionist Socialist party faithful to the ideal of national redemption and the ideal of socialism in the homeland." The resulting party, Mapai (the

Hebrew acronym for "Party of the Workers of the Land of Israel"), quickly became the dominant political party among Jews in Palestine. In 1965, Mapai merged with Unity of Labor Workers of Zion to form the Israel Labor Party. For most of their history, Mapai and the Israel Labor Party supported state economic planning and extensive social benefits.

Menachem Begin

Menachem Begin (1913–1992) was born in Poland. He was active in the Zionist movement throughout the 1930s, becoming the leader of the Polish chapter of the Betar youth movement, which insisted on the Jewish right to sovereignty over the entire territory of Palestine. When the Germans invaded Warsaw in 1939, he escaped to Vilnius, which was then under Soviet control. The rest of his family was not so lucky. He lost his parents and a brother in concentration camps.

The Soviet authorities deported Begin to Siberia in 1940. Released from Siberia in 1941, he joined the Polish army-in-exile, which was in England, and was deployed to Palestine in 1942.

In Palestine, Begin joined the underground right-wing group Irgun Zvai Leumi, which advocated the use of force, if necessary, to establish a Jewish state on both sides of the Jordan. He served as the organization's commander from 1943 to 1948. During the period of the British Mandate, Irgun Zvai Leumi committed acts of terrorism against the British army, which it regarded as illegal occupiers. The group also organized illegal immigration into Palestine. When the state of Israel was created in 1948, Irgun Zvai Leumi disbanded its military units and merged with other right-wing parties to form the Herut (Freedom) party with Begin as its head.

The Likud Party

Likud was founded in 1973 to challenge the Israel Labor Party, taking advantage of public outrage over Israel's initial losses in the Yom Kippur War. Conservative and nationalist in its ideology, Likud's primary political position was the extension of Israeli sovereignty into the territories conquered by Israel in 1967. Its support base was largely Sephardic Jews, who were poorer and less inclined to socialism than the European-born Jews who dominated Israel in the early years. Like the Israel Labor Party, Likud was a coalition party, formed of seven independent parties. At first, Likud was dominated by the Gahal bloc, which consisted of the Herut (Freedom) party and the ultra-Zionist Liberal Party.

FACT

In 1978, after some nagging by American president Jimmy Carter, Menachem Begin and Egyptian president Anwar Sadat met to discuss peace in the Middle East. The agreements they reached, known as the Camp David Accords, led to the March 1979 peace treaty between Israel and Egypt. Begin and Sadat were jointly awarded the Nobel Prize for Peace in 1978.

Likud first came to power in 1977. It ruled in coalitions with minority parties until 1983, when Yitzhak formed a "unity government" with the Israel Labor Party.

Margaret Thatcher's Capitalist Revolution

Margaret Thatcher (1925–), born Margaret Roberts, became Britain's first female prime minister on May 3, 1979. Unlike many leaders of the Conservative Party, who have typically come from privileged backgrounds, Thatcher grew up in a cold-water flat above her parents' grocery store. During her childhood, her father held a number of local political offices, including justice of the peace, town alderman, and mayor.

Thatcher was interested in politics from an early age. While studying chemistry at Oxford, she became one of the first woman presidents of the Oxford University Conservative Association. After she graduated in 1946, she worked as a research chemist for four years, reading for the bar in her spare time. In 1954, she began working as a barrister, specializing in tax law. Like many self-made successes, Thatcher believed in the power of individual enterprise and rejected the value of state support.

Thatcher first ran for Parliament in 1950, while still in her 20s. She lost, but increased the Conservative vote for the district by 50 percent. In 1959, she was elected as the Member of Parliament for the "safe" conservative district of Finchley. When she took her seat, she was the youngest woman in the House of Commons. She rose quickly within the Conservative Party. By 1970, she was a member of Edward Heath's conservative government, holding the position of secretary of state for education and science.

FACT

Thatcher's record as education minister illustrates her underlying political philosophy. During her tenure, Thatcher eliminated a program providing free milk to schoolchildren, causing opponents to call her "Thatcher the milk snatcher." On the other hand, she also created more comprehensive schools, which provide a rigorous academic education to working-class children, than any prior education minister.

After Heath lost two successive elections in 1974, Thatcher challenged him for the Conservative Party's leadership. With the backing of the party's right wing, she was elected party leader in 1975. In 1976, a speech against communism won her the sobriquet "the Iron Lady" in the Soviet press, a tag she carried with apparent pride.

Britain's "Winter of Discontent"

Thatcher led the Conservative Party to a decisive victory in 1979, following what the press dubbed Britain's "winter of discontent." In the winter of 1978–1979, inflation was hovering at 25 percent. Prime Minister James Callaghan's Labour government sought to control the rate of inflation by capping pay increases at 5 percent. Unions responded with widespread strikes that resulted in gas and food shortages, power cuts, uncollected garbage, and hospital care limited to emergency cases. An unofficial strike by gravediggers in Liverpool provided images of unburied coffins that inflamed an already exasperated public.

Thatcherism

During her first term as prime minister, from 1979 to 1983, Thatcher began by fulfilling her campaign promise to cut the power of the unions. Supported by memories of six weeks of rotting garbage and unburied coffins, the Conservative government passed a series of measures designed to limit the unions' power to strike, including laws that banned closed union shops, required unions to poll their members before organizing strikes, and made sympathy strikes illegal.

FACT

The National Union of Mineworkers' 1984 strike was emblematic of Thatcher's relationship with the unions. The mineworkers went on strike to prevent the government from closing twenty coal mines that were deemed unproductive. The strike lasted nearly a year. Thatcher refused to meet the union's demands. In the end, the miners returned to work without winning a single concession.

Having pulled the unions' fangs, Thatcher struck out at what she dismissed as the "nanny state." She introduced budget cuts for social services, such as education, the National Health Service, the social security system, and public housing. At the same time, she reduced or eliminated governmental regulations and subsidies to businesses and privatized state-owned industries and services. She also attacked inflation by limiting the amount of money printed, following Milton Friedman's principle of monetarism.

ESSENTIAL

The economic theory of monetarism holds that the rate at which an economy grows is linked to increases in the economy's money supply. Monetarists believe that the government can promote economic stability by controlling the rate of growth of the money supply.

Thatcher successfully reduced inflation, but unemployment doubled between 1979 and 1981. She was elected to a second term by a landslide; owing in part to her decisive leadership in the Falkland Islands War (1982) and to deep divisions in the Labour Party, which ran on a radical platform that critics called "the longest suicide note in history."

In her second term, Thatcher began to sell shares in companies that were previously state-owned, tripling the number of individual stockholders in the country by the end of the 1980s. The government also sold 1.5 million publicly owned houses to their tenants. Both policies brought supporters to the Conservative Party. At the same time, the disparity in incomes between the wealthy and working class increased.

In 1989, Thatcher pushed a flat rate poll tax through Parliament, which led to violent riots. Spurred by public disapproval of the poll tax and Thatcher's increasingly strident tone, Conservative members of Parliament moved against her in November 1990. She defeated her senior opponent, but did not have enough votes to retain the party leadership. Instead of contesting the election with a second ballot, Thatcher resigned from office as Conservative Party leader and prime minister on November 22, 1990, leaving behind crippling unemployment and rising welfare costs.

"Capitalism with Chinese Characteristics"

Deng Xiaoping (1904–1997) transformed the People's Republic of China from a centralized state-run economy to one dependent on private enterprises. The son of a wealthy landowner, Deng was introduced to communism during the study abroad program from hell. In 1918, at the age of fourteen, Deng and his seventeen-year-old uncle went away to high school, where they learned about a work-study program for Chinese students in France. Like other young Chinese of the period, Deng was eager to learn the skills needed to bring China into the modern world. "China was weak and we wanted to make her stronger," he wrote later, "and China was poor and we wanted to make her richer. We went to the West in order to . . . find a way to save China."

An Introduction to Politics

After a year and a half of preparation, Deng sailed for France. The program was a disaster. The students traveled to France in steerage class. Once there, they discovered that classes were pay-as-you-go and students were expected to find their own jobs. The combination of limited French language skills and high unemployment in post-war France made work difficult to find. The Chinese embassy provided a meager food allowance. Some students lived in tents on the grounds of the program headquarters.

The program was a lousy way to learn Western technology, but it provided a top-flight introduction to radical politics. Of the 1,500 students in the program, at least 200 embraced nationalism and/or communism. More than twenty of the students later became prominent members in the Chinese Communist Party, including Deng and Zhou Enlai.

Deng's revolutionary activities brought him to the attention of the French police. In January 1926, after a police raid on his apartment, Deng and some friends fled from Paris to Moscow. Compared to their experience in Paris, Moscow was heaven. The Chinese students were given adequate food, shelter, and a warm welcome. Deng enrolled in the newly opened Sun Yat-sen University, which was devoted to turning out revolutionary cadres. Five years in Paris left Deng with a lifelong taste for soccer and croissants; one year in Moscow gave him a lifelong commitment to the Communist Party.

Deng Goes Back to China

Deng returned to China at the end of 1926, where he was soon caught up in the conflict between the Kuomintang and the Chinese Communist Party. He was a leading political and military organizer in the Jiangxi Soviet and participated in the Long March in 1934–1935. He rose steadily through the ranks of the Chinese Communist Party, becoming the party's general secretary in 1954 and a member of the ruling Political Bureau in 1955.

In 1961, after the failure of the Great Leap Forward, Deng and CCP theoretician Liu Shaoqi were given the responsibility of restoring China's economy. They determined that a key to restoring agricultural productivity would be the "responsibility system": giving small work teams or households individual plots of land to farm on their own, with the understanding that they would be free to dispose of the produce after delivering a predetermined share to the state. In 1962, Deng publicly justified the choice, saying:

> *In deciding on the best production system we might have to embrace the attitude of adopting whichever method develops agricultural production most easily and rapidly and whichever method the masses desire most. We must make the illegal legal. To quote an old saying from Sichuan province . . . "It doesn't matter if the cat is yellow or black as it long as it catches the mouse."*

Mao made it clear that he didn't care whether the cat could catch the mouse or not, as long as it was Red. Deng hurried to retract his statement, leaving the "responsibility system" unimplemented.

In 1966, in the early days of the Cultural Revolution, Deng was attacked as the number two "capitalist roader." (Liu Shaoqi was denounced as the leading proponent of the capitalist road.) Deng was arrested and stripped of his CCP and government positions, though allowed to retain his party membership. After three years in prison, he was banished to a village in Jiangxi province where he and his wife worked in a tractor factory and lived under house arrest.

In 1973, Deng was reinstated to the party's leadership under the sponsorship of Premier Zhou Enlai and given the positions of first vice premier, vice chairman of the party, and chief of staff of the armed forces as if he was never out of favor. Deng became the effective head of the government during the months preceding Zhou's death, and was widely considered to be Zhou's most likely successor.

ESSENTIAL

The Gang of Four consisted of Mao's third wife, Jiang Qing, and three of her associates. Previously low- to middle-ranking officials, the four advanced to high positions during the Cultural Revolution. After the initial fervor of the Cultural Revolution subsided, they maintained their power by controlling the media and propaganda outlets and manipulating their relationship to Mao.

When Zhou died in January 1976, the infamous Gang of Four conspired to purge Deng from leadership once more. After Mao's death in September 1976, the Gang of Four were imprisoned and subsequently tried for their excesses during the Cultural Revolution. With the Gang of Four gone, Deng was rehabilitated again, this time with the support of Mao's chosen successor, an obscure regional leader named Hua Guofeng.

Deng's Reforms

In 1978, Hua resigned in Deng's favor. The party quickly accepted Deng's program of "Four Modernizations": industry, agriculture, the military, and science. The two basic pillars of the program were economic liberalization and openness to the world outside of China.

eV FACT

Known as the "four little tigers," or the "four Asian dragons," the newly industrialized economies of Hong Kong, Singapore, South Korea, and Taiwan were notable for their rapid industrialization and high growth rates from the early 1960s through the 1990s.

The most important of his reforms was a variation of the "household responsibility" system he proposed at the end of the Great Leap Forward. By 1982, communal farming almost completely vanished. Peasants saved money from farming their own plots and accumulated enough capital to start small businesses. By 1985, the number of registered household businesses totaled 11.7 million. Heavy industry remained under state ownership, but managers were given new authority and encouraged to run their enterprises effectively, rather than being limited to implementing central government planning. Inspired by the performance of East Asia's "little tigers," Deng designated "special economic zones" along the coast in 1979, offering incentives to encourage international capital to develop these areas.

Between 1978 and 1988, China's gross national product grew at an average annual rate of 10 percent. Exports increased an astonishing 2,000 percent during the same period.

eV FACT

Political reform lagged behind economic reform. In April 1989, thousands of Chinese students occupied Tiananmen Square in full view of the international media, calling for democratic reform as their grandfathers did in the May Fourth Movement in 1919. On June 4, the government sent tanks and armed soldiers to stop the protest.

Despite these changes, Deng emphasized that he did not want to abandon socialism. His goal was to create a version of "socialism with Chinese characteristics." As he explained, "after years of practice, it turned out that the old stuff didn't work."

Lech Walesa and Solidarity

In early August 1980, workers across Poland went on strike to protest rising food prices. In Gdansk, some 17,000 workers at the Lenin Shipyards staged a strike and barricaded themselves into the plant. By August 14, the strike at the Lenin Shipyard in Gdansk was losing steam. Shipyard Director Klemens Gneich assured strikers that he would negotiate for their demands if they went back to work. It was tempting, even though Gneich had not kept his promises in the past.

The strike gained new life when electrician Lech Walesa climbed over the shipyard wall, jumped onto a bulldozer, and urged the striking workers on. The reinvigorated strikers elected Walesa as the head of a strike committee to negotiate with management.

FACT

Lech Walesa (1943–) began work at the Lenin Shipyard as an electrician in 1967. He emerged as a union activist during anti-government protests in 1976, and consequently lost his job. For the next four years, he earned a living doing temporary jobs and worked with other activists to organize free, noncommunist trade unions.

Three days later, the strikers' demands were met. When other strikers in the city asked Walesa to continue his strike out of solidarity, he agreed. Walesa established an Interfactory Strike Committee that united industrial workers in the Gdansk area into a single bargaining unit. Within a week, the committee presented the Polish government with a list of demands that included the right to strike and form free unions and declared a general strike. On August 31, the Gdansk strikers and the Polish government signed an agreement that sanctioned free and independent unions with the right to strike, as well as providing greater freedom of religions and political expression.

The Independent Self-Governing Trade Union Solidarity

Delegates from thirty-two trade unions met in Gdansk on September 22, 1980. They transformed the Interfactory Strike Committee into a federation of trade unions, the Independent Self-Governing Trade Union Solidarity, with Walesa as its chairman. By early 1981, Solidarity had a membership of roughly 10 million people and represented most of the workers in Poland.

Throughout 1981, the communist government of Wojciech Jaruzelski was faced with a series of controlled strikes by Solidarity, in conjunction with demands for economic reforms, free elections, and the involvement of trade unions at the highest level of decision-making. Both Walesa and Jaruzelski were pressured into extreme positions: Walesa by more militant unionists and Jaruzelski by the Soviet Union. On December 13, Jaruzelski declared martial law. Solidarity was declared illegal and its leaders, included Walesa, were arrested. On October 8, 1982, the Polish parliament officially dissolved the union. Solidarity continued to operate underground.

FACT

Lech Walesa received the Nobel Peace Prize in 1983. Still operating underground, Solidarity members were heartened by the award. The Polish government was less enthusiastic. Fearing that he would not be able to return to Poland if he left, Walesa's wife traveled to Stockholm to accept the prize on his behalf.

In 1988, collapsing economic conditions set off a new wave of labor unrest in Poland. With no support from the USSR, demands that the government recognize Solidarity forced Jaruzelski to negotiate. In April 1989, the Polish government agreed to legalize Solidarity and allow it to participate in elections. In the free elections held that June, Solidarity candidates won ninety-nine out of 100 seats in the newly formed Polish Senate and all of the 161 seats that opposition candidates were allowed to contest in the lower house. In August, long-time Solidarity supporter Tadeuz Mazowiecki became the first noncommunist head of government in the Eastern Bloc.

Mikhail Gorbachev Opens the Door

Born into a peasant family in the Stavropol territory of Russia, Mikhail Gorbachev (1931–) joined the Young Communist League as soon as he was old enough to become a member. He spent several years driving a combine on a state farm before he enrolled in law school at Moscow University and became a member of the Communist Party. After he graduated in 1955, Gorbachev gained the attention of high-ranking Soviet officials, in part because of his work as the head of the Stavropol region's agricultural department and in part because several popular hot water spas were located in the region. In 1971, he was elected to the Communist Party's Central Committee. He became a full member of the Politburo in 1980.

ALERT

The USSR was often referred to as Russia. In fact, the Union of Soviet Socialist Republics, informally known as the Soviet Union, was a federation of fifteen Soviet Republics that were created out of the remains of the Russian empire in 1917. Russia was the dominant republic within the federation.

As a mere child of forty-nine among the eighty-somethings in the Politburo, Gorbachev became one of its most active and visible members. In the mid-1980s, three general secretaries of the Communist Party of the Soviet Union (CPSU) died in quick succession. Following Leonid Brezhnev (1906–1982) who served as general secretary from 1977 to 1982, Yuri Andropov (1914–1984) held the office for fifteen months. His successor, Konstantin Chernenko (1911–1985), died after only eleven months. On March 10, 1985, the Politburo elected its youngest member, Mikhail Gorbachev, to the post.

Gorbachev's primary goal was to rescue the stagnant Soviet economy. At first he tried the timeworn Soviet method of calling for rapid modernization of technology and greater worker productivity. It was not enough. As Gorbachev described the problem, "The very system was dying away. The sluggish senile blood no longer contained any vital juices."

In 1986, Gorbachev decided to try something new. He introduced two major economic and political policies: *glasnost* (openness) and *perestroika* (restructuring).

Implementing the new policy of *glasnost*, Gorbachev relaxed previous restrictions on freedom of speech and the press. He released thousands of political prisoners, including dissident physicist Andrei Sakharov. In 1987, the Soviets stopped jamming radio broadcasts by the BBC, the Voice of America, and the Deutsche Welle. New freedoms led to the expression of genuine public opinion—by the end of 1989, there were more than 300 independent journals published in the Soviet Union, many of them denouncing Communist Party failures.

Under the new policy of *perestroika*, Gorbachev took steps to untangle the government's legislative and executive branches from the CPSU. "We need democracy like air," he announced. In December 1988, a new bicameral parliament called the USSR Congress of People's Deputies was elected in a contested election, with multiple candidates and secret ballots. Dissidents of all kinds replaced long-standing party officials, including Sakharov, who was elected as the representative of the Soviet Academy of Sciences. In 1989, the new Congress elected a new Supreme Soviet from its ranks, with Gorbachev as chairman. Similar legislatures were established in each of the Soviet Republics.

In March 1990, Gorbachev took further steps to transfer political power from the CPSU to elected government institutions. Under his leadership, the Congress of People's Deputies elected him to the newly created post of the president of the USSR and abolished the Communist Party's constitutional monopoly on political power in the Soviet Union.

The Collapse of Soviet Communism

At the same time that Gorbachev was introducing political reforms into the USSR, he was encouraging reform in the Soviet-bloc countries of Eastern Europe.

In an ironic reversal of the domino theory, the communist states of eastern and central Europe fell one by one and were replaced by noncommunist states. In August 1989, Poland convened its first noncommunist government since 1948. A week later, the communist regime in Hungary began talks with its opposition. Massive demonstrations on both sides of the Berlin Wall brought about the collapse of the East German government in October. By the end of 1990, there were noncommunist governments in power in Romania, Bulgaria, Czechoslovakia, Albania, and Hungary.

FACT

Between 1987 and 1991, hundred of thousands of Estonians stood up to sing their way to freedom from the Soviet Union, using previously forbidden dissident songs to rally support for a nonviolent resistance movement now known as the Singing Revolution.

The decentralization of the USSR's political system and the example of new, noncommunist governments throughout eastern Europe led to the rise of ethnic and nationalist independence movements in the member states of the Soviet Union. In 1991, Gorbachev proposed a referendum on whether to hold the Soviet Union together. Six of the fifteen republics refused to participate. The Russian Republic agreed to participate, but added a second question to the referendum, asking whether Russia should establish its own presidency. Russian voters said "yes" to both proposals. Three months later, Boris Yeltsin was elected president of the Russian Republic and a treaty for a new union between the republics was under negotiation.

Faced with the end of the USSR, Communist Party hardliners rebelled. In August 1991, a group of senior CPSU officials broke into Gorbachev's vacation home and placed him under house arrest. They demanded that he declare a state of emergency. When he refused, they issued a decree themselves in the name of the State Committee for the State of Emergency. The days of compliant obedience to party decrees were over. Hundreds of thousands of citizens poured into the streets to defend the government, led by Yeltsin, who stood on top of a tank and denounced the "right-wing, reactionary, anti-constitutional *coup d'etat*." Faced with resistance, not to mention the shock of being called "right-wing" after a lifetime in the Communist Party, the coup leaders retreated.

Gorbachev resigned as the first and only president of the USSR on December 25, 1991. On December 26, the Supreme Soviet, which had ruled the USSR since 1917, dissolved itself.

CHAPTER 21

Socialism after the Collapse of the Soviet Union

At the end of the 1980s, pundits proclaimed that socialism, in all its variations, was dead, or at best irrelevant. Welfare socialism was decimated by the "stagflation" of the 1970s and neoliberalism's cult of the marketplace. The Soviet Union had committed suicide. The male industrial workers who defined the working classes for Marx and his successors no longer dominated the workforce. While traditional socialist parties shrank, new variations of socialism began to appear.

The "Third Way"

In the 1990s, many socialists began to look for a socialist approach to a world that had changed around them. The work place in Western societies had changed in fundamental ways with the entry of middle-class women into the workforce and the growth of the service sector. More importantly, globalization had reduced the capacity of any government to effectively control its economic environment. Socialist thinkers began to speak of a "Third Way" between liberal capitalism's belief in the free market and traditional socialism's belief in a centrally planned economy. At its most basic, Third Way ideology favors both economic growth and individual enterprise on the one hand and greater social justice on the other.

The Third Way has been criticized as nothing more than benevolent pragmatism. In fact, the Third Way is held together as a political philosophy by four key values:

- A belief in the importance of community, which can be seen as the old call for socialist solidarity adapted to the modern world
- A commitment to equality of opportunity
- An emphasis on individual responsibility
- A demand for organizational accountability

The Third Way has preserved socialism's commitment to equality and social welfare, but abandoned class-based politics and the ideal of public ownership of the means of production.

Tony Blair Redefines Social Democracy

The son of an attorney with failed political ambitions, Tony Blair (1953–) was twenty-two years old when he joined the Labour Party in 1975. He ran for Parliament for the first time in the 1982 by-election, placing a sorry third with only 10 percent of the votes. No one expected him to win the reliably Conservative seat and party leaders congratulated him on handling the campaign well.

FACT

In his early years, Blair was more interested in music than politics. As a boy he attended Durham Cathedral's Choristers School. At Oxford, he was the Mick Jagger–style lead singer in a rock band called The Ugly Rumors. Later, his terms as prime minister were closely associated with the cultural movement known as "Cool Britannia," including Brit-Pop and BritArt.

Margaret Thatcher called a general election in 1983 and Blair tried again. When the votes were counted, the Conservatives controlled the House of Commons, but Blair was the new representative from Sedgefield, a small mining district in northern England. At thirty, Blair was the youngest Labour MP.

In 1987, the Conservatives walloped Labour at the polls for the third time in a row and party leaders began to reconsider their basic strategy. The Labour Party was previously split between a social democratic right and a Marxist left; now it was divided between "traditionalists" who clung to the century-old socialist ideology and "modernizers" who wanted to move the party toward the political center. Blair was one of the most outspoken of the modernizers.

In 1992, the Conservatives were more vulnerable than they were in the previous three elections. The country had been in recession for eighteen months and unemployment remained close to 10 percent. Margaret Thatcher was pushed out of office by her own party members and replaced by the less-than-charismatic John Major. The polls gave Labour the lead. The polls were wrong. The Conservatives defeated Labour for the fourth consecutive general election.

"New Labour"

Blair believed that Labour lost because "society had changed and we did not change sufficiently with it." Elected party leader in 1994, Blair began to recreate Labour's platform. Under his leadership, the Labour Party took the astonishing step of distancing itself from the labor unions and changed its policies on key issues, moving closer to Conservative positions with every step.

Three months after winning the party's leadership, Blair proposed changing Clause IV of the party's constitution, which was written in 1918 by Fabian society theorist Sidney Webb. According to Clause IV, which was printed on the back of the party's membership cards, the Labour Party's mission was:

> *. . . to secure for the workers . . . the full fruits of their industry and the most equitable distribution thereof that may be possible upon the basis of the common ownership of the means of production, distribution, and exchange.*

It was a controversial idea. Former Labour prime minister Harold Wilson once said that changing Clause IV would be like taking Genesis out of the Bible. Despite objections, at the end of a nationwide campaign, Labour delegates voted to change Clause IV. The new language, twice as long and half as clear as Webb's, called for:

> *A dynamic economy, serving the public interest, in which the enterprise of the market and the rigour of competition are joined with forces of partnership and cooperation to produce the wealth the nation needs and the opportunity for all to work and prosper, with a thriving private sector and high quality public services, where those undertakings essential to the common good are either owned by the public or accountable to them.*

Blair described the party's revised position as "New Labour."

ESSENTIAL

Blair's reinvention of the British Labour Party was inspired by the work of British sociologist Anthony Giddons. A former director of the London School of Economics, Giddons is one of the theoreticians behind the concept of the "third way," which he describes as a political program not limited by the traditional left-right dichotomy.

As the 1997 elections grew closer, Blair turned further to the right, declaring himself "the entrepreneur's champion." Critics within the party objected to the form "New Labour" took. As leftist writers Leo Panitch and Colin Leys pointed out, Blair seemed to think "that socialism, if it still means anything at all, was a set of values that should guide public policy *under* capitalism, nothing more." Members of the left moaned that this wasn't the socialism they signed up for. The voters disagreed. In 1997, Blair led the Labour Party to a resounding victory. He served as prime minister for three terms and a total of ten years.

The Mitterrand Experiment

While the British Labour Party was taking a beating from the Iron Lady, the socialist star seemed to be on the rise in France. In 1981, French socialist François Mitterrand defeated conservative incumbent Valéry Giscard d'Estaing in an election for the French presidency. Mitterrand immediately dissolved the National Assembly and called for a general election. The Socialist Party of France won almost 70 percent of the seats, giving them a true majority for the first time. Mitterrand named militant socialist Pierre Mauray as his prime minister. Mauray's cabinet was made up of socialists and four communists.

FACT

A member of the Resistance in World War II, François Mitterrand (1916–1996) served as a deputy in the National Assembly almost continuously for fifty years and a minister in eleven governments under the French Fourth Republic. Under his leadership, the Socialist Party replaced the Communist Party as the leading party of the French left.

With what seemed to be a clear voter mandate for change, the socialist cabinet began a program of reforms that Mitterrand described as "the rupture with capitalism." The reform plan had a traditional socialist goal: "to free the workers from age-old oppression and to provide all those who are exploited . . . with the instruments of their own self-emancipation." In a few months, Mitterrand's government nationalized eleven large industrial conglomerates and most of France's private banks, expanded social benefits, raised the minimum wage, decentralized government administration, and raised taxes on the highest income levels.

It took Mao several years to bring the Chinese economy to a standstill; Mitterrand was more efficient in pushing through socialist reforms and accomplished the same thing in less than one year. French exports declined. The value of the franc fell and inflation rose. French investors voted with their feet and took their capital out of the country.

Mitterrand called an abrupt halt to his efforts to create a socialist France and instituted austerity measures designed to "bring about a real reconciliation between the left and the economy."

The Socialist Party lost control of the National Assembly in the 1988 elections. With two years left on his term, Mitterrand joined the socialist scramble toward the political center.

The Spread of Neo-Revisionism

Europe's mainstream socialist parties learned their lesson from Mitterrand's failed experiment. Like Britain's modernizers, the *renovadores* in Spain, *riformisti* in Italy, *nouveaux réalistes* in Belgium, and other socialist neo-revisionists of the 1980s and 1990s moved toward what Tony Blair called the "center left."

In the nineteenth century, Eduard Bernstein's Marxist revisionism accepted the possibility of reform without ever giving up hope for a socialist transformation of society. The social democrats that followed him shared that hope. When the Socialist International was founded in 1951, its Declaration of Aims stated clearly that the goal of socialism was the abolition of capitalism.

At the end of the twentieth century, *renovadores, riformisti*, and the like no longer believed that capitalism is a transitory phase in the development of humanity that will ultimately be replaced with socialism. The 1989 Stockholm Declaration of the Socialist International listed freedom, solidarity, and social justice as the aims of the movement; the abolition of capitalism was not mentioned. Neo-revisionists believe the task of socialism is to devise a regulatory framework that will support left of center social values within a thriving capitalist economy.

Market Socialism

In 1992, following the disintegration of the Soviet bloc, American economist John Roemer and Pranab Bardhan looked for a feasible socialist alternative to the Soviet economic model in a paper titled "Market Socialism: A Case for Rejuvenation." They argued that three features marked the Soviet model, which had clearly failed:

- Public or state ownership of the means of production
- Noncompetitive, nondemocratic politics
- Command/administrative allocation of resources and commodities

They claimed that competitive markets are necessary to create an efficient, vigorous economy, but that public ownership in its widest sense is needed to attain a relatively egalitarian distribution of that economy's surplus. They advocated a system that combines competitive politics and competitive allocation of resources with public ownership of the means of production.

ALERT

Traditionally, public ownership of the means of production has implied state-run industries, like British coal mines in the 1950s, collectivized farms in the Soviet Union, or municipally owned utilities. For Roemer and Bardhan, public ownership meant decisions about the distributions of profits would be made through the political democratic process even if the state does not control operation of the firms.

Market socialism is a compromise between a centrally planned socialist economy and free enterprise, in which enterprises are publicly or cooperatively owned, but production and consumption are guided by market forces rather than by government planning.

Since Roemer and Bardhan published their paper, several competing variations on market socialism have been proposed, including service market socialism, cooperative market socialism, pragmatic market socialism, municipal ownership market socialism, and bankcentric market socialism.

Some assume that publicly owned businesses would operate on a nonprofit basis. Most assume a profit-oriented system.

All share four primary goals:

- Economic efficiency
- Limited state authority
- Greater worker autonomy
- More equal distribution of primary income

All use the supply and demand of the market as a means to distribute goods, regulate prices, and allocate resources.

ESSENTIAL

Economist Oskar Lange (1904–1965) proposed the first version of market socialism in the 1930s. Lange argued that the state should own key industries, with a central planning board that adjusts prices in response to supply and demand. Conservative economist Friedrich Hayek suggested that having the government mimic market competition would be less effective than actual market competition.

Green Socialism

The fundamental idea behind Green socialism is that our industrial system, and the ideas about our place in the natural world that accompany it, are rapidly destroying the planet. The endless spiral of new needs and wants has led to demands for greater quantities of material goods and comforts. The political systems of the west, socialist and nonsocialist alike, have worked to expand production capacity. Traditionally, the socialist debate focused on how to distribute the products of industrial society more equitably. Green socialists have moved the debate to the amount and quality of what is being consumed and the kind of workday needed to produce it.

Green socialist thought rests on the work of political philosopher Herbert Marcuse and other social theorists of the Frankfort School. Marcuse questioned the Marxist idea of *homo faber*: the concept that humans are primarily working beings that create themselves through their labor. He argued that true freedom is realized through the instinctual forces of eros, or passion, and playful activity. Work requires the renunciation of instinctual pleasure. Alienated from eros by the discipline of work, the majority of the working classes have come to believe that freedom means having more and better consumer goods. While the elevation of work over eros was necessary in times of economic scarcity, Marcuse claimed this should no longer be a problem in highly developed societies. Society's challenge is to use technology to provide basic goods and services in a way that would allow everyone to bridge the gap between work and meaningful play.

Green socialists analyze the economic and political roots of the environmental crisis in terms of Marcuse's critique of *homo faber*, mass culture, and consumerism. Their proposed solutions take two basic forms: an "eco-state" that would play a major role in protecting the environment, and a loose federation of self-governing and largely self-sufficient communes.

ESSENTIAL

German-born political philosopher Herbert Marcuse (1898–1979) used Freud's theories of psychoanalysis to critique Marxism. His most important works, *Eros and Civilization: A Philosophical Inquiry into Freud* (1955) and *One-Dimensional Man* (1964), were influential in the leftist student movements of the 1960s in both Europe and the United States.

Rudolf Bahro

Green philosopher and activist Rudolf Bahro (1935–1997) wrote one of the most powerful ecological critiques of Marxism in *The Alternative in Eastern Europe: An Analysis of Actually-Existing Socialism* (1977). He pointed out that Marx assumed that socialism would be a *classless* industrial society, but an industrial society nonetheless. Instead, Bahro argued that Marxism needed "not only to transform its relations of production, but must also fundamentally transform the entire character of its means of production." Consumption is an inherent part of capitalism, which creates unnecessary and wasteful commodities at the expense of needs in its pursuit of profit. In order to reduce consumption, and industry's damage to the environment, it is necessary to transform society.

eV FACT

Rudolf Bahro (1935–1997) joined the East Germany Communist Party at seventeen. He withdrew his membership following the invasion of Czechoslovakia in 1968. As a result of *The Alternative in Eastern Europe*, he was imprisoned for two years and then deported to West Germany. He was a founding member of the West German Green Party, from which he subsequently resigned.

Bahro suggested a "Communist Alternative" to state socialism that he described as Green anarcho-communism. In addition to changing the "relations of production," socialists needed to change humanity's relationship with the environment, creating a new economy geared toward producing no more than is needed for subsistence. In addition to reducing damage to the environment, scaling down needs would allow a massive reduction in the number of hours spent working.

Because small-scale technology could not satisfy the needs of large urban populations, people should create federations of communes that could produce 90 percent of what they need, deal on a national level for another 9 percent, and for the last 1 percent deal with a world market.

Andre Gorz

Andre Gorz (1924–2007) argued that most people are stifled within the world of work. Most jobs are both boring and enslaving. Technological innovation and automation created a situation in which there is increasingly less work for people, but capitalism did not provide a framework for allowing people to work less. Consequently, the unemployed do not have the resources to enjoy a decent life and the employed do not have the time. Gorz proposed a combination of lower consumption, a reduced workweek, and a guaranteed minimum income that would allow people to pursue independent activities, including socially useful pursuits that would benefit others.

Gorz drew a distinction between *environmentalism* and what he called *ecologism*. *Environmentalism* limits itself to a call for renewable sources of energy, recycling, and preservation. *Ecologism* demands an end to the fetishism of commodities and consumption.

CHAPTER 22

"It Didn't Happen Here"

The question of why the United States never developed a mass socialist party has troubled socialist thinkers and historians since the end of the nineteenth century. As early as 1906, socialist economist Werner Sombart wrote *Why Is There No Socialism in America?*—the first of hundreds of books with similar titles published over the last century. After careful analysis, they all come up with variations on "America is different."

"American Exceptionalism"

The phrase "American exceptionalism" was first used by French aristocrat and liberal Alexis de Tocqueville (1805–1859) in his two-volume masterpiece, *Democracy in America* (1835–1840). De Tocqueville traveled to the United States after the Paris Commune of 1830 in order, he said, to see "what a great republic is." He came to the conclusion that "The great advantage of the Americans is to have arrived at democracy without having to suffer democratic revolutions, and to be born equal instead of becoming so."

Since de Tocqueville, "American exceptionalism" has been used by virtually every shade of political thought to explain America's political history. Socialist thinkers attributed the lack of a viable socialist party in the United States to various aspects of "American exceptionalism," the most important of which are discussed in this chapter.

Americanism: Liberty, Equality, and Justice for All

British Prime Minister Margaret Thatcher didn't say it first, but she said it best: "Europe was created by history. America was created by philosophy."

Unlike the countries of Western Europe, America's national identity is bound up in a shared ideology, sometimes called *Americanism*. The Enlightenment ideals of the rights of man and the social contract, the political heritage of British constitutionalism, and the radical tradition of religious dissent blended together into a potent ideological mixture of individualism, populism, egalitarianism, and a healthy suspicion of central authority. The idea of individual rights, no matter how badly executed, was built into America's system of values from the beginning in the Declaration of Independence:

> *We hold these truths to be self-evident, that all men are created equal, that they are endowed by their Creator with certain unalienable rights, that among these are life, liberty and the pursuit of happiness.*

European socialist parties gained strength in the course of fighting for fundamental political rights. Americans enjoyed those same rights long before industrialization created an urban working class, including the right of association and white male suffrage. States that originally had property qualifications for voters dropped them by 1830. By 1840, two mass-based political parties, the Democrats and the Whigs, lured 85 percent of all adult white men to the polls with "walking around money" and alcohol. When socialist parties arrived in America in the late 1840s, the big democratic jobs were done.

ALERT

> The Marxist ideal of government-controlled modes of production didn't appeal to either the American Federation of Labor or the Industrial Workers of the World. Both groups believed government-owned industry would be harder for workers to fight than private companies. As AFL president Samuel Gompers said, "What the state gives, the state can take away."

To a great extent, the socialist movement had little appeal in America because many of the goals of socialism, with the major exception of government control over the mode of production, aspired to what Americans believed they already had: a democratic society in which all men were equal before the law.

Diversity Versus Solidarity

In the ethnically and culturally homogenous countries in which socialism was born, working-class solidarity made intuitive sense. (At least until World War I, when many socialists discovered they were British, French, or German before they were socialist.) In the United States, wave after wave of immigration created a working-class split by religious, ethnic, and racial diversity. In the 1970s, when middle-class women entered the workplace in great numbers, the addition of gender further complicated the mix.

In 1911, during socialism's American golden age, the United States Immigration Commission reported that three-fifths of American wage earners were of immigrant origin. The divisions were deep and complicated: Native-born workers allied against immigrants, "old" immigrants from Britain and Northern Europe allied against "new" immigrants from southern and eastern Europe, and European Americans of all kinds allied against Asians and freed black slaves. The same organizations that fought for legislation benefiting labor also fought to have immigration restrictions passed on the grounds that a flood of unskilled and poor newcomers would pose an economic threat. This fear was largely unfounded. Each wave of new immigrants took the lowest paying jobs, allowing those present before them to move up the social and economic ladder.

ESSENTIAL

America's long-standing ambivalence about immigration was an impediment to the adoption of socialism. Until the 1960s, recent immigrants dominated American socialism; first Germans, who were America's enemy in both world wars, and later Eastern Europeans, who were associated with Soviet Russia. As a result, Americans tended to see socialism as inherently un-American.

The Opportunity for Social Mobility

Nineteenth-century socialists saw America as a new country that was not burdened with attitudes, institutions, traditions, or hereditary privileges left over from a feudal past. Although there were enormous discrepancies in wealth, there were no rigid class distinctions. A man could rise as far as talent and luck would take him. If he was born in America, he could rise from log cabin to the White House, like Andrew Jackson and Abraham Lincoln. An immigrant could climb from penniless weaver's son to become the "richest man in the world," like Andrew Carnegie.

As Friedrich Engels noted, America was a nation "without a permanent and hereditary proletariat. Here everyone could become, if not a capitalist, at all events, an independent man, producing or trading with his own means, for his own account." After 1862, even men without the means to buy land could earn a farm with their own labor, thanks to the Homestead Act of 1862.

FACT

The Homestead Act of 1862 gave a United States citizen, or intended citizen, who was willing to live on the land and improve it, the right to claim 160 acres of undeveloped federal land. Between 1862 and 1934, homesteaders earned the deeds to 270 million acres of federal land. The last claim under the Homestead Act was filed in 1979.

Marx and Engels noted as early as 1847 that the American government's efforts to give men the opportunity to settle on free land and become farmers undermined the development of socialist ideals. The majority of Americans believed they were living in a society of equal opportunity.

The Two-Party Electoral System

Parliamentary political systems allow minority parties to make a real impact on national politics. Governments are formed based on a simple legislative majority. If the party with the largest number of seats doesn't have a majority, it must form a coalition with one or more smaller parties. (This leads to occasional ideological oddities, like Winston Churchill's combined Conservative and Labour government in Britain during World War II, or the so-called "Unity governments" combining Labor and Likud in Israel.) Because a prime minister holds his position at the discretion of the party, a minority party in a coalition government has the power to topple a government by withdrawing its votes.

ALERT

Between 1900 and 1912, when the Socialist Party of America was at its height, socialist candidates won thousands of municipal offices, 150 seats in the legislatures of eighteen states, and two seats in the House of Representatives. Despite success at the local and state level, the Socialist Party never made an impact in a presidential campaign.

In contrast, the winner-take-all nature of the presidential electoral system means that third parties are seen as having little chance to affect national elections. (The most successful socialist candidate for president, Eugene Debs, won only 6 percent of the vote.) Voters often perceive voting for a third party as throwing their vote away, or fear that voting for a third party will enable a candidate they dislike to take office. The only way a third party can win a presidential election is for there to be a major split in one of the two dominant parties.

Sometimes, successful third parties are absorbed into one of the major political parties. For the most part, third parties affect national politics when the major parties adopt elements of their platforms. Instead of being absorbed into a larger party, America's socialist parties have tended to splinter into smaller microparties. On the other hand, socialist programs were adopted and adapted by mainstream Democratic politicians from the time of the New Deal up until the emergence of "Reagan Democrats" in the 1980s.

ESSENTIAL

> American socialists were hampered in the political system by their own intransigence. Where leaders of the British Labour Party and the German Social Democrats repeatedly abandoned unpopular programs and even Marxist positions in pursuit of larger goals, American socialists have clung to ideological purity.

Despite the odds against them, third parties have not always fared badly in presidential elections. In 1924, Wisconsin congressman Robert LaFollette won 17 percent of the popular vote and carried Wisconsin running on the Progressive ticket. In 1968, Alabama governor George Wallace won 14 percent of the popular vote and five southern states on the American Independent ticket in 1968. Texas businessmen Ross Perot won 19 percent of the popular vote running as an Independent in 1992. In each of these cases, the party was built around a single charismatic leader, something American socialism has lacked since Eugene Debs.

Modern Misconceptions about Socialism

Over the last hundred years, Americans have been both baffled and frightened by socialism.

Red Scares

Periodic "red scares" have shaped America's domestic and foreign policy at times of national crisis. In 1919, Attorney General A. Mitchell Palmer was convinced that socialists were plotting to overthrow the government. Without evidence, he arrested thousands of communists, socialists, and anarchists, most of whom had trouble organizing a small political party—let alone a revolution—and held them without trial.

In 1938, the House Committee on Un-American Activities (HCUA) was formed under the chairmanship of Texas congressman Martin Dies, Jr. Originally intended as a tool for investigating possible German-American spies and the activities of the Ku Klux Klan, under Dies's leadership HCUA focused on the possibility that the American Communist Party had infiltrated the Federal Writers' Project and other New Deal programs. Dies's tactics were soon attacked by those who saw HCUA's activities as a way of blocking Franklin Roosevelt's progressive programs without leaving a voting record that their constituents could track. HCUA's most vocal critic, New York congressman Vito Marcantonio, himself accused of ties to the American Communist Party, told members of the Committee in 1940:

> *If communism is destroyed, I do not know what some of you will do. It has become the most convenient method by which you wrap yourselves in the American flag in order to cover up some of the greasy stains on the legislative toga. You can vote against the unemployed, you can vote against the W.P.A. workers, and you can emasculate the Bill of Rights of the Constitution of the United States; you can try to destroy the National Labor Relations Law, the Magna Carta of American labor; you can vote against the farmer; and you can do all that with a great deal of impunity, because after you have done so you do not have to explain your vote.*

ALERT

Joseph McCarthy wasn't responsible for the infamous Hollywood blacklist. In 1947, the House Committee on Un-American Activities investigated possible communist influence in Hollywood. The original blacklist, known as the Hollywood Ten, consisted of ten witnesses who refused to answer committee members' questions. Eventually more than 300 actors, directors, and screenwriters were blacklisted by the movie industry.

In the early 1950s, Senator Joseph McCarthy used similar tactics when he claimed members of the American Communist Party had infiltrated the government. Playing on American fears of the spread of Soviet-style communism, he used his power as the chairman of the investigation subcommittee of the Committee on Government Operations of the Senate to accuse thousands of people of disloyalty, subversion, and treason with little regard for evidence.

Modern Misconceptions

Socialist is once again being used as an epithet, hurled with the same lack of precision that Mao's Red Guards used when accusing someone of being a "capitalist roader." In the past, "red scares" have been based on the fear that "they" were conspiring to destroy the United States. Today, the popular understanding of socialism is still shaped to a great degree by the Cold War, which was often described in terms of a battle to the death between good (capitalism) and evil (communism). As a result, many people equate socialism with an attack on American values. In fact, both right-wing populists and American socialists often quote from the Declaration of Independence and the Bill of Rights when arguing their positions.

Misconception #1: Socialism and Communism Are the Same Thing

As the last twenty-one chapters have demonstrated, socialism wears lots of different red hats. While all communists are socialists, not all socialists are communists. Communism is a specific version of socialism based on Marxist-Leninist ideology. Soviet-style communism is a specific historical manifestation of communism. Most socialists today are opposed to Soviet-style communism, which is not surprising given that the Soviets themselves abandoned it.

Misconception #2: If the Government Pays for It, It's Socialism

Extreme antisocialists groups, such as the Future of Freedom Foundation, consider any government-owned, -funded or -subsidized operation to be socialist. In fact, governments paid for public works, standing armies, and public services long before Thomas More dreamed up Utopia. Just think the Great Pyramid, the Great Wall of China, the Taj Mahal, the Roman legions . . .

Misconceptions #3 and #4: "It Didn't Happen Here" Versus "America Is a Socialist State"

The people who say "It didn't happen here" and the people who say "America has been a socialist state ever since [fill in the blank]" make the same basic mistake. They assume that a political system is either capitalist or socialist.

Long time Socialist Party spokesman Norman Thomas once said:

> *The American people will never knowingly adopt Socialism. But under the name of "liberalism" they will adopt every fragment of the Socialist program, until one day America will be a Socialist nation, without knowing how it happened.*

America's mainstream political parties have adapted ideas from the socialist platform for many years, including Medicare, the minimum wage, Social Security, and the eight-hour day. The United States, like much of the world, has a mixed economy that includes elements of both capitalism and socialism.

The Tricky One: Nationalized Medicine Is Socialism

Nationalized medicine is definitely an idea that has long been espoused by socialist parties worldwide. Every country that has called itself socialist or had a social democrat or labor party majority in its government has adopted some form of nationalized medicine.

FACT

The first presidential candidate to advocate universal nationalized health insurance was Henry Wallace, who served as Franklin Roosevelt's Vice President from 1941 to 1945. The Progressive Party candidate in 1948, Wallace also advocated an end to the nascent Cold War, an end to segregation, and full voting rights for African Americans. He won only 2.4 percent of the popular vote.

It is probably accurate to describe universal healthcare as having its roots in socialism, just like Medicare and Medicaid. Whether that's a bad thing is a question outside of the scope of this book.

APPENDIX A

Glossary

Alienation

The Marxist concept that as workers lose control over the conditions and products of their labor, they also lose control over their lives.

Ancien Régime

The political and social system based on the idea of the absolute monarch, particularly as it developed in France in the two centuries before the French Revolution. The term is sometimes applied to the rest of Europe during this period.

Attainder and Forfeiture

In English law, the legal extinction of civil rights for a person convicted of treason or a felony. Once a person was attainted, he lost all his goods and property to the crown.

Bourgeoisie

In Marxist theory, the capitalist class that will oppose the proletariat in class struggle.

Capitalism

An economic system based on market competition and the investment of capital in business by private individuals.

Class consciousness

In Marxist thought, the awareness on the part of one social class that it is distinct from, and antagonistic to, other classes in society.

Class warfare

In Marxist theory, the struggle resulting from the conflicting interests of the bourgeoisie and the proletariat that will bring about the socialist revolution.

Constituent assembly

A legislative body elected for the sole purpose of writing a constitution.

Differential rent

An increase in rent that occurs because of changes in social conditions rather than the efforts of the landowner.

Egalitarianism

The belief in equal political, economic, and legal rights for all citizens.

False consciousness

The idea that workers could be co-opted by the perceived possibility of upward mobility into supporting a social system that was against their own interest.

Gradualism

The concept of moving toward the socialist state through a series of reforms rather than revolution.

The "Iron Law" of Wages

The concept that wages are tied to the cost of food and that real wages will never rise above the cost of subsistence.

The Labor Theory of Value

The idea that the value of a product is based on the amount of labor needed to produce it.

Laissez-Faire *Economics*

Literally, "leave it alone." The principle of government noninterference in economic affairs, and the idea underlying Adam Smith's doctrines of free trade and the self-regulating marketplace.

Microparty

A political party that has too small a membership to have an effect on regional or national elections. Also known as a "minnow party."

Mode of production

Both the skills and technologies a society uses to produce wealth and the way in which it organizes labor.

Nationalization

The process by which the government takes control of an industry that was previously owned by private investors.

Participatory democracy

The idea that all citizens are directly involved in all important decisions.

Plebiscite

A direct vote in which the entire electorate is invited to accept or refuse a measure.

Populism

A political program or movement that champions the common people, usually defined in contrast to an elite. Populist movements generally combine elements of both the right and the left.

Poverty-Trap

A situation caused by means-tested social welfare benefits or tax laws that discourages people from trying to improve their situations for fear of losing their safety nets or reducing their disposable income.

Primogeniture

A form of inheritance in which the eldest son inherits all or most of a father's property.

Privatization

The act of selling a government-owned industry to the private sector.

The "Propaganda of the Deed"

The anarchist idea that violent action is the most effective form of propaganda for the revolutionary cause.

Social Contract

The concept that people form government by voluntarily giving up some liberties in exchange for security.

Stagflation

The simultaneous occurrence of an economic recession and inflation.

Subsistence wage

The amount needed to pay for the minimum necessary for survival.

Surplus Value

The difference between the cost of labor and the value that labor produces.

Universal Manhood Suffrage

The concept that all adult males in a society have the right to vote.

Utopia

An imagined perfect society. Literally "no place."

Vanguard of the Proletariat

Lenin's theory that a small, tightly disciplined socialist party will lead the proletariat to revolution.

Voluntarism

Samuel Gompers's theory that workers should rely on voluntary organizations to defend their interests rather than on the state.

APPENDIX B

Further Reading

Berman, Sheri. *The Primacy of Politics: Social Democracy and the Making of Europe's Twentieth Century.* New York: Cambridge University Press, 2006.

Buhle, Paul and Nicole Schulman, ed. *Wobblies!: A Graphic History of the Industrial Workers of the World.* New York: Verso Books, 2005.

Busky, Donald F. *Democratic Socialism: A Global Survey.* Westport, CT: Praeger, 2000.

Ely, Geoff. *Forging Democracy: The History of the Left in Europe, 1850–2000.* New York: Oxford University Press, 2002.

Gay, Peter. *The Dilemma of Democratic Socialism: Eduard Bernstein's Challenge to Marx.* New York: Collier Books, 1962.

Gray, Alexander. *The Socialist Tradition, Moses to Lenin.* New York: Longman's Green and Co., 1946.

Kropotkin, Peter. *Memoirs of a Revolutionist.* Originally published 1899.

Marcus, Steven. *Engels, Manchester and the Working Class.* New York: Random House, 1974.

Muravchik, Joshua. *Heaven on Earth: The Rise and Fall of Socialism.* San Francisco: Encounter Books, 2002.

Sassoon, Donald. *One Hundred Years of Socialism: The West European Left in the Twentieth Century.* London and New York: I. B. Tauris, 1996.

Thompson, E. P. *The Making of the English Working Class.* New York: Vintage Books, 1966.

Wilson, Edmund. *To the Finland Station: A Study in the Writing and Acting of History.* Originally published in 1940.

Index